ALSO BY NICHOLAS EPLEY

Mindwise

A LITTLE MORE SOCIAL

A LITTLE MORE SOCIAL

How Small Choices Create Unexpected Happiness, Health, and Connection

NICHOLAS EPLEY

ALFRED A. KNOPF
New York 2026

A BORZOI BOOK
FIRST HARDCOVER EDITION PUBLISHED
BY ALFRED A. KNOPF 2026

Published by Alfred A. Knopf, a division of Penguin Random House LLC,
1745 Broadway, New York, NY 10019.

Library of Congress Cataloging-in-Publication Data
Names: Epley, Nicholas, author
Title: A little more social : how small choices create
unexpected happiness, health, and connection / Nicholas Epley.
Description: First hardcover edition. | New York : Alfred A. Knopf, 2026. |
Includes bibliographical references and index.
Identifiers: LCCN 2025042373 (print) | LCCN 2025042374 (ebook) |
ISBN 9780593319543 hardcover |
ISBN 9780593319550 ebook
Subjects: LCSH: Loneliness | Belonging (Social psychology) |
Social isolation | Social history—21st century
Classification: LCC BF575.L7 E65 2026 (print) | LCC BF575.L7 (ebook) |
DDC 158.2—dc23/eng/20260206
LC record available at https://lccn.loc.gov/2025042373
LC ebook record available at https://lccn.loc.gov/

penguinrandomhouse.com | aaknopf.com

Printed in the United States of America
2nd Printing

The authorized representative in the EU for product safety and compliance is Penguin Random House Ireland, Morrison Chambers, 32 Nassau Street, Dublin D02 YH68, Ireland, https://eu-contact.penguin.ie.

For Lindsay,
who reaches back

Contents

Preface: Social Enough Animals?

> Man is by nature a social animal. . . . Anyone who either cannot lead the common life or is so self-sufficient as not to need to, and therefore does not partake of society, is either a beast or a god.
>
> —ARISTOTLE, *Politics,* 350 BCE

There's a fundamental paradox at the core of human life. On the one hand, we're highly social creatures whose happiness, health, and success depend on having positive relationships with other people. On the other hand, we're often reluctant to reach out and actually *be social* in the ways that connect us positively with other people. We avoid talking with strangers. Once talking, we stick to small talk rather than connecting more deeply. Or more often we avoid talking altogether and keep our social distance by typing to each other. When we feel grateful, we keep it to ourselves. When we need help, we're reluctant to ask. When we know someone who needs our support, we hesitate to reach out. Every day there are opportunities, big and small, to reach out and connect with others that we choose not to take. Aristotle was right: We are indeed social animals. But then why do we so often choose to be *un*social?

This paradox struck me like a lightning bolt one morning on my way into work. That day began like most others for me, commuting on a train to my office at the University of Chicago, where I work as a professor of behavioral science. I boarded the train with my neighbors from the

South Side of Chicago, many with familiar faces but unknown names. We trudged down the aisle in single file until peeling off at the first row with an open seat along the window, our own little acreage of solitude. People got on at the next stop, and the next, and the next, heads bowed in silence on the hunt for their own isolated acreage of solitude.

Eventually the train car filled up. A fiftyish-year-old African American woman wearing an elegant red hat had no choice but to take the last available spot next to me (a larger-than-average, middle-aged, curly-headed, hatless white guy). We then started our thirty-minute ride into Hyde Park, where I would get off, all of us ostensibly social animals sitting cheek by jowl, staring at our phones or our knees or blankly into space, completely ignoring each other in silence. Alone, together.

I was suddenly struck by the oddity of our daily routine. That morning I was in the midst of writing an early chapter of my first book, *Mindwise,* that described our unique but imperfect capacity as human beings to understand the minds of others. To an extent that seems unmatched by any other species on the planet, our brains are equipped for social connection, with an outsized cerebral cortex specifically built to understand other people and to reward us with a chemical bath of happiness at any hint of a positive social connection. This is why connecting with other people—even strangers—is one of life's most consistently enjoyable experiences and why being isolated and disconnected is among life's worst.

And yet here we all were—me included—trudging off to work carrying one of the most socially capable brains on the planet, encased within a body made happier and healthier by connecting with others, going through what most surveys indicate is the worst part of our day (commuting), keeping completely to ourselves. Is this the best way to spend these moments, day after day after day?

That morning I decided to test a different approach. As a psychologist, I try to understand human behavior using experiments, but this time I decided to put myself into an experiment. Instead of ignoring the person who just sat down next to me, I would try to connect.

A flood of concerns instantly ran through my head: Maybe she's not interested in talking to me? What do I say? Will she think I'm a creep trying to hit on her? Do I really want to seem like *That Guy*? *That Guy* is the one who talks endlessly on a long flight. Nobody wants to be *That Guy,* including *this* guy. But would the next thirty minutes really be better for either of us if I spent that time doomscrolling the news or checking email rather than reaching out and treating this stranger like a friend?

The silence felt like a literal wall between us. Nevertheless, the experiment must go on. *Gulp.* "I love your hat . . . I have one just like it," I finally said with a big smile and a small laugh.

Sometimes when you stop to really pay attention, you notice things that you might have missed otherwise. I've spoken to strangers countless times, as I imagine you have. I just hadn't focused on it that carefully. Sometimes you meet nice people, and other times they're not so nice. Sometimes conversations are great, and other times they're not so great. Sometimes I'm in the mood to talk, and other times I'd rather sleep or work. My observations were all over the place. At the time, I thought that whether opening up to someone is nice or not depends on whom you're talking to, what you're talking about, and how you're feeling at the moment. But giving *this* precise moment in *this* conversation such careful scrutiny left me feeling startled by the power of those opening words. "I love your hat" clearly isn't in the Conversation Starter Hall of Fame, but in that context, where the compliment was genuine, the interest in connecting authentic, and my smile big enough to show through the corners of my eyes, uttering those words felt like flipping on someone's power switch. *Boom! Let there be life.*

My seatmate's response did not remotely resemble my pessimistic fears. She turned to me, lit up. Her face had morphed from an almost lifeless neutral expression to a bright smile as she laughed right along with me. I followed my mediocre opener by asking if she was excited about her day ahead, then what she did for a living, and how long she had lived in the area. Taking a genuine interest in her also made her curious about me. This reciprocating interest led to talking about families and careers, whether we were happy where we were or were hoping for something different (she wasn't very happy and felt stuck in her job). I told her about the research I conducted, and about the experiment I had just enrolled us in. She agreed that it was odd how often we choose to ignore each other. She thought this tendency might be a relatively recent development, that people don't talk to strangers "these days" because parents tell their kids to be afraid of strangers, or because everyone is addicted to their phones.

My memory of our exact words has faded, but my memory of how the conversation made me feel is crystal clear: It was great. Perhaps more important, it was *surprisingly* great. What struck me so powerfully that morning was the large gap between my pessimistic expectations about how she would respond if I reached out and her actual response. The pessimism that normally led me to keep to myself on most days now seemed sadly misplaced.

Of course, this conversation didn't leave me feeling happier for the rest of my life, or even the rest of the day, because our emotions are fleeting. It did, though, make an otherwise dull and boring thirty-minute commute meaningfully better than it would have been otherwise. And what is a happy life other than a string of positive moments? We often think of happiness as being something that's fairly stable over time, like height, but it actually fluctuates the way any emotion does. Being consistently happier requires behaving in ways that bring happiness routinely.

The insight that hit me like a lightning bolt that morning was that I had the power to make a moment better by being a little more social, and in the process could make someone else's moment better, too. How many other commutes had been more mediocre than they needed to be? How many other nice people had I failed to meet? What if I was a little more social a little more often?

"Thank you so much for talking with me this morning," she said with a smile as big as the one I initially greeted her with.

Hello? . . . Maybe no

I'm far from the first person to have wondered whether we're friendly enough for our own good, but that morning was the first time I had put the belief that was keeping me from reaching out to the test so deliberately. Looking around at a trainful of people who were also avoiding each other day after day made me wonder if my misplaced pessimism might be fairly common. I started asking my friends and family for their opinion: Would you be better off if you reached out to other people like I did on the train that morning more often? Their typical response was some version of "Hell no!"

Clearly, avoidance was more the rule than the exception. Some of my colleagues at the University of Chicago even brought up exceptionally unlikely possibilities about reaching out: kidnapping, robbery, physical assault. In fact, one even referred to talking to strangers on the train as "talking to the serial killers." Elon Musk seems to hold the same fears, hating public transportation because "there's like a bunch of random strangers, and one might be a serial killer."[1] To solve this clear and present stranger danger, Musk created the Boring Company to dig new subway systems that would move people in small pods from one location to another alone, thereby avoiding any serial-killer encounters.

My friends weren't building their own subway systems, but they certainly had some anxiety about reaching out. They also thought that if we were better off engaging with others more often, then we'd already be doing it. That could be true, but there are also many things we'd be better off doing that many of us are not already doing, including eating less, sleeping more, and exercising somewhere north of never. Maybe sociality is like these other activities? Perhaps we're not social enough for our own good?

Mistakenly Seeking Solitude

My experience and a billionaire's fears hardly count as compelling data. To start testing whether our expectations about social interactions are on the mark or off, we'd have to conduct an actual experiment. Seeking the perfect spot for that experiment is what led Juliana Schroeder (my always-ambitious collaborator) and me to the underground entryway of the Homewood, Illinois, train station. There, next to a sign advertising a "commuter study," and offering a $5 Starbucks gift card for participating, is where our real research began.[2]

After they agreed to participate in the experiment, we asked commuters to guess how positive their commute would be that morning if they just did whatever they normally did on their commute (this is our control condition), if they just kept to themselves and enjoyed their solitude on their commute (this is our solitude condition), or if they tried to make a connection to the person who sat down next to them by having a conversation. If you think that enjoying your solitude sounds about as close to heaven as you'll get on a commuter train and that being asked to talk to a stranger sounds a little closer to hell, then you're not alone. These commuters, on average, also thought they would have the most positive commute if they just kept to themselves in solitude or did whatever they normally did, and thought they would have the least positive commute if they tried to talk with a stranger. It's no surprise, then, that nearly everyone on the train chooses to sit in complete silence day after day. If you thought that talking to someone would be less pleasant than keeping to yourself, then you'd choose to keep to yourself, too.

However, when we put these beliefs to the test by actually asking people on the trains to do each of these things,[3] these beliefs were not only wrong, they were in the opposite direction of what really happened. Instead of having the most positive experience while keeping to themselves in solitude, our commuters actually had the most positive experience when they tried to connect with a stranger in conversation and the least positive when they kept to themselves in solitude.[4] What our commuters imagined was reaching out to talk with someone who didn't really want to talk to them, thinking they'd have little to talk about, meaning that they'd be better off just keeping to themselves. What our commuters actually found was someone who was generally more willing to talk than they had expected, with more to talk about than they had guessed. They got to know each other a little bit, talking about their lives and their families and their jobs. One pair with kids going to college shared their experiences on college visits. Others talked about their shared hobbies or their plans for the day ahead.

It wasn't the content of their conversation that really mattered here, but rather the unexpected power of the conversation to create a warm connection when one person reached out to try. What was once a cold, nameless stranger on the train was now Ralph ("a VERY nice man who reminded me of a kind caring grandpa"), or Debbie (with three kids, who loves watching sports and gardening), or Pat (who was celebrating her birthday), or Jackie and Patricia (who "were fun to talk to"). Most interesting here is that the commuters didn't anticipate how nice it would feel to turn a random stranger into a known acquaintance beforehand. Reaching out wasn't just positive; it was *surprisingly* positive.

Seeing this result, to me, felt a little like what I imagine Galileo must have felt after peering through his telescope and noticing that the universe didn't look the way everyone thought it looked. I started to see a potential resolution to the paradox of highly social people nevertheless choosing to be nonsocial. Here on these trains was a space where almost everyone was actively avoiding an opportunity to reach out and connect with each other, not because it was actually making this moment better, but because we mistakenly *thought* that trying to connect would make the moment worse.

Undersociality

These experiments weren't flukes but rather the tip of a very large iceberg coming into view. They inspired what has now been more than a decade's worth of research trying to understand why we can be overly pessimistic about our social interactions, why it matters for our well-being, and even why it matters for the societies we live in. This research has moved far beyond the narrow confines of my commuter trains and into almost every aspect of our social lives, from the choices we make to approach or avoid strangers and acquaintances, to how openly and honestly we manage our relationships with friends and our closest family.

This research has also come full circle and seeped into every aspect of my personal life. As I imagined after my commute that morning, no research that I have ever read about or been involved with has changed the way I live my own life more than this. Although I've always been somewhat social and outgoing, I also experienced intense anxiety meeting new people or speaking in professional settings. I lost twenty pounds in the weeks leading up to my first job interview for a professor position because I was so nervous I could barely eat or sleep. I could also see many instances where it would be easy for me to reach out that I was choosing to avoid. I still miss opportunities now, and sometimes make mistakes reaching out to others, but testing my expectations to align them with reality has made me more sociable—friendlier, kinder, and more open and honest with other people—than I would be otherwise.

This research also changed how I reacted in a time of crisis when pain struck my family. On July 11, 2016, six months into my wife's pregnancy, we lost our daughter, whom we had already named Sophie. Three months before her death, Jen and I had been shocked to learn that Sophie had Down syndrome. That shock didn't last long because we chose, almost entirely because of my own pessimistic fears, to connect with other families who were already raising children with disabilities in order to learn about their experiences. Every family we contacted wasn't just willing to talk; they were delighted to talk. These conversations taught me so much about the pleasures and pains these parents felt, and also about the similarities we'd find between raising children with and without disabilities. Every family we talked to would use the word "blessing" to describe their child. I also learned from these conversations that my fears about raising a child with this particular disability were likely misplaced. Jen and I could do this, together.

After learning so much and committing so deeply to raising a child with an intellectual disability, losing our unborn daughter was devastating, easily the worst thing that's ever happened to either of us. Jen and I mourned Sophie's death in a state of limbo for months, not knowing what to do next. For several years at that point, my colleagues and I had been finding many more examples of cases where we, as social animals, seemed to be overly reluctant to reach out and connect with others deeply and meaningfully. In my personal life, these findings suggested to me that we could do more in our family than I might have otherwise imagined.

So one morning I suggested to Jen that we could consider adopting a child if she felt ready. We had grown our family this way before, and we had gotten ourselves prepared to be new parents again. Jen was already ahead of me, having learned of opportunities to adopt a child with Down syndrome in China, where children with disabilities can face very difficult lives. She asked if I would be open to doing that.

This option was full of uncertainty and doubt for me, but again the results I kept seeing of people underestimating the positive impact of social connection kept popping into my mind. It surely sounds odd to think that the cold statistics of experimental results could affect my thinking about the future of our family in this way, but for me—a person who had seen thousands of data points from other people and who believed those data points revealed something important about human nature—it brought a sense of data-driven courage and strength. Yes, we could do this.

Roughly one year later, in March 2018, Jen and I boarded a plane bound for China with our four other children. We were reaching out to Lindsay: two years old, born to a mother we'll never know or meet, with big rosy cheeks, dark eyes, and a relentless smile despite her difficult start in life. Lindsay reached back. She's been exactly the blessing that every parent we spoke to said that she would be.

Raising Lindsay has been far from easy, of course, because all children bring unique challenges into their parents' lives, and children with disabilities bring additional challenges. But she is also amazing in so many ways that have broadened my perspective on the power of connection almost beyond prior recognition. I shudder now at the thought of how close we could have come to letting my fears keep us from bringing Lindsay into our lives.

Learning about how our overly pessimistic expectations can create misplaced barriers that harm our social lives and compromise our well-being has fundamentally changed how I live my life. I'm a better person to other people than I used to be. In return, being a better person to others has made my own life better as well. I wrote this book because I think it could change the way you live your life for the better, too.

This book is about *hello?* It is about the split second that precedes nearly every social interaction you ever have where you make a choice about whether to reach out and connect with another person in some way or hold back and keep to yourself. These social decisions are among the most important you make in your daily life because they determine the quality of your relationships, which in turn has a major impact on your happiness, your health, and your success.

The message from this research is both optimistic and empowering, but you won't come to believe it or to see the opportunities you have to be a little more social in your own life unless you actually go out and practice it in the real world. Fortunately, unlike more punishing self-improvement goals like exercising more or eating better, practicing to become a little more social is a surprisingly positive experience.

The first step to making sociality a habit is to explain why it's worth even bothering to try. Centuries ago, Aristotle recognized that we are fundamentally social beings, but in the centuries since, psychologists have been discovering new depths to the power of sociality that I can't imagine Aristotle himself would ever have imagined. In the next chapter I'll explain why sociality is a need on par with eating and sleeping, why it's likely to be far more important for your happiness than even money, and why living a life with more love in it gives you a life that is both happier and longer.

PART I

Why?

Why is social connection so important for our well-being, but also something we so often choose to avoid?

1

Homo Socialis

> No enjoyment equals the satisfaction we receive from the company of those we love and esteem; as the greatest of all punishments is to be oblig'd to pass our lives with those we hate or contemn.
>
> —DAVID HUME, *A Treatise of Human Nature*

In February 2022, a life-threatening storm sent police in Prestino, Italy, to check on Marinella Beretta's "small home in the midst of myriad other houses." Marinella was home, but the police were too late. Her withered skeleton was sitting at the kitchen table. Some other risk had taken her life more than *two years* earlier.

Marinella died not only completely alone but also completely unnoticed since her neighbors last reported seeing her in September 2019. No family had come or called to check on her. No friends emailed to find out why she didn't show up for some event or another. Marinella had lived so independently that nobody noticed her absence anywhere, in any capacity, for more than two years. "The mystery of Marinella's invisible life behind the closed gate of her cottage teaches us a terrible lesson," reported the Italian newspaper *Il messaggero*. "The true sadness isn't that others didn't notice her death. It's that they didn't realize that Marinella Beretta was alive."[1]

It's hard to imagine that someone could die so completely alone in today's world, but it's nearly impossible to imagine it happening at almost any previous point in human history. Daily life for our ancestors was, by necessity, deeply social. People lived most moments of their entire lives surrounded by family and neighbors, whether they wanted to or not. Simply staying alive required routine interaction, bound together not by impersonal exchanges of money but by the social threads of reciprocity. You scratch my back and I'll scratch yours. Life wasn't easy, but you didn't die unnoticed at your kitchen table.

Times have changed. Thanks to countless technological advances, we are now more independent, and spending more time by ourselves, than ever before. The number of people living alone in the United States, for instance, has more than tripled over the last century, from 7.7 percent in 1940 to 27.7 percent in 2020.[2] In many parts of the world, you could wake up alone in your home on any given day, eat breakfast bought online and delivered touch-free to your doorstep, entertain yourself by surfing the internet or watching television, go wherever you want in your car or on public transportation, and pay for whatever you need with a credit card, all without ever having to actually talk to another human being. No back-scratching required.

The benefits of independence are instantly obvious: You can live where you want, do what you want, and avoid almost any interaction you don't want. The cost of independence is that we can now choose to live our lives feeling more isolated and alone than was likely at any point in human history. According to the British historian Fay Bound Alberti,[3] descriptions of loneliness as we think of it today didn't show up in English-language books until the early 1800s but have been skyrocketing ever since.[4] Even the meaning of loneliness seems to have evolved over time. Before 1800, Alberti finds, the rarely used terms "lonely" and "loneliness" were generally used to describe the physical state of being alone rather than the psychological state of feeling disconnected. Although it's possible that English speakers before 1800 were somehow unable to feel lonely, that seems preposterously unlikely to me. More likely is that it was such a rare experience that people didn't write about it.[5]

Not so today. Loneliness is now such a popular concept that dictionaries provide not just one definition but two, including both the traditional meaning that psychologists refer to as social isolation and the more modern psychological state of feeling disconnected.[6] In 2023, the U.S. surgeon general declared loneliness an epidemic. Roughly 45 percent of Americans in 2018 reported experiencing some degree of loneliness on a regular basis, and 58 percent reported feeling that they always or sometimes feel as if nobody knows them well.[7] This was even before the COVID-19 pandemic forced many into isolation, an event that seemed to impact loneliness among younger Americans the most. A survey of nearly twenty-five hundred Americans conducted late in 2021 found that 79 percent of people aged eighteen to twenty-four reported feeling lonely to some extent compared with only 41 percent of seniors aged sixty-six and older, a flip in the typical demographic patterns of older people being lonelier observed before the pandemic.[8] One study comparing scores on the gold standard used by psychologists—the UCLA Loneliness Scale—found a steady increase in loneliness among young adults since it was first used in 1974, an increase that is roughly comparable in statistical terms to having the height of the average person increase by three inches over the last four decades.[9] Whether you'd call an increase of three inches over that time period a tallness epidemic might be open to debate, but you'd definitely notice that "kids these days" were towering over their parents.

Your Stone Age brain wasn't built for this. It's impossible to understand the full cost of making mistakes in our social lives without understanding how deeply sociality is woven into the fabric of our being. From serving as a basic need on par with eating and drinking to shaping our brain size to determining our self-esteem and sense of identity, social connection is the stitching that holds our lives, and our societies, together. We are *Homo socialis.*

Social Needs

That loneliness feels painful tells us something very basic about what we need to survive and thrive. Our bodies, after all, aren't in the habit of sending us spam messages. When we're feeling good, that's a signal that something is going well and maybe should be done more often.

When we're feeling terrible, that's a signal that something is wrong and probably needs to be changed. The reason drinking a tall glass of water when you're thirsty feels great is the same reason a big hug from a good friend when you're sad feels great: It's your brain's reward system telling you that this is a good thing.[10] This is why the opposite of loneliness feels like happiness.

The reason our brains are built to work this way is fairly obvious. For most of human history, being alone or ostracized for any meaningful length of time was essentially a death sentence. Those capable of maintaining strong social connections were likely to both live longer and pass on these cooperative traits by having more children. Even Darwin recognized the evolutionary value of prosociality, noting that "selfish and contentious people will not cohere, and without coherence nothing can be effected."[11] Indeed, survey results indicate that people who are consistently selfish even today also make less money and have fewer children.[12] Put simply, a human brain that makes social connection a top priority survives longer and succeeds better than one that does not.[13]

For much of the twentieth century, though, psychologists failed to recognize social connection as a basic human need, treating it instead as a luxury good or as sentimental baggage that distracted us from really important needs like eating and sex. Abraham Maslow, a psychologist best known for his theory that motivation operates on a "hierarchy of needs," designated belonging as a mid-level need in his hierarchy that we cared about only after we felt safe and well fed, relegating it to bronze-level status in motivation's Olympics. Behaviorists in the early twentieth century went even further, speculating that children cry for their mothers not because they need social connection but because they need something else, like food or warmth. They even speculated that a perfect child could be raised alone in a box as long as it was kept comfortable and well fed, without ever requiring human contact.

Nonsense. These theories were disproven by scientists the moment they were actually tested. The opening sentence of one review paper from 1976—just over thirty years after Maslow published his theory—describes the situation as an "interesting paradox": "The theory is widely accepted, but there is little research evidence to support it." The authors later clarify that by "little research evidence" they really meant "no evidence."[14] Although Maslow was right to note that our needs go far beyond the basics of sex and sustenance, we don't seem to pursue them in the ordered or hierarchical fashion he suggests, but rather pursue a small set of fundamental needs on an as-required basis.

There's no better illustration of the simultaneous pursuit of basic needs than the image below of a young rhesus macaque acrobatically clinging to its soft and warm "cloth mother" while feeding from the cold steel of its "wire mother." This image comes from Harry Harlow's famous research on the importance of love. Harlow found that young rhesus monkeys raised with a "wire mother" that provided food, but no physical sense of love or connection, didn't grow up to live happily ever after but rather withered away and died young. You can hear Harlow's contempt for the psychological theories of the time in his summary of his own work: "It takes more than a baby and a box to make a normal monkey."[15] It certainly takes more than a baby and a box to raise a normal human being, as Harlow's contemporary John Bowlby observed. His study of perfectly well-fed orphans who were nevertheless wasting away in cribs untouched and alone during World War II found that many were "gravely damaged for life."[16]

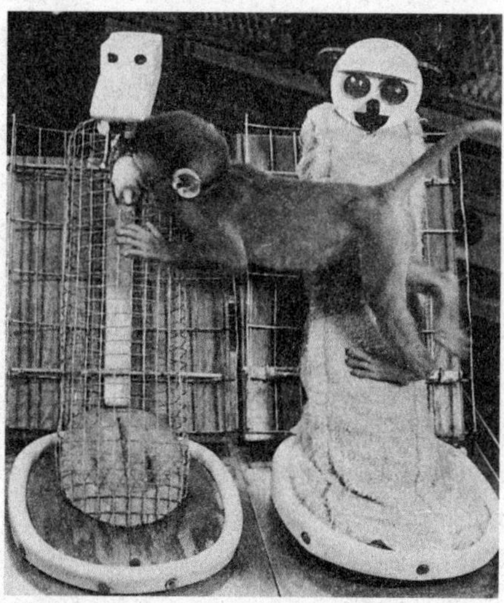

Harlow Primate Laboratory, University of Wisconsin—Madison

Our social needs don't end after infancy. You can feel their fundamental importance in the voice of a financially stable but desperately lonely woman quarantining alone after a divorce at the start of the COVID-19 pandemic: "I had a home, money, an isolated location to quarantine—I was safe by every measure. But my partner, who promised to protect me and our children, had disappeared overnight. [My friends] wept with me on the phone, but I woke up every day facing the fear and pain on my own. I decided not to drink, . . . but I also found it hard to eat. Within weeks I had shed 20 pounds."[17] Desperately wanting to connect can keep you from having much interest in eating.[18]

You can also see the importance of social needs in our neural architecture, where the drive to connect with others relies on the same reward structures as the drive to eat, sleep, or have sex. Your brain's signal for craving friends is the same as its signal for craving food.[19] What's more, the system that governs your drive to connect is the same system targeted by highly addictive drugs like heroin, cocaine, and fentanyl. It's often said that love is a drug, but that's just a metaphor. The literal truth is that some drugs are addictive because they make you feel like being loved.

You can even count the importance of social needs by tallying up the successes of hundreds of men who participated in the Study of Adult Development, a longitudinal study that followed hundreds of Harvard sophomores for their entire lives starting in 1938. The goal was to identify the traits that would create good leaders. The researchers who created this study had not even considered that relationships might be important for much of anything, and included these social variables only as an afterthought. The social variables, however, ended up being the strongest predictors of flourishing throughout life, more important than income, occupational success, and both physical and mental health. George Vaillant, the researcher in charge of the study for more than forty years, summarized its primary findings quite simply: "The only thing that really matters in life are your relationships with other people."[20]

Social Brains

Human connection may be a core need, but that doesn't mean it's easy to satisfy. People are complicated. They are wonderful sources of support in some moments but sources of intense pain in others. Managing relationships is a complicated coordination game requiring us to stay attuned to the thoughts, feelings, and beliefs of everyone from family members and friends to acquaintances and strangers. As the comedian Jim Gaffigan joked in a way that every parent can appreciate, "Other people's children's birthday parties are the most joyful events you will ever resent having to attend."[21] Keeping track of whom to trust, whom to cooperate with, who said what, who knows what, who did what, is all—to put it mildly—extremely complicated.

Our brains reflect this complexity. In fact, the human brain stands out in the animal kingdom for its relatively gigantic neocortex, the fat part of your brain just above your eyes right where the band of your hat would sit. These additional neurons are very costly, lengthening pregnancy and dependency in development. This additional brainpower gives us sophisticated social thinking, which is one attribute—possibly *the* attribute—that sets us apart from our nearest primate relatives. In one especially ambitious experiment, researchers compared the intellectual performance of 105 human toddlers with that of 106 adult chimpanzees and 32 adult orangutans on what amounts to two different IQ tests.[22] One was a physical IQ test that involved reasoning about objects, such as being able to keep track of where a reward is located in a shell game. The other was a social IQ test that involved reasoning about other minds, such as tracking another's gaze to monitor what they're thinking, or learning by watching someone complete a task. The results were clear. When it came to reasoning about physical objects, the human toddlers were neck and neck with the chimpanzees and orangutans, getting around 70 percent of the questions right. But when it came to social intelligence, the human toddlers crushed the primate competition, getting around 80 percent of the social IQ questions right compared with only around 40 percent for the chimps and orangutans. If you reach for a glass of water in front of a human toddler and miss it, the child is capable of reading your mind to know that you *wanted* a glass of water, and can even hand it to you if you don't pick it up yourself. You can miss a glass of water in front of a chimpanzee all day long, and they will do almost nothing.

Homo sapiens means "wise hominin," but this translation doesn't tell us what human beings are uniquely wise about. We're uniquely wise about other people.

Social Senses

If something is valuable, then you monitor it closely and maybe even put an alarm on it, like a security camera in your home or an antitheft alarm in your car. Social relationships are essential to our health and happiness, and they come with an alarm system as well. In fact, I bet you can trigger your social alarm system using only your imagination. Let's try it.

Imagine yourself back in high school for a moment. The person you've always had a crush on pulls you aside and asks, "Would you go to the dance with me on Friday?" Makes you feel good about yourself, doesn't it? Now imagine the role reversed with you finally getting up the courage to ask your high school crush to go to the dance and they say, "Nah, I'd rather not." Feels awful even to just imagine it, doesn't it? I'm with you. I remember finally working up my courage in high school to ask a girl I had a crush on for years out on a date, only to be turned down because—and I quote from memory—"I have to get my hair cut that night." *Ouch.* I've been happily married for twenty-nine years as I write this sentence and recalling that moment *still* hurts.

Our extreme sensitivity to acceptance and rejection has led psychologists to argue that our deepest sense of ourselves—our self-esteem—is actually our social alarm system monitoring how our relationships are going. Like a fuel gauge in your car monitoring how much gas you have, self-esteem is a *sociometer* in our brains that keeps track of what others think of us.[23] If self-esteem really operates this way, then it should spike when we get signals that other people are thinking well of us, and plummet when we get signals that others are thinking poorly of us. This explains why getting positive feedback like gratitude and compliments feels so good, and why getting criticized or insulted feels so bad. It also explains why public speaking so routinely takes the No. 1 spot on our Greatest Fears List: Our public behavior is judged by others, and could be judged negatively, and hence rings the alarm bells on our sociometer.[24]

The deeply social nature of our self-esteem isn't a new phenomenon. In 1902, the sociologist Charles Cooley suggested that we "live in the minds of others," with a "looking-glass self" that is largely a reflection of how we think others see us.[25] Similarly, Morris Rosenberg, the sociologist who in 1986 published the most widely used measure of self-esteem in existence, considered self-esteem a "barometric self-concept" that would rise and fall in response to our sense of how others evaluate us. "At any given instant," Rosenberg wrote in the 1980s, "a person's self-respect may be high, but in the following moment an unkind word, a gentle frown, or a slight setback may cause it to plunge sharply."[26]

The purpose of our sociometer—our self-esteem—is to steer us into situations that keep us positively connected to others, and away from situations that leave us disconnected or rejected.[27] This doesn't mean that our sociometer functions with perfect accuracy. Far from it, in fact, because our beliefs about what others think of us are prone to such a wide variety of mistakes and false alarms that I'll spend the rest of this book explaining how they can harm our well-being.

For now, though, what's important to remember is that our highly social brains carefully monitor how we think we're appearing in the minds of others precisely because those connections are so important to us.

Social Happiness

Okay, but how important is *so* important? To put the importance of relationships in perspective, let's do some comparisons about what actually brings happiness and what does not.

In 2010, two eventual Nobel Prize winners, Daniel Kahneman and Angus Deaton, published a newsworthy analysis addressing an age-old question: Can money buy happiness? To find out, they analyzed responses from roughly 450,000 Americans to a well-being survey conducted daily in 2008 and 2009 by Gallup.[28] Some questions asked people to report how happy they were *in* their life by asking whether they felt certain emotions the previous day (or not), including positive emotions (happiness, smiling, enjoyment), negative emotions (worry, sadness), and stress (yes or no). Another question asked people to indicate how happy they were *with* their life on a ladder that ranged from 0 (the worst possible life for you) to 10 (the best possible life for you). Along the way, this survey also asked people to report how much money they made each month.

So, does making more money make people happier both in their life and with their life? The answer is obvious to anyone who has ever been poor: Of course it does! Those who made more money also reported more well-being on every measure compared with those who made less money. There are, though, three caveats. First, each additional dollar brings a little less happiness (the biggest effects of income on well-being come from getting out of poverty).[29] Second, the precise impact of income on well-being depends on what you're measuring (it's smaller for momentary mood than overall life evaluation). Third, the effects of income on well-being are actually not as big as you might imagine. For instance, roughly 90 percent of people making around $160,000 reported feeling positive emotions, but roughly 80 percent of those making only $20,000 reported feeling positive emotions, too. That 10 percent matters, but it's also not massive. Roughly 60 percent of people making around $160,000 per year reported not feeling stress the day before, but 55 percent making $20,000 or less also reported not feeling stress. Money eases misery, without question, but as you've probably heard a thousand times, there's much more to happiness than money. How much more, exactly?

To find out, Kahneman and Deaton compared the effect of money against the wide range of other things that were also measured, such as whether you have a college degree or not, whether religion is important to you or not, whether you have health insurance or not, and whether you were answering the survey on a weekend or a weekday.

The short story is that being above versus below the median income had a fairly small, but positive, effect on every measure of well-being, as did most of the other variables measured in ways that you can probably guess.[30] What stood out, though, was social isolation: whether someone reported spending the day alone or not. The difference in positive mood reported between those who spent the previous day alone versus with others was more than *seven times larger* than a fourfold increase in your income. Opine as we will about the value of occasional solitude, these results indicate that spending a day completely alone is a bummer, on par with the pain of spending a day with a headache.[31] For Kahneman, the conclusion was clear: "Emotional happiness is primarily social. The very best thing that can happen to people is to spend time with other people they like. We find loneliness is a terrible thing. So is extreme poverty. But loneliness, regardless of how rich you are, is a very bad thing."[32]

Indeed, in the first study comparing the happiest people in surveys with the least happy, social relationships stood out like a beacon.[33] "The very happy group," wrote the psychologists Ed Diener and Martin Seligman, "differed substantially from the average and the very unhappy groups in their fulsome and satisfying interpersonal lives," meaning they had better friendships, they had stronger romantic relationships, and they spent more time with others but less time alone. No other variables they measured—including personality, religiosity, finances, physical attractiveness, use of tobacco and alcohol, objective numbers of positive and negative events, time spent in other activities (such as sleeping, watching TV, or exercising)—predicted happiness as well as social relationships.[34] Having positive social relationships won't ensure your membership in the Happiest People Club, but having bad relationships will keep you out of it.

You can even see the importance of social connection over the course of any given day. The things that tend to make us feel best are positive things we do with other people. One study, for instance, asked just under one thousand working women to write down everything they did the previous workday, from the moment they woke up to the moment they fell sleep, and indicate how positive and negative each activity made them feel. The results are in the figure below. Toward the top of the list were social activities that generally connect you in positive ways with other people, with "intimate relations" (how scientists write about sex) being the most consistently positive thing someone might do on a workday. If we treat sex as the most positive experience on any given day (perhaps especially on a workday), then we can calculate the ratio of positive to negative feelings that each of these other events gives us by comparison, which is shown above the bars in the figure below.[35] Coming in a close second, however, is socializing, clocking in at about 85 percent as positive as sex. As you move to the right side of the figure showing less positive experiences, you also see fewer social experiences, with working and commuting bringing you only 54 percent of the positive feelings that you get from "intimate relations."

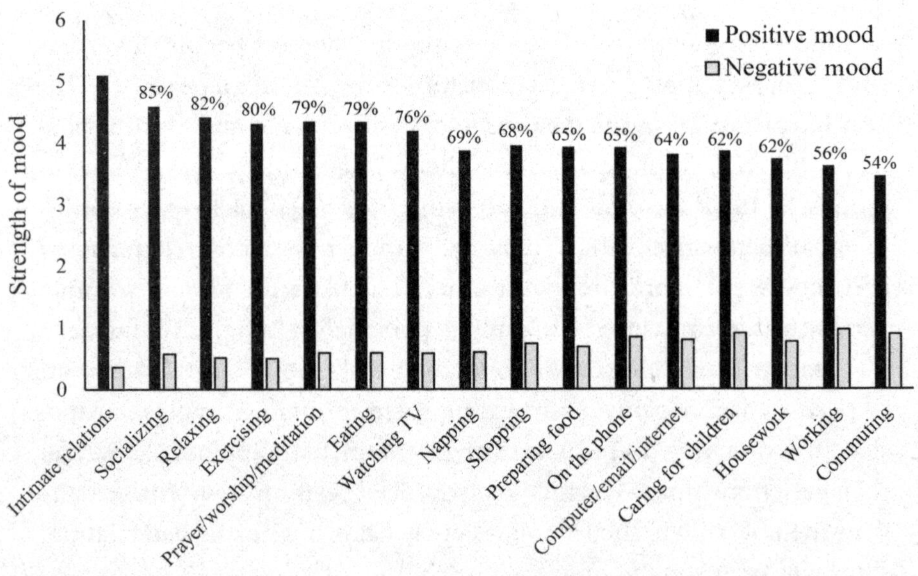

This figure shows the amount of positive and negative mood reported for each category of activities. The ratio of positive to negative mood from each activity compared with "intimate relations"—the most positive overall experience people reported over the course of their day—is shown in the percentages above each category. Re-created from Kahneman et al. (2004).

A closer look at this figure also reveals one activity that seems a little out of place in a "more social is more positive" pattern: caring for children. There it is, just a tiny bit worse than emailing but on par with housework.

Wait. Really? Aren't children the one thing that parents love most, the apple of our eye and all?

Yes, of course. One's children are among the few things most people would reflexively risk their lives to save. But if you've ever taken care of kids, whether your own or others', then you also know that it's not all snuggles and snack cakes. Jen and I have five children, meaning I can speak with some conviction about this. The most joyful experiences I've ever had have come from time with my kids. My heart still races when I remember the time our son Habtamu hooked a corner kick in a *Bend It Like Beckham*–style goal while playing eighth-grade soccer, or the overwhelming moment when our daughter Tsion rang the bell at Lurie Children's Hospital in Chicago to signal the successful end of her cancer treatment. But then the most difficult experiences I've ever had have also come from time with our children. Children aren't a stable high for our emotional lives; they're a world-class roller-coaster ride.

The "taking care of children" row highlights the obvious fact that simply being with other people isn't necessarily wonderful. It's what you're doing with other people that really matters. Social experiences are best when goals are aligned, fun is had, relationships are strengthened, and connections are formed. This is also why friends consistently emerge in surveys as the people we like being with the most. It's not that friends are necessarily the best people to be with, but rather that what we do most often with friends—socializing, playing, connecting—are more positive experiences than what we usually do with work colleagues, strangers, or even our spouses. When one group of researchers factored out the specific activity, essentially examining how positive people felt doing the same activity with different people, they actually found that time spent with children was the most positive and meaningful.[36] If all parents had to do were fun things with their kids, as we tend to do with friends, then parenthood would be uniformly delightful. It would also be called Being a Grandparent.

"Be a grandparent" is hardly welcome advice for anyone wanting to have a better day anytime soon, but understanding the importance of positive social connections for our well-being suggests a more timely method: Do the things that connect you in positive ways to others. Being kind to someone, connecting with a stranger in conversation, acting friendlier when you're around others, passing along a compliment, expressing gratitude when you feel it, reflecting on your appreciation for others, and even just saying hello to a barista or bus driver are all activities that scientists find reliably increase our happiness.[37] These social activities tend to make you feel good because they boost your sociometer by increasing your social value in the eyes of others.

These social activities also run against common "self-care" advice that encourages people to live a better life by turning inward, focusing more on "me time" and satisfying our own desires and needs. Our inherent sociality, however, suggests that a better way to make yourself feel better is to turn outward and try to make someone else feel better instead. One groundbreaking experiment tested these two approaches directly by recruiting people on a college campus, asking them how they felt, and then handing them an envelope containing either $5 or $20 and instructing them to spend it either on themselves or on another person. Any cynic would readily predict that those who spent money on themselves would be happier, but in this case the idealist would be more accurate. Those instructed to spend their money on other people—such as buying someone a coffee or lunch—felt significantly more positive after their spending spree than before, whereas those who spent on themselves felt a little less positive (regardless of whether they were spending $5 or $20).[38] Additional research replicating these results in cultures ranging from farmers in South Africa to Pacific Islanders on Vanuatu has made it clear that spending money on others, compared with spending on yourself, feels especially good in just the ways you might expect would crank up your sociometer: when you feel more connected to the person you're helping, when it feels as if you've freely chosen to act friendly rather than being forced or required to do it, and when you can see the positive impact of your social act on the other person.[39] To paraphrase the authors of this research, if money's not bringing you happiness, maybe you're not spending it right.[40]

Social Health

Governments the world over have been running public service campaigns for decades encouraging us to exercise more, eat better, and smoke never, but the research I've covered so far suggests that if governments really wanted us living better lives, they'd encourage us to be nicer to each other, too. In fact, some of the most eye-opening research I've ever come across suggests that strengthening your social relationships might have as big an effect on your physical health as the standard public service targets, if not an even bigger one. The first of these analyses, published in 1988, found that being isolated from others (versus connected) was as big a risk factor for poor health and even death as smoking a pack of cigarettes a day or not exercising.[41] Over time the pattern has become even clearer: Negative relationships or being disconnected is actually a bigger risk factor for death—sometimes much bigger—than risks such as smoking or being obese.[42]

Being alone and feeling alone are potentially deadly, but those causes never appear on someone's death certificate.[43] Instead, social disconnection is a distant killer, increasing more immediate risks of death rather than killing you directly. Being alone means there's nobody there to help you in the times you really need it, and nobody there to encourage you to take better care of yourself.[44] In Chicago, a major heat wave in 1995 pushed the heat index to a staggering 126 degrees Fahrenheit, buckled roads, melted the electrical grid, cutting power for at least forty-nine thousand households, and officially killed 465 people (although the actual number is probably closer to 739, the number of deaths above the norm for that week). In his book *Heat Wave: A Social Autopsy of Disaster in Chicago,* the sociologist Eric Klinenberg revealed that this heat wave overwhelmingly killed people living alone, especially poor elderly Black men who had nobody around to help them when their apartments became ovens.[45] Forty-one people died so completely alone that their bodies were never claimed. Every single one of those souls lost their lives precisely because they were alone, but not one had "alone" on their death certificate.

Feeling alone is an even more invisible killer than being alone because it gradually nudges people toward "deaths of despair" like suicide or drug and alcohol use, or slowly compromises our health until we are eventually weakened enough that we succumb to some other malady. That painful feeling that comes with loneliness is your body's way of pushing you to reconnect with other people, but it's also a physiological stressor that can diminish almost every aspect of your health. As the Yale psychologist Laurie Santos put it in one podcast, if loneliness had a health warning the way cigarettes do, it would sound like this: "May cause increased inflammation, disrupted sleep, abnormal immune responses, depression, anxiety, higher stress levels, early cognitive decline, alcoholism, cardiovascular disease, stroke, Alzheimer's, diabetes, suicide, and even early death."[46]

Having positive social support, in contrast, can reduce stress and strengthen your immune system. In one experiment you'll be happy not to have been part of, volunteers were injected with the cold virus just before spending the weekend isolated in a hotel room. These injected volunteers were less able to fight off the infection if they felt as though they had little social support, and also if they spent relatively little time in loving physical contact—hugging or holding hands—with another person in the two weeks before the study began.[47] Getting the cold shoulder from other people may make it more likely that you'll actually catch a cold.

And although no coroner will ever indicate that someone died of a lonely heart, a lonely heart is indeed a broken heart, subject to a level of stress that the heart of someone who is well connected is not. Those who report feeling lonely sleep less, have higher blood pressure, and are more likely to suffer from chronic heart disease that leads to heart attacks and strokes.[48] One study that tested an intervention to combat these cardiovascular risks found that asking older adults to spend money on others (versus on themselves) was just as effective in reducing blood pressure as the medicine they were taking for it.[49] Being well connected with others isn't just a good feeling; it's also good medicine.

Aristotle recognized centuries ago that social connection was so essential to our existence that he considered friendship a moral virtue. "For without friends," he argued, "no one would choose to live, though he had all other goods."[50] Have we really needed countless experiments, brain scans, and death records to confirm what was so obvious to Aristotle? Isn't the importance of other people for our well-being obvious?

In some ways, it is. "Invest in your social relationships, it will be a form of happiness," points out Daniel Gilbert, a psychologist at Harvard University and one of the world's leading happiness researchers. "There is utterly no secret to the kind of things that make people happy, but if you list them for people, they go, 'Yeah, that kind of sounds like what my rabbi, grandmother, my philosopher have said all along. What's the secret?' The answer is there is no secret. They were right."[51] To some psychologists, discovering that the secret to happiness isn't really a secret is a little deflating. Reflecting on the obvious implications of his own research, Daniel Kahneman said, "I'd feel embarrassed to give that as advice—'improve your relationships.' But obviously if people are going to get happier, it's going to come to that."[52]

Unfortunately, social connection can be the kind of thing you know is critical at one moment but then forget as you're going through the daily grind of life. If social connection is so obviously important for our well-being, then why do so many of us buy homes out in the suburbs that trap us alone? Why do so many families now sit around the dinner table staring at their phones rather than connecting with each other? And why, at the end of the classic film *It's a Wonderful Life,* does the guardian angel, Clarence, need to remind George Bailey, "Remember no man is a failure who has friends"?

Because, as the research I'll describe to you in the next chapter shows, what really matters isn't if we can nod our heads dutifully when our grandparents tell us that relationships are all that matters in life, but rather if those thoughts occur to us when we're actually choosing whether to reach out and engage with others or to hold back and avoid social interactions. All too often, that wisdom about the value of social relationships doesn't influence the actual choices we make. All too often, we mistakenly choose to make ourselves unhappily alone.

2

The Choice

> We make ourselves a place apart
> Behind light words that tease and flout,
> But oh, the agitated heart
> Till someone really finds us out.
>
> —ROBERT FROST, "Revelation"

You make *the choice* so easily and routinely that it almost becomes invisible. You stop at a crosswalk and smile, saying hello to the person walking by. You're at lunch with an acquaintance and bring up something deep and meaningful, like their hopes for the future. You have a kind thought come to your mind about someone, and you decide to share it as a compliment without hesitation. You have an ongoing problem with someone you love that's eating away at you and decide to have the open and honest conversation right now. Or, you make *the choice* differently. You ignore the person next to you, stick to small talk, keep your compliment to yourself, or put off the hard conversation with someone you love.

The precise details behind each instance of *the choice* vary, but its basic features are simple: Do you choose to approach another person and connect in some well-intended way, or do you choose to avoid the interaction and stay more disconnected? Do you, in the words of Robert Frost, choose to reach out so that someone really finds you out, or do you hold back and make yourself a place apart?

Jessica Pan, a science journalist living in London, was definitely a person who chose to make herself a place apart. As she describes in her book, *Sorry I'm Late, I Didn't Want to Come: One Introvert's Year of Saying Yes*,[1] Jessica once burst into tears of horror after walking into a surprise birthday party, and for years afterward would wake up on the morning of her birthday and half-jokingly whisper to her husband, "If you throw me a party, I will murder you." Watching masses of revelers at musical festivals on TV makes some people feel bad about missing out, but it made Jessica feel relieved. When given opportunities to connect with others, especially strangers, Jessica chose to do what "any shy introvert worth their salt has invariably done . . . throw the ringing phone across the room, faked being sick, walked into a networking event and immediately backed out, and pretended not to speak English when approached in a bar."

Jessica's habit-forming history of choosing avoidance explains why her voice carried the distinct tremor of panic when she called me one day to ask for advice. She was about to embark on a yearlong experiment of living as an extrovert and was in need of some reassurance that she wasn't going to ruin her life. Jessica had read about our research but thought that the concept of talking to a stranger on a train sounded "insane." She was not the type of person, she thought, who would enjoy talking to random people. Instead, she dreaded and therefore chose to avoid most interactions. Nevertheless, for the sake of a journalistic experiment, Jessica had decided to try spending a year seeing what would happen if she made *the choice* differently. At one point this plan had sounded like a good idea to Jessica. Now it sounded like a terrible mistake.

For most of her life, Jessica didn't second-guess how she made *the choice*. Then she hit a bad year. Jessica lost her job and felt stalled in her career, and had her best friend move away. Stable pillars of her life were crumbling. Jessica had written articles about the importance of social connection for happiness and health. She knew all the data we've covered so far. She also knew that her life could be different because she had seen it in her husband, who is "of a different breed," with no anxiety around other people. Jessica had also seen a different life through her father, who chooses to talk to anyone at any time about anything ("He has no filter," she told me). She wondered what would happen if she started acting a bit more like them, approaching more and avoiding less. "Would it offer up a world of life-changing experiences?" she mused, or wind up leaving her "in the woods, eating weeds and only communing with wolves until she died of malnutrition, alone but kind of happy that she never had to engage in small talk about Bitcoin ever again"?

Those fears were now front and center in Jessica's mind while she was on the phone with me, seeking some reassurance that she wouldn't be rejected a dozen times a day, that she would figure out how to carry on a conversation once she chose to start one, and that she didn't have to get stuck in inane small talk with strangers. Pacing the room while holding my cell phone, I felt like a therapist for the first time in my life.

Jessica was pessimistic about how her year of choosing differently would turn out, but I was optimistic. I thought the fears that were holding her back were *overly* pessimistic, and that she would come to feel both more optimistic and more empowered once she started testing her fears. Jessica's desire to be more sociable, coupled with doubts about how her interactions would turn out, highlights how social connection is a choice governed by two potentially competing psychological forces. These forces essentially create two voices in our heads, one encouraging us to reach out and approach other people and another encouraging us to hold back and avoid them. Understanding how these forces operate also gives us insight into how the voice holding us back can sometimes speak too loudly, keeping us from being social enough for our own good.

The source of my optimism came from watching the field of psychology go through the same debate about how to make *the choice* using experiments that Jessica was going through in her own mind, yielding results that surprised even the researchers themselves. To see the foundations of this scientific debate, we can go further back to the mid-1800s, with two notes, each neatly divided into two columns.

Darwin's Choice

After returning from his trip to the Galápagos, Charles Darwin wasn't just pondering the origins of our species. He was also pondering one particularly important instantiation of *the choice:* whether or not to reach out and ask his cousin Emma Wedgwood to marry him. Like Jessica, Darwin was hearing the competing voices of approach and avoidance in his head as he figured out his future. Thankfully for us, Darwin took this choice seriously enough to write his thinking down, giving us a window into the details of human decision making. He did not, however, seem to take his deliberations so seriously that he expected psychologists would be dissecting them nearly two centuries later: The first of his two notes was scribbled on the back of a letter from a friend.[2]

Darwin divided his first note on April 7, 1838, into two columns, one titled "if *not* marry," and the other titled "if marry." Darwin's initial thoughts made the "not" ledger seem considerably more appealing: travel to Europe and North America, take summer vacations, "study affinities." His thoughts in the "marry" column, in contrast, were downright dreary: needing to work for more money, no travel, no summer tours but instead trapped "in London like a prisoner," and "no books" due to the increased expenses he expected from being married. At this point, avoidance was winning out. Darwin seemed destined to live as a bachelor.

A couple of months later, Darwin's mind had shifted. "This is the Question," he circled at the top of his second note, with the approach and avoidance columns again added beneath it. This time, "marry" seemed to be in the lead: "Children-(if it Please God)—Constant companion, (& friend in old age) who will feel interested in one." The challenges of constant work had also dawned on Darwin: "God, it is intolerable to think of spending one's whole life, like a neuter bee, working, working, and nothing after all.—No, no won't do." Although "not marry" continued to have its charms—"Freedom to go where one liked . . . Conversation of clever men at clubs—Not forced to visit relatives"—Darwin had made up his mind. "Marry-Marry-Marry Q.E.D.," he wrote to signify the end of his deliberations before moving to the next obvious question: "When? Soon or Late?"

Fairly soon, it turned out. Darwin proposed on November 11, 1838, on what he called "The Day of Days!" She accepted. He was elated. The couple remained together until Darwin's death nearly forty-three years later, raising ten children over the course of their marriage. Emma was at Darwin's bedside to hear his last words: "I am not the least afraid to die."[3] The outcome of Darwin's conflicted choice seemed good for all involved.

The particular details of Darwin's thinking are interesting, but the thought processes underlying those details are what matter for our purposes. Within Darwin's two columns, we can see three essential features of all social decisions. First, there is a struggle between the two basic goals that guide any decision: the pursuit of positive outcomes and the avoidance of negative ones. Second, these motivations are not fixed but fluctuating. The forces of approach and avoidance can play tug-of-war in your mind from one moment to the next, or from one context to another. Finally, *the choice* is guided not by how a decision will actually make you feel but rather by how you *think* a decision will make you feel. Darwin's marriage proposal could not be based on his actual experience of being married to Emma, because his experience was in the future. His proposal could only be based on his belief about what the future would be like if they married. Choosing to propose did not mean that Darwin *knew* they would both be happy in marriage, only that he *expected* they'd be happy. When I was talking with Jessica Pan, she was experiencing the same thought processes. Her fears of choosing to live a more outgoing life were based not on actually being more outgoing but rather on her expectations about what being more outgoing would be like.

This last observation might seem obvious, but it's easy to forget when we're actually making a choice and our expectations are so clear that they feel like a fact rather than a bet. However, that our choices are bets on the future helps to explain why different people make different bets, and why our bets can vary from one moment to the next or from one context to another. Psychologists have learned that the two forces governing our motivations to approach and to avoid—known technically as BAS (the behavioral approach system) and BIS (the behavioral inhibition system)—are largely independent systems in our brains. These systems are like an old married couple who constantly work together, often with considerable bickering. If the factors that guide these two voices in our minds are well aligned with reality, then we weigh the odds correctly in an educated bet and make our social decisions wisely. But if they are misaligned, as research I'll cover in this chapter suggests they can be, then one force can affect our decisions more than it should and lead us into making predictable mistakes.

Two Masters

You don't have to be contemplating marriage to appreciate how some choices can feel like a mental tug-of-war. When you get home Friday night after a long week of work and are deciding whether to head out to a party to meet some new people or stay home and watch TV by yourself, you might feel as if you are of two minds. One mind is focused on how pleasurable it might be to get together with some new people, while your other mind is thinking how painful it will be to start up a bunch of awkward conversations. One mind is pushing you to go out and connect, while the other is encouraging you to sit down on the couch and keep to yourself.

Of course, you only have one brain, so you can't literally be of two minds, but the feeling of conflict does reveal a deep truth about how our brains work: The parts assessing the benefits of taking some action are largely distinct from the parts assessing the costs. Each system can provide its own unique input, with the approach system indexing the degree of pleasure or likelihood of positive outcomes and the avoidance system indexing the degree of pain or negative outcomes, just as in Darwin's two columns. Your approach system encourages you to head out to meet some new friends because you've almost always enjoyed doing so in the past. Your avoidance system, in contrast, reminds you that you can't be sure how interesting *this* party will be and watching TV instead would surely be easy so it's probably best to stay home by yourself. Jeremy Bentham even used the imperial sensibilities of late eighteenth-century Britain to humanize these two forces: "Nature has placed mankind under the governance of two sovereign masters, pain and pleasure. . . . They govern us in all we do, in all we say, in all we think."[4]

The key insight is that these "two masters" do not have to agree on *the choice*. Sometimes they see eye to eye and your decision will be obvious: all benefit and no cost, or no benefit and all cost. In these cases, you won't feel any conflict at all. At other times, though, these two masters might be telling us very different things. One is telling you to go ahead and reach out, while the other is telling you to hold back and avoid an interaction. In these cases, you're in the midst of an approach/avoidance conflict.

These two systems govern almost every aspect of how we evaluate our social lives, including what we notice and attend to, how we interpret what we're attending to, how we remember the past, and even how we evaluate ourselves.[5] When we're approach oriented, people seem safer. We tend to notice more opportunities to reach out and connect, evaluate them more positively, remember past social events more positively, and feel more optimistic about our chances of making new friends and maintaining our current relationships. When we're more avoidance oriented, in contrast, people seem scarier. We tend to notice reasons to be afraid of them, remember our past social interactions being more negative, and are more pessimistic about our ability to make future friends or keep our current ones.

It's hard to overstate the importance of these two forces in our lives. A common view among psychologists, in fact, is that all human behavior can be reduced to the resolution of approach and avoidance forces.[6] It's easy to see why. What more fundamental process is there? Every living organism on the planet has some capacity to approach seemingly pleasurable stimuli and avoid punishing ones, from the most minuscule single-celled bacteria to the most massive gazillion-celled blue whales. Survival is all but impossible without it.

Uncertain Masters

This all sounds simple, as if wisdom were no more complicated than ninth-grade algebra. Deciding whether to go on a second date, attend a party, talk to a stranger? Just sit down and take Darwin's strategy to the next level: Consider the pros, consider the cons, identify the importance of each pro and con as well as its likelihood, and then crunch the numbers to see the option with the best expected outcome. Easy does it.

Until, of course, you actually try to do it. Two fundamental challenges make it hard to get *the choice* exactly right. The first challenge: It's not obvious what the numbers should be. Set aside something as difficult as Darwin's marriage proposal or Jessica's decision to live a year as an extrovert and focus on simpler social decisions. Do you really know how a conversation with an old friend you haven't talked to in a while is going to go, or how your partner will respond to an apology, or how a stranger will react if you give them a compliment? Even seemingly simple social interactions are enormously complicated and therefore hard to anticipate perfectly. We even waffle on these calculations from one moment to the next, seeing benefits of engaging in one moment and then deciding it's probably not worth it in another. Adding even more complexity, the assessment we make when a social interaction is far off isn't necessarily the same as when *the choice* is *right now*.

The second challenge: Different people seem to have different opinions about what the numbers should be. The thought of having a deep and meaningful conversation with an acquaintance, for instance, might seem like an exciting opportunity to make a new friend to some people, but as a dreadful opportunity to have an awkward conversation to others. And how do we factor in the more extreme possibilities, like the rare but real possibility that a stranger we'd try to talk with would steal from us, or sexually assault us, or physically harm us? This isn't a math problem; this is a debate.

Where do these differences between us come from? One obvious answer is that different people like and enjoy different things so that our approach and avoidance tendencies are guiding us in the direction that's exactly right for each of us. Those who choose to be more outgoing are happier engaging with other people, while those of us who are more reserved are happier keeping to ourselves. However, recognizing that our social choices are guided not by how our interactions actually turn out but rather how we *think* they'll turn out raises a different possibility. It could be that we're making different choices because of what we *think* we'll enjoy rather than what we *actually* enjoy. Had Jessica Pan's self-reported personality as a shy introvert—a "shintrovert," as she called herself—come from actually being happier by being more avoidant, or from an overly active avoidance system that had routinely led her to think she'd be happier by being more avoidant?

Let's take on these two challenges one at a time.

Approach and Avoidance Moments

In five minutes and thirty-two seconds, Amanda Gorman went from being famous in poetry circles to being famous in almost every circle. Her mesmerizing performance of her poem "The Hill We Climb" at Joe Biden's 2021 presidential inauguration was a worldwide sensation that—by her own account—almost didn't happen. Although she was initially thrilled at the thought of performing, the voice in her head encouraging her to avoid it got louder and louder as she got closer to actually making *the choice:* Do I agree to give this presentation or not? "The truth is I almost declined to be the inaugural poet," she wrote. "Why? I was terrified."[7]

Surely being asked to deliver your poem at a presidential inauguration has to be among the highest honors any poet could receive, and Amanda was the youngest person ever asked. Gorman's approach system should have been firing all its neurons simultaneously, and it was, at first. But then, like a sleeping grizzly bear getting poked in the eye, her avoidance system woke up and roared as the actual time to make the decision neared. Now her excitement at the thought of reading the poem was fighting with her emerging panic about actually doing it. She wasn't worried about her ability. She knew she could deliver her poem. Her fears were distinctly social. How would people react? "I had insomnia and nightmares, barely ate or drank for days," she wrote, even writing to close friends and family that she was "most likely going to pull out of the ceremony." Time slowed as anxiety built before she had to make *the choice.* "The night before I was to give the Inaugural Committee my final decision felt like the longest of my life," she wrote.

Gorman is an extraordinary talent with a perfectly ordinary mental conflict. In general, the closer you get to some decision or event, the stronger *both* approach and avoidance motivations can become. When you're trying to achieve a goal where your approach motivations are dominant and reasons to avoid are weak or nonexistent, then you work harder the closer you are to achieving that goal. The "first step is the hardest" whenever you're trying to change something, whether it's to exercise more, eat less, or connect with others more often, at least partly because you become more motivated when you're just about to achieve a goal.[8]

In conflicts like Gorman's, with strong approach and avoidance motivations arising simultaneously, the dynamics get more interesting. At a distance, your approach system is in charge, highlighting benefits, likely successes, and reasons to be optimistic. But when the decision or moment is imminent, your avoidance system gets stronger, drawing your attention to reasons to be pessimistic. These dynamics help to explain why we sometimes "chicken out" or "get cold feet" at the last second.

You can see this pattern clearly in one experiment in which university students were asked to guess how well they'd do on a series of cognitive ability tests either later in the semester or in a few minutes from *right now*.[9] When the test was to be taken some time later, confidence was high. These students thought they would score in the 68th percentile, on average, a figure that is impossibly above average. But students about to take the test *right now* were considerably less confident, predicting that they would score in the 51st percentile (on average). The reason for this gap became clear when the students explained their estimates. Those who imagined taking the test some time later were more likely to describe reasons they would succeed and less likely to mention reasons they might fail, compared to those who were about to take the test *right* now.

Jessica Pan told me she went through the same time course of approach followed by avoidance before almost every social interaction she had, whether talking to a stranger on a train or in a coffee shop, or hosting a dinner party for friends and acquaintances. At a distance, the calm, cool, and collected voice of her approach system told her that everything would be fine, but then just when she needed to make *the choice* to open her mouth to say hello, the avoidance system would start screaming to keep to herself. "I hated doing it," she said, speaking about her attempt to be a little more social. More specifically, "I hated the moment right before doing it. That moment was really, really scary for me."[10] Those fears right at the moment when we need to reach out are exactly what would keep us from doing the things that we know at other times would be good for us.

Fortunately for Amanda Gorman, she overcame her fears at the moment she needed to and agreed to speak. When the time came to walk to the podium, fully committed and unable to back out, her approach system was fully in charge: "As I stepped up to the podium to recite, I felt warm, as if the words waiting in my mouth were aflame. . . . I haven't looked back."

Approach and Avoidance People

The two masters of approach and avoidance not only create conflicts that can vary from one moment to the next in our own minds but also create what seem like approach and avoidance debates between different people. Some people are at-ease approachers: outgoing, talkative, and up for anything. You know the type: first on the dance floor, talks to everyone, and is assertive enough to lead fish out of water. Others are more socially anxious avoiders, as Jessica Pan was. These people would choose to be almost anywhere other than a dance floor, would generally stay quiet except around family and friends, and are generally more inclined to let others take the lead in social settings.[11]

If these two tendencies sound like other personality traits you've heard of with different names, then you're exactly right. The two independent systems of approach and avoidance were initially suggested as the biological mechanisms underlying the personality traits of extroversion and neuroticism, which are two of the five traits that psychologists over the last century have identified as stable and consistent enough to look like routine habits, or personality traits. People higher in extroversion tend to think of themselves as more outgoing, sociable, talkative, assertive, and energetic, while those on the opposite end of this spectrum are introverted and generally think of themselves as more shy, reserved, and calm. As you can surely guess based on this description, those higher in extroversion are also consistently more approach oriented, especially toward other people, while people lower in extroversion—that is, introverts—are less approach oriented.

In contrast, people higher in neuroticism—sometimes referred to now as negative emotionality—tend to report feeling more stressed, nervous, worried, and afraid, whereas those on the opposite end are more calm and at ease. The tendencies associated with higher levels of neuroticism are all avoidance oriented, whereas those at the opposite end of this spectrum are less avoidance oriented.[12] Those who are high in extroversion and low in negative emotionality are the most likely to make *the choice* by going ahead and reaching out to connect with another person. Those who are low in extroversion (that is, introverts) and high in negative emotionality, in contrast, are the most likely to make *the choice* by avoiding social interactions.

So What?

So here we are in this unfolding story: How we make *the choice* to approach or avoid others varies across moments and also varies across people. This isn't surprising. What we want from one moment to the next changes, and people seem to want different things. So what? If we're all consistently choosing what we actually like and what makes us happier as different types of people, then personality traits like extroversion and neuroticism shouldn't be related to our happiness and well-being.

This is where our story takes a surprising turn.

Although the scientific study of well-being is relatively young, emerging in the late 1970s and the 1980s, one result was crystal clear from the very beginning: Extroversion is strongly correlated with happiness. In fact, extroversion is positively correlated with every other measure of subjective well-being that psychologists assess, too. The decades since have only reinforced these results to the point where many papers now start by summarizing the connection between extroversion and well-being as "one of the most noteworthy and robust findings in personality psychology."[13]

Indeed, extroversion and neuroticism are consistently the strongest personality predictors of a person's well-being. One meta-analysis that aggregated results from 347 studies conducted with more than 120,000 people from around the world found that the average correlation between extroversion and happiness was 0.49.[14] To put the size of the correlation in perspective, the correlation between the heights of fathers and sons is roughly 0.50, while the correlations typically identified by psychologists are in the 0.2–0.3 range. A correlation of 0.49 is big. In this meta-analysis, extroversion was also positively correlated with experiencing more positive emotions and fewer negative emotions. Extroversion is also positively correlated with broader measures of well-being, including satisfaction with one's life and the reported quality of one's life, although these correlations with broader measures of well-being are generally a little weaker. Put simply, those who are more approach oriented tend to have more positive lives. In contrast, those who are more anxious and avoidance oriented, as measured by neuroticism, report experiencing more negative emotions and fewer positive emotions and are both less satisfied with their lives overall and less happy in their lives at any given moment.

It's easy to imagine that these relationships might be limited to particular countries or cultures that especially value high-energy, approach-oriented, individualistic behaviors, such as the United States, whereas other cultures may be more oriented toward rewarding introversion. There is a little truth to this, but the emphasis here should be on the word "little." In one large study of nearly sixty-five hundred people from thirty-nine countries, the relationship between extroversion and the amount of positive emotion people reported feeling was indeed larger in the United States than it was outside it, but the correlation was still positive and very large outside the United States as well.[15] The correlation was also larger in more individualistic cultures, where more value is placed on attaining personal goals, than in relatively collectivistic cultures, where more value is placed on attaining goals that are good for a group. However, the connection between extroversion and well-being was again very strong in both cultures and the differences between them were relatively small. Around the world, those who are more approach oriented also report being happier.[16]

The relationship between extroversion and positive emotions even held during the COVID-19 pandemic, in places where our social lives were restricted to six-foot separations and Zoom calls. Far from being an introvert's heaven and extrovert's hell, as many had imagined when it all began, those who were more extroverted continued to connect with others more often in whatever ways they could, and as a result continued feeling happier and more satisfied with their lives. These COVID-19 connections included spending more time engaging with people online or on the phone, and even violating shelter-in-place orders to stay more connected in person.

Indeed, one of the leading happiness researchers in the world, who also happens to be quite extroverted, confided in me one evening at dinner that they had made it through the lockdown period by creating a pod of friends who would get together to party on a regular basis so as to avoid the misery of isolation. Another leading happiness researcher—also quite extroverted—told me that their spouse built a shelter on their deck so that they could get together with small pods of friends outside even when it was cold because they knew the consequences of being isolated. As you might imagine, this did put extroverts at a slightly elevated risk of contracting and spreading COVID-19, but these effects looked to be small and inconsistent across studies. However extroverts were getting together, they were choosing to do so in ways that were both relatively safe *and* uplifting.[17]

Perhaps more important, this relationship between extroversion and well-being emerges not only when you look across people with different average levels of extroversion (what psychologists refer to as personality "traits") but also when you look across moments within a person's day (what psychologists refer to as personality "states"). These moments matter a lot for our well-being because the vast majority of variability (typically around 80 percent) in our behavior comes from the states we're in rather than our traits.[18] When researchers send people text messages several times a day and ask them what they're doing and how they are feeling, they consistently find that people report feeling more positive when they are doing something that is more extroverted, and report feeling less positive when they are doing something that is more introverted. In a typical day in my life as a professor, for instance, I feel more positive and energized when I'm up in front of a class than when sitting alone writing in front of my computer. What may be especially surprising is that researchers find, in one study after another, that this is true regardless of how extroverted or introverted people report themselves to be.[19] Even introverts report feeling more positive when they're acting outgoing and extroverted.

If the approach and avoidance debate happens both within people and between people regarding what will make them happy, the approach-oriented side seems to have the better argument, even if it's not always winning the debate within your own mind.

So . . . Why?

Yes, really. I know. That being more approach oriented, or extroverted, consistently leaves even introverts feeling more positive seems odd, or maybe even unsettling. When I share these results in conversation or in class, it sometimes leaves people feeling a bit defensive, especially if you think about personality traits as describing something about the type of person you are rather than about the choices you tend to make and the habits you've therefore developed. Indeed, an MBA student of mine who raised her hand after learning of these results only half jokingly said, "As an introvert, I feel a little under attack right now!"

My student's sentiment is not unusual. I felt the same way when I first learned about this research, as did a small army of psychologists who initially reacted to these results with great skepticism. This skepticism lasted decades as psychologists tested how reliable these effects were, tried to explain why these effects might emerge, and also went on a long hunt for potential costs of being more approach oriented.

The correlation between approach-oriented behavior and happiness observed in large-scale surveys just scratches the surface of several decades of research. The first study I know of that directly tested how introverts and extroverts feel over the course of a day was published in 2002.[20] This study captured the emotional lives of a group of people for thirteen days using the cutting-edge technology of the time: a PalmPilot. Everyone first completed a personality survey that measured their extroversion as a trait. They then went through what sounds like a spamming nightmare. For the next two weeks, each person was pinged five times every day at random moments and asked to indicate how extroverted they had been over the last hour and how positive they felt. To measure extroversion, each person indicated how talkative, energetic, assertive, and adventurous they had been acting. To measure how positive they felt, each person reported how excited, enthusiastic, proud, and alert they felt over the last hour.

The goal was to test whether anyone in the study consistently felt more positive while being more introverted. Somewhat amazingly, nobody did. Instead, *every single person* reported feeling more positive, on average, when they were acting more extroverted. Another study measured how 136 people ranging from eighteen to eighty-nine years old felt over the course of nearly sixty thousand social interactions, and again found that people felt happier when they were acting extroverted, regardless of how extroverted or introverted people scored on a standard personality test.[21] If you're surprised by this, then you've got good company because the researchers were surprised as well. "Contrary to our expectations and long-standing conceptual notions," the researchers wrote, "the congruence of personality traits and social context characteristics did not seem to have a consistent effect on momentary happiness." Nonacademic translation: Much to our surprise, people were happier when they were acting more extroverted regardless of how extroverted they typically were.

These results clearly suggest that we might be able to make ourselves feel better throughout the day if we chose to act extroverted more often, regardless of how extroverted or introverted we normally consider ourselves. As one group of researchers gently put it, "Because of the positive association between extraversion and well-being, . . . one might wonder whether it would be advisable for everyone to act more often in an extraverted way?"[22] Really? Would going about your day choosing to be more extroverted make you feel happier?

Many psychologists have now conducted exactly this kind of test, and the general conclusion is clear: Yes, acting extroverted tends to make people feel more positive. One of these tests, for instance, asked a group of 131 undergraduates to act more extroverted than they might otherwise every day in one week, and to act more introverted every day in another week, with the order of the weeks varying randomly.[23] Recognizing that extroversion can sometimes sound more socially desirable on a survey, these researchers took pains to use neutral language in their instructions, asking people to act as talkative, assertive, and spontaneous as they could in their extroverted week, and as deliberate, quiet, and reserved as they could in their introverted week. Three times per week, each person reported how they felt. At the end of these two weeks, the results were that people—regardless of their levels of extroversion—reported feeling more positive moods, less negative moods, more connected to others, more competent, more satisfied with their lives, and, to a lesser extent, happier in their extroverted week than in their introverted week. Even the lead researcher on this experiment, the behavioral scientist Sonja Lyubomirsky, was taken aback by the results. "The surprise," she said, "was that we found the biggest effect sizes we've ever had on any intervention, for both introverts and extroverts. So the introverts, just as much as the extroverts, got happier when they acted extroverted."[24]

Surely, though, there must be some fairly obvious cost to acting more extroverted, perhaps especially when it doesn't come as naturally for someone. Researchers had the same thoughts, sparking a now decades-long research-driven hunt to find those costs. That hunt, often again to the surprise of the researchers themselves, has largely come up empty. For instance, maybe acting extroverted is exhausting, and it must be especially exhausting if you're introverted because it's more uncommon and unfamiliar. This certainly seems plausible. One research group who both shared this intuition and tested it across several experiments, though, learned that people actually tend to feel *more* energized immediately after acting extroverted regardless of their personality type, with the feeling of fatigue generally coming a few hours later. This pattern of energized and fatigued, though, hit extroverts and introverts with the same intensity and time course in their experiments.[25] Feeling tired and wanting some quiet time to recover after an evening socializing does not make you uniquely introverted; it makes you a human being.

Maybe, though, acting extroverted is mentally taxing and distracting, essentially making you less smart if you generally act more introverted? This again seems plausible. Acting like someone you're not might require you to be so focused while you're putting on a show that you're mentally exhausted afterward and not able to think very clearly. Researchers again, however, had the same thought but found no evidence for it when they actually tested it. Replicating the typical findings, the people in their experiments again felt more positive after being instructed to act extroverted in a small group conversation, but they did not find any evidence that this diminished their capacity for thinking when carefully tested immediately afterward. Again we hear the familiar refrain of surprise in the researchers' own words. "Our studies," they wrote, "were sound in that they replicated very clear mood differences across experimental conditions. . . . However, even in this context, we found no evidence to suggest that introverts suffer costs when acting extraverted."[26]

Undeterred, the hunt continued. Sure, researchers wondered, acting extroverted might leave you feeling happier, but maybe acting in a way that's contrary to your typical personality would have other previously unmeasured costs on well-being, such as making people feel inauthentic? This theory again makes great intuitive sense, but when multiple groups of researchers actually tested how "authentic" people feel after acting extroverted or introverted, they found that acting extroverted actually leads people to report feeling *more* authentic, again regardless of their personality type.[27] The reason, it seems from these studies, is that people feel more authentic when they're feeling good, and being more outgoing and extroverted tends to make us feel good.[28]

Maybe, though, acting more extroverted feels good when you do it once or twice, like camping or cocaine, but the costs emerge over time when you keep doing this regularly? You might feel happier choosing to be more outgoing during an hour-long dinner, but maybe it would become unpleasant if you tried being more outgoing every day, especially if you generally acted more introverted? As one research group that was also onto this hypothesis put it, "Whereas the large majority of research has focused on the short-term benefits of extraverted behavior, we hypothesized that counter-dispositional extraversion might have well-being related costs in the long run due to the accumulation of costs following from acting out of character."[29] However, when researchers actually tested how people feel when acting more or less extroverted than normal over a period of ten days in one experiment and over five months in another, they found "no support for this hypothesis." Instead, what they found was that acting more extroverted led people to feel more positive, whereas acting more introverted led people to feel less positive, again regardless of their personality and regardless of how long these stretches of behavior lasted. Acting extroverted isn't like camping or cocaine that's good for a while and then becomes negative; it's more like coffee: generally pretty good every day you choose to have it.

The hunt for costs of acting extroverted on well-being has not, though, come up completely empty. It has identified one critical barrier for anyone to actually experience the positive impact of being more approach oriented on their well-being: actually choosing to do it. Like any habit, being more approach oriented gets easier to do when you practice it more often, and it's harder to do if you're not practicing it as a habit regularly. There is only one high-quality experiment I know of which found that being asked to act more extroverted worked less well for introverts. In this experiment, being asked to act more extroverted for a week increased happiness for most people (especially the most extroverted), but it had no meaningful impact on happiness for those who were the most introverted. Why not? Because those who were the most introverted didn't actually follow the instructions to act more extroverted. Whatever fears were holding the most introverted people back in their social lives also kept them from trying something different in the experiment. Like the benefits of physical exercise, the benefits of social exercise that come from reaching out and connecting with others only come if you choose to do it.[30]

"Would introverts be better off if they acted more like extraverts?" one group of researchers asked in the title of one of their papers. If by "better off" you mean feeling more positive both in your life and with your life, then the answer is clear: in all likelihood, yes. In fact, the answer seems to be yes for anyone, regardless of how introverted or extroverted you typically choose to be.

So . . . Why Not? The Case for Optimism

The research I've covered in this chapter makes it clear that sociality isn't just a matter of what we like and dislike; it's also a matter of what we *think* we'll like and dislike. If you make choices routinely enough based on what you think you'll like, then eventually your thoughts will create habits that become the defining features of your personality. The intuitive story that extroverts like connecting with other people while introverts don't just isn't supported by the evidence. Personality doesn't describe the kind of person you are; it describes the kinds of choices you tend to make, and therefore the kinds of experiences you tend to have and the habits you tend to form. It's not that extroverts are happier being more sociable while introverts are happier keeping to themselves. Instead, extroverts are more likely than introverts to make *the choice* to approach others a little more often, and their increased happiness and positive emotion in life shows it.[31]

So why, then, don't more of us take the easy opportunities we have to be a little more social? The answer I'm going to spend the rest of this book explaining is that the expectations that can guide our approach and avoidance systems often lead us to make a systematic mistake: We tend to underestimate how positively the social interactions that enhance our well-being are going to turn out. Put another way, the voice in our heads encouraging us to hold back and avoid interacting with other people can be a little too loud, and we can listen to it a little too often.

Whether that avoidant voice comes to us in the very moment when we're making *the choice,* as I experienced that morning on my commuter train, or more regularly as a habit, as it was for Jessica Pan, the risks of social interaction that we imagine and that guide how we make *the choice* are bigger and scarier than reality typically warrants. Avoiding truly unpleasant interactions makes you wise, but avoiding pleasant interactions out of mistaken fear is foolish. It can lead us to miss brief moments of positive social interactions that make our days feel better, to miss out on friendships that could be long lasting, and to generally feel overly lonely in our lives. It leads, I believe, to making choices that you might later recognize as mistakes for both your own and others' well-being.

I knew all of the work that I've covered in this chapter so far and the decades-long journey from doubt to understanding that psychologists have gone through when Jessica was on the phone expressing her own doubts about acting more extroverted. This is where my optimism for her year of living a more extroverted life came from, and the reason why I could encourage Jessica to simply try to reach out a little more often and take note of what happens. Either our phone call or the commitment that comes from signing a book contract was enough to get her started. And indeed, over the course of her year of choosing to be more social, Jessica Pan learned that the beliefs that had been holding her back from reaching out were overly pessimistic. This didn't mean reaching out to others constantly, of course, but turning down the volume on the avoidance voice a bit meant she was reaching out a little more often than before, and feeling consistently better as a result. After her year was over and her book was published, we talked again to discuss how her year had gone and how she was living her life differently now, with nothing but the sound of calm in her voice.

It was very hard, she told me, to get started. She described how every choice to interact put her on high alert with an intense fear that it would be awful, from talking to a man on a London train platform to baristas in coffee shops, only to find that her actual interactions ranged from okay to amazing, but never matched anything close to what she had feared. She bonded over a shared love of *30 Rock* with a new friend on a train and described how talking to baristas in her favorite coffee shop was "a total lifeline" during the COVID-19 pandemic, even if it was only a minute or two of banter. After years of writing nearly every day in the same café owned by "a really beautiful Vietnamese French woman, Kim," whom she both loved and was totally intimidated by, she finally started up a conversation after the owner noticed an article she had written in the newspaper. "I was so scared to talk to her," Jessica told me. "She seemed to know everybody and was best friends with all of her customers, except for me even though I came into her café every day."

Now they're great friends, not just the kind who follow each other on Instagram, but "proper friends." Kim even gave Jessica her toddler's old baby clothes when Jessica was expecting her own child a few years later. Jessica says she thinks about this a lot—how much she would have missed if she hadn't reached out to talk to Kim. She was so certain that other people would be annoyed or irritated if she tried to engage that she avoided talking to strangers even if she saw them every day. "Now I realize they're not annoyed, but rather often like talking to people." Making decisions to be a little more approach oriented when she felt safe to do it actually made Jessica feel safer in her community because she knew people around her. "It's just nice to establish community. It's nice to see a familiar face. You don't lose anything, and it adds a lot to your day."

In fact, Jessica's year of extroversion changed her so much that she started working part time in an indie bookshop in London, where the main part of her job is chatting with customers and making book recommendations. She told me, "I was feeling isolated working from home alone as a writer, and every day I'd walk by this bookshop and wonder what it would be like if I could work there. Out of the blue, I sent them an email, and a few weeks later I started my first shift there. I absolutely love working there. My entire job is basically being friendly and getting to know the local customers. It's a role I previously would have assumed I'd absolutely hate, but it's the highlight of my week now."

Not everyone was willing to engage in conversation when she tried, of course, but even those cases were nothing like what she had feared. "That was a huge lesson for me," she said of trying to talk to people who weren't that interested in talking back, "because nothing bad happens and you're totally fine." But even those experiences are rare. Despite considering herself an extreme introvert, Jessica learned that when she tried to talk with someone new, they were almost always happy to talk back. This insight was empowering. "I honestly found that I'm very successful at striking up conversations if I try to do it," she told me. "I'm rarely rejected."

When I pressed her for a number—so how often are you actually rejected when you try to talk to someone?—she pointed out that she tries to choose new people to talk with somewhat carefully and then said, "I don't get rejected." A zero percent rejection rate when she wanted to connect with someone was not the figure Jessica had in mind before she started her year of living more extrovertedly. Jessica told me that the year has changed the way she lives her life. By changing how she made *the choice*, she changed her social habits. She even changed her personality, because personality indicates not the kind of person you are but rather the kinds of choices you typically make and the habits you therefore develop. Among many changes, "I talk to strangers all the time now," she told me. "It's not weird."

One of my most prized possessions is a copy of Jessica's book that she signed for me with the inscription "Thank you for changing my life." Of course, it wasn't me who changed Jessica's life. She did it, completely on her own. I just invited her to test whether the voice in her head that was encouraging her to hold back from connecting with others might turn out to be a little bit wrong. What Jessica learned from treating her beliefs as bets on the future rather than as accurate facts of life was that the gaps between her beliefs about social interactions and her actual experience could be massive. Referring to the benefits of making *the choice* differently for a year, she wrote, "It was more than I could have ever hoped for when I started." This is the same gap I also experienced that morning when I talked with the stranger in a red hat on my own train. This gap isn't unique to Jessica and me, but rather a common feature that shows up again and again in a variety of different situations.

That such a gap could exist might seem rather odd. Where does it come from? After all, we talk to people every day. We share compliments, give thanks, and work through conflicts. We have shallow conversations and deep conversations. We make friends and lose friends. We fall in love and are sometimes thrown out of it. If there's anything we should be able to learn about, it's social interaction. We can't look into the future, but don't we have enough experience from the past to know how our social experiences are likely to turn out, or at least not to be overly pessimistic about them?

No. The problem is that we don't actually have enough experience, or at least the right kind of experience, to get our expectations about social interaction perfectly aligned with reality. This isn't for a lack of intelligence or wisdom or cleverness on anyone's part. Anticipating the outcomes of social interaction is a *really hard* problem for at least three reasons. First, the outcome of any social interaction is inherently uncertain. Second, our own perspective also differs in predictable ways from the other person we're interacting with, meaning that we can easily misunderstand how someone else is likely to respond to us. Finally, the feedback we get from our social experiences is systematically biased in a way that can keep us overly pessimistic. Once our expectations about social interactions are set, they can guide our behavior in ways that keep us from actually testing them.

When our beliefs dictate the experiences that we have, then the world is not a kind learning environment that gives us perfect insight into the minds of others or corrects our mistakes when we make them. Instead, as I'll describe in the next chapter, the world becomes a confusing learning environment that allows overly pessimistic expectations to thrive.

3

Unexpected Values

> The whole of science is nothing more than a refinement of everyday thinking.
>
> —ALBERT EINSTEIN[1]

I was alone and facing a boring four-block walk to my office one morning when an instance of *the choice* walked up next to me. A couple of inches taller than I am, with a long graying beard and even longer graying hair, he looked like an Orthodox monk who would prefer weeks of solitude in a desert monastery over a moment of conversation with me any day. His expression was stern, with a resting face best described as grinchy. He was also in the midst of putting his right earbud in at the moment I noticed him, after already putting in his left one, the technological equivalent of a "Do Not Disturb" sign.

Because we were both getting off the same commuter train, it seemed likely that I'd see him again. I was inclined to strike up a conversation that might make our walk more enjoyable, but then he didn't look interested in talking. There it was, *the choice,* a split-second decision to approach or avoid.

I'm sure you can understand my reluctance to reach out in that moment, but how wise was that instinct? I've certainly put in my headphones even when I'd have been happy to talk if someone else wanted to. I've also been told that my own face can look pretty darned grinchy when my mind is wandering. At worst, I thought he'd ignore me. At best, I knew the power that simply reaching out to other people in a positive way can have.

This is just one of countless examples of *the choice* we make to reach out and connect in a positive way with another person or hold back and avoid them. This example also highlights the core challenges we face to varying degrees when trying to make *the choice* wisely. We can't look into the minds of those around us to really know their thoughts and feelings in the moment, or transport ourselves into the future to know how these interactions will actually turn out. The best we can do is choose based on what we expect will bring the best outcome.

This expectation, however, isn't a fact. It's just our best guess. Even though there are few things we spend more time thinking about than other people, there are also few things we think about that are more complicated, meaning that our expectations of social interactions can sometimes be mistaken. For several reasons we'll cover in this chapter, our guesses can also systematically distort our view of the future in ways that leave us overly pessimistic. This can warp our expectations of how someone is likely to respond when we reach out to them, how it is likely to unfold, and even how the interaction will leave the other person feeling after it's over.

I knew of these distortions through the research my colleagues and I had conducted over the prior decade, along with related research from other behavioral scientists. Einstein was right that science is "a refinement of everyday thinking," and the research I'd been involved in had profoundly refined my thinking about other people in the same way that Jessica Pan's yearlong social experiment had refined her thinking. These data points have moved my expectations in a more wisely optimistic direction. I knew it was a good bet that talking would make the four-block walk positive for both of us. So, I reached out.

"Good morning, I'm Nick, and we haven't met before," again confirming that I'm nothing special with opening lines, but my outstretched hand and big smile showed that my friendliness was genuine.

And then—*boom!*—there it was again, just as I had seen that morning on the train years before: the switch. As if I'd reached around to his back and flipped on his power button, he came to life. His grinchy expression turned instantly into a smile even bigger than mine. His face changed so much that he almost looked like a different person.[2] His right hand immediately tucked his earbud back into his pocket while his left hand pulled out his other earbud as he went to grab my handshake. "Hello!" he said with an unexpected French accent and a friendliness that reached back to me as positively as I had reached out to him.

As we walked, the conversation flowed surprisingly easily due to my interest in getting to know him. I learned that he had moved to the same town I live in, had kids in the same schools that I did, worked at the same university that I do, and grew up connected to the countryside in the same way I was (albeit on different continents). We had far more in common than I would have guessed based only on appearances. Instead of my peeling off to my office after four blocks, we moved off to the side and kept talking for a few minutes more. He's now a friend I'm happy to have met, but whom I could have avoided if I had let undue pessimism guide that instance of *the choice*. Avoiding that conversation would have been a mistake for my own well-being. By avoiding the conversation, I also would never have learned that I had made a mistake.

Why are our social expectations so often pessimistically biased, and why do they persist? Where do these mistakes come from?

From at least three places: exaggerated uncertainty, mismatched perspectives, and confusing environments.

Exaggerated Uncertainty

To say that we dislike uncertainty when making choices is like saying the Wicked Witch of the West dislikes running in the rain. In fact, we sometimes like the worst possible outcome even more than an uncertain outcome, a phenomenon behavioral economists have not so creatively dubbed the uncertainty effect.

To see this effect, imagine yourself at a bookstore and you notice an employee in the middle of the store offering a $50 gift certificate that has to be used within the next two weeks. The employee says you can offer what you think it's worth, and if the employee likes the price, then the gift certificate is yours. Certainly, a gift certificate with a tight deadline is worse than one with no deadline. You might not be sure if you can get to the store in the next two weeks, and you don't want to waste your money. So, what would you be willing to pay for it? When one group of researchers asked people this question in a similar scenario,[3] the average was $26.10. The gift card isn't worth the full $50 because of the time restriction, so people are willing to pay about half of its face value, on average. That seems reasonable.

Now imagine that the employee offers you a gamble, holding up two gift cards that have to be used in the next two weeks, one worth $100 and one worth $50. What you can buy now is the chance to flip a coin and decide which gift card you get. Heads, $100. Tails, $50. How much would you be willing to pay for the coin flip?

Again, these cards aren't worth their full cash value because of the two-week restriction. However, surely this coin flip is worth more than the $50 card because you've now got a 50 percent chance of getting $100. However, when the same group of researchers asked people how much they'd be willing to pay for an uncertain win of either $50 or $100, the average was only $16, roughly $10 *less* than they were willing to pay for the $50 card alone. *What?* Offering $10 less for a gift card that has a 50 percent chance of being worth $50 more seems beyond unreasonable.

It's not that people misunderstand the problem, are confused by the probabilities, or aren't aware that $100 is more than $50. Subsequent research has ruled out these obvious explanations.[4] Instead, the mere uncertainty of not knowing what you'll get—$50 or $100—is so negative that it makes the definitely better but uncertain option seem worse.

The implication of the uncertainty effect for your social life is clear. Other people may be the greatest source of our happiness and well-being, but they can also be the greatest sources of our pain and misery. Every social interaction includes some degree of uncertainty and therefore risk, including physical, relational, or financial risks. Perhaps most common is the reputational risk that someone might think poorly of you if you say the wrong thing, give the wrong gift, compliment in the wrong way, or ask for help at the wrong time. When Jean-Paul Sartre wrote the line "Hell is other people" into his play *No Exit,* his character was referring to the social pain that comes from having other people judge you negatively, and also from the mere possibility that someone *might* be judging you negatively.[5]

Our aversion to uncertainty moves from a nudge to a shove when we also exaggerate the actual amount of uncertainty that exists in our social interactions. A key challenge is that the back-and-forth nature of any social interaction makes it especially hard to anticipate where an interaction might go. This complexity might make the range of possible outcomes seem especially large; an interaction could go anywhere! In real life, though, the actual range of plausible outcomes may be surprisingly narrow due to what is arguably the strongest and most universal of social norms: reciprocity.[6] You scratch my back and I'll scratch yours.

It's easy to imagine, for instance, that the grinchy-looking stranger could have responded to my hello in a wide variety of ways. He could have pretended not to hear, given me the middle finger, pulled out a gun, or screamed, "Hallelujah, someone's finally talking to me!" In real life, though, when you reach out in a positive way to talk with someone, the results are fairly predictable: They tend to talk back. It's also easy to imagine that opening up and having a deep conversation could lead to a wide range of reactions from another person. In real life, though, opening up to another person typically leads them to open up to you in return. And it's easy to imagine that you'd struggle to find something in common with a random stranger because we don't show all of our life's experiences, interests, or beliefs on our foreheads. In real life, though, when you say something, it usually prompts your conversation partner to think of something related, meaning that conversation seeks out our similarities. Trying to find something in common with a stranger might seem like finding a needle in a haystack, when it's actually like trying to find a needle in a haystack *with a magnet*.

How a social experience unfolds is therefore not as uncertain as we might imagine, generally ending up in a way that is consistent with how it began. If you reach out and treat someone like a friend, then they're likely to reach back and treat you like a friend in return. If you treat someone like a stranger and ignore them, then they're likely to ignore you right back. This means that you have an enormous amount of power to influence how it turns out. If you'd like people to smile at you, smile at them first. If you'd like someone talk with you, try talking to them first. If you'd like people to be nice to you, start by being nice to them.

The problem is that we tend to underestimate the power we have to shape our interactions, leaving us with a greater sense of uncertainty than is warranted. Just as magnetic forces are invisible to the naked eye, so are the features of a conversation that can pull people together. We tend to think of each other like marbles rather than magnets: as independent objects that are indifferent to one another rather than as objects whose interaction tends to pull toward each other. Failing to fully appreciate the power of reciprocity means that the range of outcomes we can imagine is wider than the actual outcomes we experience.

Consider an experiment I have now run with more than four thousand people that I'll describe more in chapter 6. In this experiment that I usually run in large presentations, I pair up people in the audience with someone they don't know to have a deep and meaningful conversation for about fifteen minutes based on several questions I give them, including "What are you most grateful for in your life?" and "Can you tell me about one of the last times you cried in front of another person?" After the conversation, I ask people to report their experience in the conversation, such as how awkward it was and how enjoyable it was, on scales that range from 0 (not at all awkward/enjoyable) to 10 (very awkward/enjoyable).

It's easy to imagine that a deep conversation with a stranger like this could go almost anywhere, from being really awkward and unpleasant if you have nothing to talk about, to being really positive if you're open and honest with each other. Indeed, when I asked a separate group of people to predict the percentage who gave each response on the scale below, people expected that the responses would span the entire range of the scale, as you can see in the relatively flat gray line below. People expected roughly 6 percent of people would find the conversation to be not awkward at all, while 15 percent would say it was very awkward, with largely similar percentages of people giving every response in between. Notice, however, the steep sloping black line that shows the percentages of people who *actually* gave each response, which shows that the actual range of experiences is really quite narrow. A little over 30 percent give a response of zero, indicating that it wasn't awkward at all, and more than 90 percent reported that their conversation was at the midpoint of this scale or below. People imagined that conversations would range across the entire spectrum of awkwardness. In reality, most weren't awkward at all.

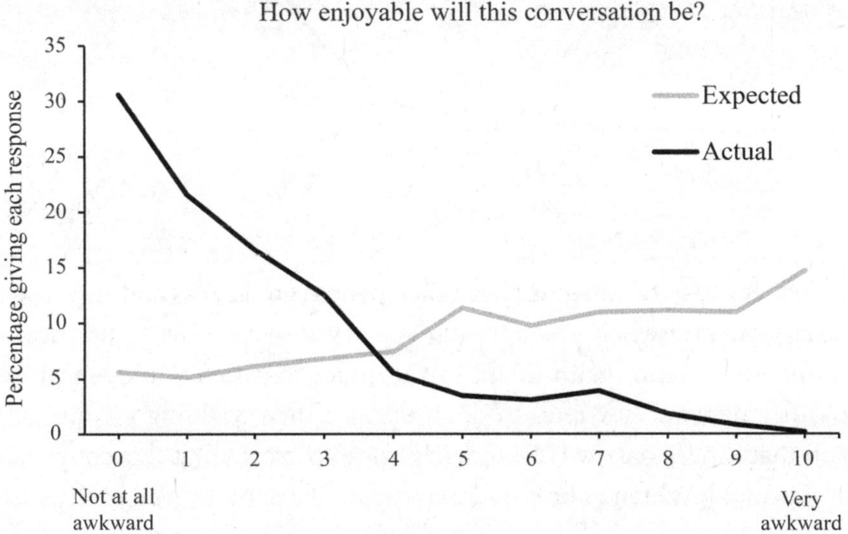

You see the same pattern in the next graph, but reversed, for how enjoyable people expected versus actually experienced these conversations to be. The gray line is relatively flat, with people expecting that enjoyment would range across the entire spectrum of the response scale, expecting that 10 percent would give the lowest two response options and only 12 percent would give the highest. In fact, people's actual enjoyment of these conversations again did not vary as much as people imagined, with more than 30 percent giving the most positive rating and not a single person giving the lowest two ratings. This again means that the imagined range of enjoyment was much larger than the actual range.

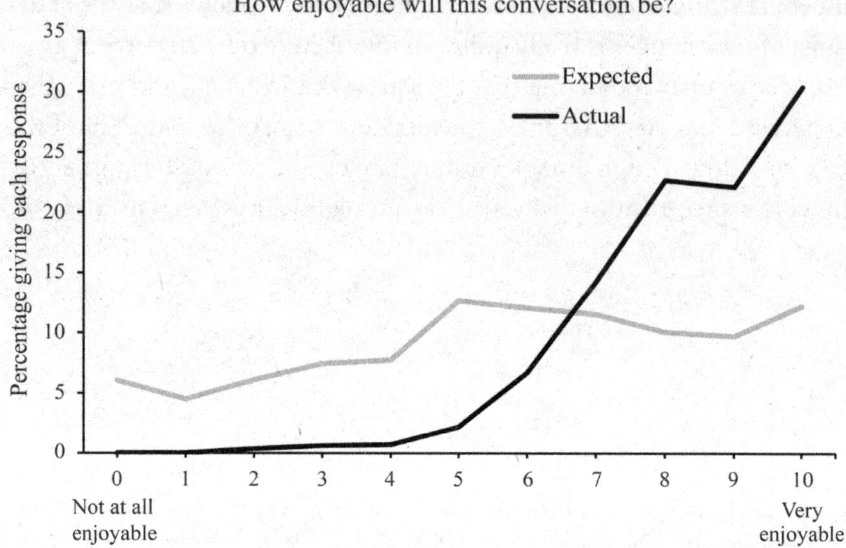

Yes, it's easy to imagine that other people could respond in a wide variety of ways when you open up and try to have a deep and meaningful conversation with them. But in practice, when you open up to another person, they tend to open up in return, yielding a conversation that ranges narrowly from fairly good to great. That this conversation would brighten your mood isn't much of a gamble; it's a pretty sure thing.

The Stanford psychologist Jamil Zaki once likened our fear of social interactions to our fear of sharks: far too extreme for most of us, in most contexts.[7] "Shark attacks," he said, "turn out to be basically the least common way you can die, but [they] loom large in our imagination and change our behavior in a way that we don't really need to change it." It's not that everyone in the world is wonderful, kind, and delightful to talk with. They are not. Some social interactions will be terrible. It's also not that you should ignore the possible range of risks you might face in your life. Some people can be sharks and should be avoided. It's also not that everyone's risks are the same. Some people are definitely more vulnerable, and some situations are definitely riskier than others. However, failing to appreciate the power of reciprocity can lead you to underestimate how positively almost anyone will respond if you reach out positively to them first. Fearing the presence of sharks might keep you from reaching out to surprisingly friendly people around you.

Mismatched Perspectives

The second source of misplaced pessimism stems from the different perspectives we have when we're evaluating ourselves versus others. There are, after all, two minds involved in this interaction. The problem is that we tend to evaluate ourselves based on a different, and often harsher, standard than we judge others. We evaluate ourselves on our competence. We evaluate others on their warmth.

This difference in perspectives is perfectly exemplified in an iconic scene from the movie *Jerry Maguire*. In this scene, Jerry (played by Tom Cruise) rushes to the home of his now-separated wife, Dorothy (played by Renée Zellweger), in the hopes of saving their troubled marriage. After the most successful day of his career as a sports agent, Jerry realized that a relentless focus on his work had led him to neglect the most important thing in his life—his wife. Even his biggest professional achievement left him feeling empty because he wasn't sharing it with her. Bursting into their home prepared to profess his love in a private moment, he instead finds their living room full of women there for a divorce support group. "Hello, hello," Jerry calls out, trying to break through the din of conversations, "I'm looking for my wife." In front of a now stone-cold silent room of women, his wife stands up while he stammers to find the right words. "This used to be my specialty . . . I was good in a living room. They'd send me in there, and I'd do it alone. And now I just . . ." Jerry eventually gets to the meaning of what he's there to do: "I miss my . . . I miss my wife. . . . I love you. You complete me. And I just had . . ." But Dorothy doesn't need more words. "Shut up," she says. "Just shut up. You had me at hello." Jerry's perspective was focused on how poorly he was expressing his love to his wife, but Dorothy couldn't have cared less about how articulate he was. What mattered to her was the love Jerry showed the moment he showed up for her.

This discrepancy between Jerry's anxiety and Dorothy's acceptance highlights two fundamental dimensions of social judgment that psychologists often call the Big Two: competence and warmth.[8] Competence was on Jerry's mind: How could he find exactly the right words to win his wife back? In general, competence includes our evaluations of how capable, effective, or smart someone is. It makes good sense that Jerry was focused on his competence, because he was trying to do something effectively. Jerry's competence was not, though, on Dorothy's mind. Instead, she cared about Jerry's warmth. Warmth refers to social qualities of how friendly, kind, trustworthy, and likable someone is. This relative difference in focus on competence versus warmth when we're reaching out versus being reached out to is not just a movie fiction. It's a common feature of social interaction because of the difference between how we evaluate ourselves and how we are evaluated by others. It's also a difference that can lead us to be overly pessimistic about some of our social interactions.

The Big Two of competence and warmth guide our social evaluations because they help us to answer two basic questions that we have about each other. Evaluating warmth helps us answer whether a person has good or bad intentions. Evaluating competence helps answer whether someone is capable enough to implement their intentions. Naturally, warmth is the first thing we want to know about someone as we determine whether they're a friend who can be trusted or a foe who should be avoided. Only after we've answered that do we think about how competent someone is.

Our sense of someone's warmth isn't just what comes to mind first; it also dominates our overall evaluations of them, determining how much we like them. This means that our sense of another person's competence can enhance our sense of another person's warmth, but doesn't override it. Someone who is kind and smart, for instance, seems saintly. Someone who is cruel and smart, in contrast, seems sinister.[9] Our sense of someone's warmth determines whether our overall evaluation is positive or negative, while our sense of competence intensifies that evaluation. We also assess someone's warmth more quickly than their competence. If you look at a picture of someone's face, you'll typically be able to assess how trustworthy the person seems faster than how smart the person seems. In fact, your sense of someone's trustworthiness after seeing a picture of their face can come to your mind within a hundred milliseconds, which is literally as fast as the blink of an eye.[10]

You're also more likely to agree with other people about how nice and trustworthy someone is than you are about how smart and capable they are. This is because the signals of someone's warmth are clearer for us to recognize than signals of someone's competence.[11] Even children as young as three can quickly spot whether someone seems nice or not in the same way that adults do, and only later develop a sense of whether someone seems smart or not.[12] It's no wonder that when I ask my kids how their teachers are at the start of every school year, I never hear of how talented they are in teaching trigonometry or Tolstoy. Instead, I hear how nice, or sometimes not nice, they are.

Of course, the amount of attention you pay to another person's warmth versus competence will vary depending on the context you're in. As William James explained in the very first psychology textbook ever written, "Thinking is for doing," and what you're trying to do affects how you think about other people.[13] When you're hiring someone for a job, you'll think more about how competent they are than when you're trying to make a new friend. What's surprising, though, is how much warmth continues to dominate our evaluations regardless of the context we're in. If you're picking a financial adviser, you obviously want someone who's good at finance, but the first thing you still need to know is whether this is someone you can trust or not. Even in places where you'd think that someone else's capabilities, expertise, and performance would dominate our evaluations, we might still be trying to make sure someone can be trusted, meaning that attributes related to competence can still play second fiddle to our sense of someone's warmth.

Consider seeking out someone to give you career advice. Surely you'd expect that it wouldn't matter much whether the person was nice and encouraging. Mostly you'd care whether they knew what they were talking about and could give you good advice. You wouldn't be alone in your expectation. When researchers asked people to rank a list of attributes they thought they would value most in a career adviser, those related to competence (expertise, constructive criticism, and advising experience) took the top ranks while the attribute related to warmth (how positive they seemed) was ranked as the least important.[14] The same effect also emerged when a separate group of people were asked to rank the importance of these same attributes when selecting a celebrity coach on the reality TV singing competition *The Voice*. On this show, each artist sings for a group of four famous coaches on their first episode. If two or more of the coaches—including famous singers like John Legend, Adam Levine, Reba McEntire, Gwen Stefani, and Usher—are interested in advising the artist, the artist decides which coach to work with. Again, people imagining what attributes they would value most in a coach ranked competence ahead of warmth, with expertise taking the top-ranked position and warmth taking the last-ranked position.

This all makes sense in theory. But what happens in real life when you hear someone like Pharrell Williams tell you, "Where do I begin with your tone? Your voice is like silk"? Do you actually choose the most competent adviser, or do you go with the one who's the most encouraging and lifts your self-esteem like a hot-air balloon? To find out, researchers looked at four of the first five seasons of *The Voice* to see which coaches the 119 artists who had interest from two or more coaches selected. They found that the strongest predictor of an artist's choice was the coach's warmth: how positive and encouraging the coach was when talking to the artist. Although the coach's expertise, defined by how similar the coach's own music genre was to the artist's genre, came in a close second place in predicting the artist's choice, none of the other competence-related attributes mattered. Even when someone's expertise would seem to be most important, warmth can be not only powerful but *surprisingly* powerful.

However, as prominent as warmth might be when we've evaluating other people, it is not as prominent when we're thinking about ourselves. Other people are trying to figure out whether you're a kind, decent, and trustworthy person to be around, but you largely take that for granted about yourself. When Jerry Maguire was trying to win back his wife, he knew he loved her, and so his warmth wasn't on the top of his mind. Instead, he was trying to figure out exactly what to say, therefore focusing on his competence.

To see this focus on competence when thinking about ourselves, try to remember the last time you considered starting a conversation with a stranger (or imagine trying to do it now). I'm betting that moments before starting this conversation, what was running through your mind was what you'd talk about and whether you'd be able to carry on a conversation rather than how friendly you seemed. When you think about reaching out to express your support to someone who is going through a tough time, you're likely focused on whether you're actually able to help them more than on how kind and caring you'll seem to the person you're reaching out to. When you think about passing along a compliment to someone, you're likely thinking about whether this is the right time to deliver it rather than how nice the compliment is. And when you feel grateful to someone and want to share your appreciation, the first thing that's likely to pop into your mind is how on earth you get the words right to express how you actually feel, not how nice it is to express gratitude at all. In "This One's for You," the country-music singer Luke Combs sings of this concern in his heartfelt expression of gratitude toward his friends. "I told you all I'd write you a song," Combs sings. "Pour my heart in a melody to keep you singin' along. This might not be the right time and these might not be the right lines to prove or say what I'm trying to, but this one's for you."

It's easy to see how these differing perspectives—how we evaluate our own actions versus how others evaluate us—can lead us to hold systematically pessimistic biases in social life. If someone writes you a song, pouring their heart in a melody to keep you singin' along, do you really think you'd care whether they were singing at just the right time or with just the right lines? Is there ever a *wrong* time for someone to sing you this song? Obviously, what you'd care about most is their warmth: the gratitude and love they're showing you. And yet if you're the one singing the song, like Combs, you might instead be overly worried about your timing or your tune.

I can empathize with this feeling. For our twenty-fifth wedding anniversary, I made a recording of myself singing the song that I thought best represented how I feel about my marriage to Jen—Ben Folds's song

"The Luckiest"—to a slideshow of pictures from our life together. I'm even cringing just telling you about this because I am not a great singer by any stretch of the imagination. I felt excrutiatingly awkward while making it. Only knowing about the perspective gap between warmth and competence gave me the courage to send it to her. Based on her reaction, I think I had her at hello.

The things we do to reach out and connect to others tend to be very high in warmth. If, though, you're primarily focused on your competence when reaching out to others, then you'll probably underestimate how positively another person will feel when you make *the choice* to approach them. Failing to realize that we look at ourselves through a lens of competence while others are evaluating our warmth can leave us underestimating just how positive reaching out can make others feel.

Confusing Environments

Exaggerated uncertainty and mismatched perspectives can explain why we might underestimate how positively our efforts to connect will turn out in any single case, but they don't explain why we might continue making the same mistakes over and over again. Surely we interact with other people enough to learn what it's like. Why could pessimistic biases endure?

If the world was always a kind teacher, then we would learn almost perfectly and eliminate these biases from our minds. A kind teacher would make it easy to learn what reality was like by providing evidence that more closely resembled a scientific experiment, where we compared our beliefs about the world with reality, examining how accurate our beliefs are regardless of what those beliefs might be. A kind teacher would look like the world that Jessica Pan lived in for a year where she made *the choice* to approach others whenever she could: talking to people on trains when time allowed, reaching out to her favorite coffee shop owner each time she visited, and even doing stand-up comedy when the opportunity arose. A kind teacher would look like the experience I had with my grinchy-looking stranger when I tested my expectations by reaching out with a "hello," allowing me to learn how he would actually respond.

But if our expectations guide how we make *the choice,* leading us to approach others when we think it might be positive but to avoid them when we expect it to be negative, then the world becomes a confusing teacher because we miss out on learning from the experiences we avoid. The data from our experiences no longer reflects reality. If, for instance, you believed that talking to someone will be unpleasant, then you'd likely avoid them and would lose the ability to test if your belief was right or wrong. Just as the hockey great Wayne Gretzky recognized that "you miss 100% of the shots you don't take," you also miss the chance to learn from the social connections you choose not to make.[15] Overly pessimistic expectations can persist in this confusing environment because you miss having the experiences that could correct them. The optimism that encourages us to make *the choice* by reaching out to connect with someone stands the chance of being corrected, but the pessimism that encourages us to avoid someone does not.

Your beliefs about other people can also affect how other people treat you, further confirming pessimistic expectations even if they are somewhat mistaken. For example, imagine that you and a good friend are starting a new job at different companies and each trying to figure out how friendly people in the company are. Your friend is pretty optimistic about people, and therefore walks around the office smiling and saying hello to each person they meet. All around the office your friend goes—hello . . . hello . . . hello—learning from each interaction. Imagine that you, though, are a little more pessimistic and therefore decide to sit in your office and see who pokes their head in to say hello. There you sit—waiting . . . waiting . . . waiting—noticing and learning as you go. At lunch you meet to talk about what you've learned. Who do you believe is more likely to think that their co-workers are friendly? Your friend, who reached out to say hello whenever they could, or you, who held back and watched how often others said hello to you first?

I see the rather obvious answer play out through our youngest daughter, Lindsay, every day when I'm with her. Lindsay has no filter on saying hello to anyone and everyone she comes across, flipping the switch on nearly every person who hears her voice, bringing them to life with her huge smile and loud "hello." It's amazing to see how powerful this little bundle of hellos can be.

You might think that a student would recognize that what they learn will depend on what book their teacher gives them, but psychologists have found time and time again that it's hard to recognize when the information we're given to learn from through our everyday experience tells the whole truth or a partial truth.[16] When your beliefs about how others might respond are guiding your decisions about whom to reach out to and whom to avoid, then they're also constraining the data in ways that make it a confusing source to learn from. If you think others don't want to engage or connect with you, it can be difficult to recognize that you might be bringing that very behavior out in others. When you're dealing with a confusing teacher like that, it's hard to learn that your beliefs might be wrong.

In his Nobel Memorial Prize in Economics address, one of the champions of human rationality, Gary Becker, argued that rationality doesn't require that people be omniscient in a world full of confusing learning environments, but it does require people to be consistent by acting in line with their expectations. "The [rational] analysis," Becker said, "assumes that individuals maximize welfare as they conceive it. . . . Their behavior is forward looking."[17] Being forward looking, though, isn't the same as actually knowing the future. This means that fully rational people can act in line with their expectations, but still make systematic mistakes. Uncertainty about how someone else might respond can leave our present selves blind to the power of reciprocity when we reach out to connect with another person, and evaluating ourselves primarily in terms of our competence can make us forget that someone we reach out to cares primarily about how warm and friendly we seem to be. These biases can create overly pessimistic conceptions that could then keep a fully rational person who acts on these beliefs from collecting the data necessary in their own life to correct them.

These biases don't blind us to reality, but they can color our conceptions of it in a pessimistic direction that might keep us overly avoidant in life. As I'll describe in the next chapter, if we're overly avoidant, we'll tend to keep our social circle small, connecting with family and friends we already know but not with strangers, even when it might be safe, easy, and surprisingly positive to do so.

PART II

Why Not?

If connecting with other people is so important for our happiness, our health, and even our longevity, then why aren't we doing it more often? Why do we avoid connecting with strangers when easy opportunities are all around us? Why do we choose to connect over media that connects us poorly with others rather than choosing more effective media? Once connecting, why do we so often get stuck in conversations that aren't as deep and meaningful as they could be?

4

Hello, Stranger

Keep on smilin', 'cause
when you're smilin'
The whole world smiles
with you.

—FRANK SINATRA

Claire Feuer was only fourteen when she woke up in the middle of the night and learned the surprising power of reaching out and connecting with a stranger in conversation. She was awakened that night by the sound of a helicopter and the sight of police lights flashing on the ceiling of her small Brooklyn bedroom. Confused, she got up and noticed that the door from her room to the backyard was open. Turning back after shutting it, she saw a person—a "figure," she told me—standing in the corner. As a father myself, it was chilling to hear her calmly relate this experience to me a decade and a half later. "Dad, is that you?" she asked. Her father, Loren, was the only other person home. The man didn't respond. "Oh, you're the plumber, you're here to fix the bathroom?" she stammered in confusion. Still no response. Finally realizing she was facing an intruder in her house, she told me that her body went into "complete shock." "Okay, this is it," she thought.

At that moment, Claire had to make *the choice* almost instantly: Stay and engage with this man, or run like hell? The solution, she said, "just hit me: have a conversation."

If you think that sounds like a no-good-horrible-terribly-bad idea, then I'm with you.

Nevertheless, Claire persisted.

She began by setting some ground rules. The man agreed not to hurt her or her father. Then, she said, "something switched." Just as I had seen when I engaged with my red-hatted fellow commuter, and with my grinchy-faced stranger, Claire's kindness toward the stranger led him to respond kindly in return. By taking control of how the interaction started, Claire was using her power to change how it ended. She started the conversation by asking what his favorite color was (blue) and what he liked to do with his friends (play basketball). "I think what I was doing," Claire recalled, "was trying to find the human in him, and for him to realize that I, too, was human." After talking for some time, she heard her father, Loren, walking down the hallway, at which point she asked the man to wait while she explained the situation to her father. Loren then walked into Claire's bedroom, told the man he couldn't stay, walked him out the front door, and then called the police to tell them where their suspect was. Loren and Claire never learned why the police were after him, but they suspected trespassing or burglary. Claire has never been able to get in touch with him but wished she could, "because it changed the trajectory of my life."

That change came from realizing that she had what felt like a superpower. She learned that reaching out and approaching others, even in potentially scary situations, had a surprisingly powerful impact on how others responded to her. A little more than a decade later, Claire got tired of looking around New York City, where she lived, and seeing so many "silent spaces" where people rarely connected with each other. She decided to try using her superpower to change those spaces by talking to strangers whenever she was able to do so, including in the silent space she knew best: the New York City subways. Claire said it took her fifteen minutes to get up her courage to have her first conversation with an artist who looked kind and interesting, but she's learned with experience that she doesn't need as much courage as she initially thought. "It turns out that so many people are willing to talk when you try. It's kind of incredible. People can't stop talking. So that's what led me to start the Subway Social Club."[1]

Yes, that's right. What Claire learned about her social superpower at fourteen led her to start what I believe is the first and only Subway Social Club of New York City, complete with buttons you can wear to identify yourself as a member. "When you ride," she wrote in a package that contained my own honorary club buttons, "you'll find as your evidence supports, that New Yorkers are a friendly bunch."[2]

Reaching Out Reaches Back?

Come on now. New Yorkers on the subway are a friendly bunch? Is Claire crazy?

She's not.

How many times has Claire been kidnapped, robbed, or assaulted after reaching out to someone?

Never.

Maybe she's riding some special train line you've never heard of, full of a new type of human being you've never met?

If you're skeptical about Claire's experience, then this possibility might be right. Not because of the people who happen to ride Claire's trains but rather because of what she brings out of them. Claire still encounters the manspreaders, seat hoggers, and cell-phone gazers engrossed in their screens. She's also aware that the odds of a bad interaction are different when someone comes up to talk with her from when she picks someone somewhat randomly to talk with, because someone who approaches her is more likely to have an ulterior motive than someone she reaches out to randomly. She doesn't go overboard and talk to everyone all the time, of course, but has a lower threshold than most do for reaching out when she's easily able, and when she feels safe.

"I don't force conversations," Claire said while explaining that she actively keeps an eye out for opportunities to uplift someone with a friendly "hello." Keeping an eye out for opportunities also means that she spots more opportunities than she might otherwise. "I have a thing for tattoos," she told me, so she compliments people on them when she can. Sometimes Claire notes that her conversations are contagious. "I think my favorite types of conversations are ones when I start talking to someone, and then you see other people looking at each other, and then they start talking, too." What she knows that many don't is that these conversations are likely to be really nice, and so she takes the opportunities she's given to make moments in her life better by being a little more social.

Although Claire's experience when she was fourteen is extreme,[3] I was not surprised to hear her story about the trains in New York because Juliana Schroeder and I had observed the same things in our research on the commuter trains in Chicago. But the experiment I described in the preface was just one experiment in one context. To test whether we would observe the same surprisingly positive experience of connecting with strangers in other "silent spaces," we conducted our next experiment in a place that seemed even less inviting for connecting with strangers: Chicago city buses. As on the trains, we asked people commuting into our laboratory for this study either to do whatever they normally do while riding the bus (our control condition), to keep to themselves on the bus (our solitude condition), or to try to connect with someone in conversation on the bus (our connection condition).

Once in our lab, we asked them to tell us how positive they felt and how productive their commute had been. We then compared the bus riders' experience with a separate group who imagined how positive and productive they'd feel in each of these conditions. The figure below shows that we found the same things on the buses that we did on the trains. People imagined that talking to a stranger would leave them feeling the *least* positive and the *least* productive, whereas those who actually went out and had a conversation with a stranger on the bus reported feeling the *most* positive and no less productive.

Getting this result—that connecting with a stranger was surprisingly positive on both trains and buses—suggested we might be discovering a general pattern rather than just a one-off quirk. We weren't alone. Other researchers were finding similar patterns. Romantic couples in one experiment imagined that they would enjoy a conversation

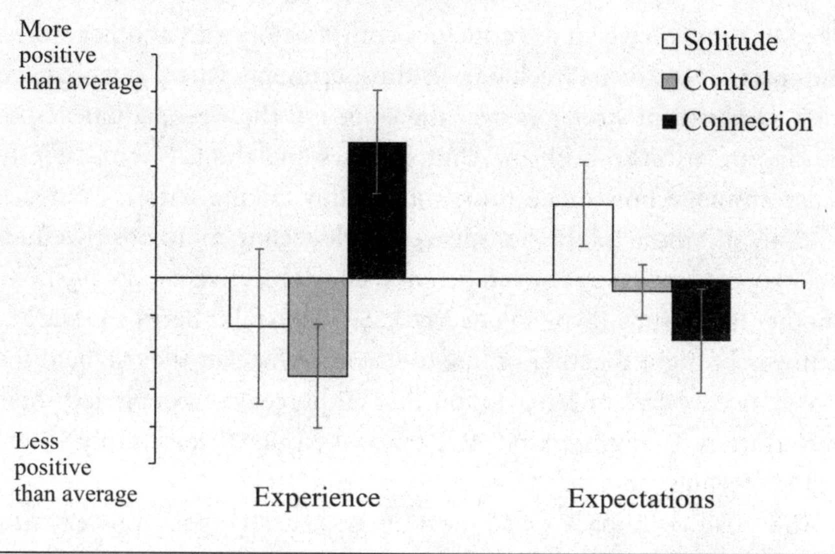

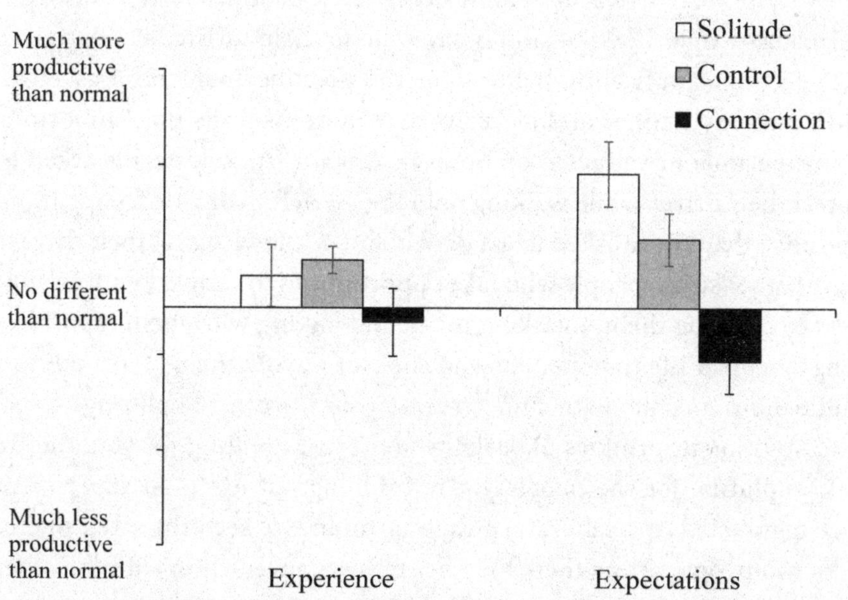

with a stranger less than talking to their own partner, but they actually enjoyed them equally.[4] Undergraduates in another experiment imagined that they would enjoy having a conversation with a person of the same race more than talking with someone of a different race, but they again enjoyed them equally.[5] In workshops where people were asked to simply have an introductory conversation with another workshop participant or in weeklong field experiments where people have one with different strangers over the course of the week, adults across the age spectrum in both the United States and the U.K. consistently underestimated how much they would enjoy talking with a stranger.[6] Not only did these interactions leave people feeling more positive than they expected, but they also left people feeling objectively more positive. Another large study involving nearly 3,257 video talks between random strangers brought together online to discuss whatever they wanted for at least twenty-five minutes found that 67 percent of people left their conversation feeling more positive than when they began. Only 9 percent left feeling more negative.[7]

The positive impact of connecting with a stranger even extends to very brief interactions. In an experiment conducted in Vancouver, Canada, people asked to simply say hello to their barista in a Starbucks left feeling significantly better after the greeting than those asked to just grab their coffee and leave (as they more typically do).[8] In a similar experiment conducted on buses in Ankara, Turkey, people asked to greet their driver while walking onto the bus left their ride feeling more positive than those asked to get on without acknowledging their driver.[9] In another study, people who take opportunities to connect with strangers by greeting them, thanking them, and talking with them report living a happier life than people who choose to avoid them.[10] Sprinkling a little more sociality with strangers into your life can be uplifting.

Additional sprinkles of sociality aren't just uplifting for you; they're also uplifting for the people you're reaching out to. In an experiment we conducted in a laboratory waiting room, we secretly asked one of the two people sitting there to either have a conversation with the other person in the room or keep to themselves.[11] We found that those who were talked to in the waiting room were just as happy with the conversation as the people we asked to start the conversation. We also found that people who were ignored in the waiting room by the other person felt just as mediocre as the people we asked to keep to themselves. Both the surprisingly positive pleasure of connecting and the pain of being avoided are contagious.

I have taken these results to heart over and over again. Although I don't ride the city buses often, I strike up conversations whenever I'm taking the bus from the Midway airport parking lot in Chicago to the terminal, making an otherwise dull ten minutes friendlier while also learning about the interesting places where people are going. I take the same opportunities when standing in line somewhere, sitting in a waiting room somewhere, or being driven in a cab or rideshare somewhere. Once you start looking, you'll start spotting silent spaces all around you that you can make better by being a little more social.

Reaching Out Surprises You Back

Simply looking for opportunities to make silent spaces a little more social won't make you reach out to connect with strangers more often if misplaced pessimism is what's holding you back. As we discussed, that pessimism can stem directly from the inherent uncertainty of what will happen when you reach out to a stranger. But what is it, exactly, that we're uncertain about? Identifying the source of potentially misplaced pessimism is the key to figuring out when you might try to overcome it.

One possible source is what springs to mind when you imagine reaching out to connect with a stranger. Instead of the typical experience you have when you talk to someone new, what might actually come to mind more often are the bad experiences you've had that you would prefer to avoid ever having again. If so, then our expectations about an upcoming interaction could be biased in the direction of our bad experiences rather than based on our typical experiences. Indeed, psychologists often find that extreme experiences stick in our memories better than typical experiences, particularly extreme negative experiences. This is also true of the experiences that we hear about. "Area Woman Makes New Bus Friend" will never make a news headline, but "Area Woman Robbed at Gunpoint on Local Bus" will always land on the front page.

Although this kind of "negativity bias" can certainly play some role in our pessimistic expectations, it didn't seem to be the main reason why people thought they'd be happier keeping to themselves on trains and buses in Chicago. In additional experiments where we asked people to predict how they would feel if they had a conversation with someone on the train or bus, they predicted that their conversation would be more similar to the predictions of those we asked to imagine a best-case scenario than it was to those we asked to imagine a worst-case scenario.[12] When our commuters imagined talking with a stranger, they actually expected it would be somewhat positive.

Instead, our overly pessimistic expectations come from an earlier point in the interaction: We start out thinking others wouldn't want to talk to us in the first place. It was the fear of rejection, rather than the fear of a terrible conversation, that created overly pessimistic expectations. When we asked people on the trains and buses in Chicago to tell us what percentage of other riders would be willing to have a conversation if they tried to start one, they estimated less than 50 percent, on average (46.4 percent on trains and 44.6 percent on buses, to be exact). Like getting your bike over a speed bump at the top of a hill, people seemed to think the conversation would be hard to start but easier once it got going. These beliefs about the difficulty of starting an interaction, though, seemed to be mistaken. Nearly everyone who returned our survey on the trains and buses reported being able to talk with the first person they approached. A few people told us they were unable to talk to another person because nobody sat down next to them on the train, or because they couldn't find someone who they thought wanted to talk and therefore didn't try. But most people had little or no trouble starting a conversation when they actually tried. Reaching out turns out to be a surprisingly powerful way to encourage someone to reach back positively to you.

It's easy to understand why you might be overly concerned about being rejected if you tried to start a conversation with a stranger. If someone sitting right next to you isn't talking to you, then it's pretty simple to infer that they don't *want* to talk to you. You might sit in silence, disconnected from other people, because you're not interested in connecting with others, but you might also sit in silence even when you'd be happy to talk because you think others aren't interested in connecting with you.[13] Indeed, our bus and train riders in Chicago were overwhelmingly of the latter type: happy to talk but reluctant to start. If everyone on the bus held those beliefs, or even if just most people did, then you would end up with an entire bus full of people who are happy to talk with their neighbors but never say a word.

Our lives spent in the presence of other people have more opportunities for social connection than we seem to realize because we fail to recognize the superpower of reciprocity that Claire Feuer experienced when she was fourteen. When you reach out to someone in a genuinely positive way, you change that person in a way that reduces the risk of rejection. When you reach out to connect, the person you reach out to tends to reach back.

Reaching Out Teaches You Back

There's even more benefit that comes from connecting with strangers that we miss beyond the glow of warm fuzzy feelings. After all, conversations don't just connect; they also teach. "Everyone you will ever meet knows something you don't," noted Bill Nye, the Science Guy.[14] The person next to you on the airplane has visited places you've never been. The person next to you in the grocery line has had experiences you've never imagined. The office colleague you've never spoken to has hobbies you didn't know about. However, none of what someone else knows is visible just by looking at them because their knowledge resides invisibly inside their skull. How can we realize what we're not learning when we don't know what others have to teach us?

I had no idea, for instance, when an elderly couple sat down next to me on a flight from Chicago to Washington, D.C., that the woman had grown up on the border of Vietnam and met her husband during the Vietnam War, and that she now teaches English as a second language to immigrant families struggling to make it in the D.C. area. I also had no idea that her husband sitting next to her along the aisle had become a nuclear scientist after his time in the service and later became one of the very few Americans to have gone to North Korea to examine its nuclear capabilities as part of a delegation from the U.S. Department of Energy.[15] I had no idea when I got into a Washington, D.C., cab one day that the driver had grown up only five miles from where two of our adopted children were born in Ethiopia and that he could tell me much more about what daily life was like there (or that he might be able to translate a song I remembered and sang to him from the back seat of his cab). I had no idea that the man standing behind me in a TSA line at an airport one day had graduated more than fifty years before from the same MBA program that I now teach in. I could go on and on with stories like this. Bill Nye is right. Everyone you will ever meet knows something you don't, but we don't learn what others have to teach us if we keep to ourselves.

This may seem obvious in the abstract, but our research suggests that it's not so obvious in real life.[16] For instance, in one experiment we conducted in a botanical garden, we paired up strangers who happened to be visiting at the same time, gave them one of two sets of prompts to discuss, and then asked them to have a short conversation with each other lasting roughly ten minutes. One set of prompts was rather mundane, including "Tell me what you do for a living" and "How do you like to spend your free time?" The other set of prompts was potentially more interesting, including "Tell me about an interesting person you know or who you've met" and "Tell me about an interesting place you've visited." Before the conversation, we asked everyone how much they thought they would learn both about the person they were talking to and about things in general. After the conversation, we asked them how much they actually learned. It didn't matter whether we asked people to talk about mundane or interesting things. In both cases people reported learning more than they expected to.[17]

Again, the source of our misplaced doubt is failing to anticipate the power of reciprocity, in this case by misunderstanding how reciprocity operates in the midst of a conversation. After all, a conversation is a cooperative effort between you and the person you're talking with. What you end up talking about isn't a random selection of topics, but rather is selectively pulled from the topics you both have at least some interest in. One person says something, and the other tends to think of something at least somewhat related in response. If you were to sit down and have a conversation with me, we might wind our way into talking about this book because we've both read it, but if I was to talk with anyone who hasn't read this book, then we'd talk about our families or our hobbies or some other overlapping sliver in our Venn diagram of mutual interests.

However, as we covered in chapter 3, these magnetic forces of social interaction seem hidden, such that our expectations are rather insensitive to the back-and-forth responsiveness inherent in conversation. In one experiment, for instance, we weakened the power of reciprocity to guide conversation to areas of mutual interest by asking people in one condition to stick to a single topic (in this case, talking only about the United States), and compared this with open conversations that could move to any area of interest. Before the conversation, people didn't think this variable would matter, because they expected to learn just as much in both types of conversations. However, when people actually had their conversation, they learned much more when the topic was open because the conversation could be steered to topics of mutual interest. People also expected to enjoy both types of conversations equally, but actually enjoyed the open conversation more. This meant that people were especially likely to underestimate how much they'd learn and enjoy in an open conversation with a stranger.[18] Not knowing where a conversation might go and failing to appreciate how responsiveness can steer it in a mutually interesting direction is what can leave us mistakenly thinking that an unstructured conversation with a stranger might go nowhere interesting at all.[19]

Reaching Out Likes You Back

Another source of uncertainty about reaching out to a stranger is the impression that you'll leave on the person you're talking to. Nobody wants to be a bore. The Scottish enlightenment philosopher David Hume even believed that the powerful impact our conversations can have on others elevated the status of being a good conversationalist to a moral virtue. "It may be affirmed in general," Hume argued, "that all the merit a man may derive from his conversation (which, no doubt, may be very considerable) arises from nothing but the pleasure it conveys to those who are present." Because "a cheerful good-humour'd companion diffuses a joy over the whole company," Hume reasoned that the qualities that make someone friendly in conversation "naturally beget love and esteem, and answer to all the characters of virtue."[20]

Being a good conversationalist might be a moral virtue, but it might seem hard to achieve that saintly status if you doubt your own conversational ability. A little over a hundred years after Hume's claim that good conversation is virtuous, the very first book I know of offering advice on *how* to be a good conversationalist opened its 1867 edition by simply affirming that "it is unnecessary to expatiate on the uses, advantages, and pleasures of conversation" because they "are obvious, and are universally felt and admitted." It even labeled the ability to carry on a good conversation a "rare and precious gift, possessed by very few indeed."[21]

Much has changed since Hugo Reid penned this advice in the 1800s, including no longer needing advice about how to have good conversations in stagecoaches, but the view of good conversation skills as being a "rare and precious gift" seems to have changed fairly little. Public speaking is still regularly included among people's biggest fears, and carrying on a conversation with a stranger continues to have the same challenges it has always had. You have to figure out how to start and how to stop, what to talk about and what to avoid, how to handle awkward silences when they arise, and how to avoid being any of the thirteen different types of conversational bores that Hugo Reid spent half of his book describing (including "The Bully," "The Jabberer," "The Joker," or perhaps worst of all, "The Mute," who chooses not to talk at all).

This presumed challenge of being a good conversationalist could lead to some real insecurities about your own abilities in this department. In fact, although people typically rate themselves above average, often even in the top 10 percent, on any desirable ability (such as "leadership"), research indicates that this statistically impossible degree of self-confidence vanishes when people are asked about their conversational abilities. Just think about yourself for a minute. On a percentile scale that goes from 1 (I'm at the very bottom) to 100 (I'm at the very top), with 50 being right in the middle, how would you say you stack up against others in terms of your ability to initiate and carry on a rewarding conversation with a stranger? In a world where above average is now average, I'm betting you might feel somewhat inadequate. I certainly did before the research I've described in this chapter got me routinely talking to strangers. Indeed, when one group of researchers asked people this question, the average estimate people gave for themselves was profoundly average (49th percentile). It also paled in comparison to the statistically impossible scores people gave themselves for their own reading ability (78th percentile), walking ability (73rd percentile), and job performance (73rd percentile). Out of twenty abilities, in fact, conversational ability was the only one that *did not* yield an average that was significantly above average. With the grade inflation that occurs in our own minds, this is the equivalent of giving ourselves a D in conversational skills.[22]

Is this pessimism warranted? Probably not. Although some of us are certainly better at carrying on a conversation than others and most of us could surely become better with both planning and practice, it also seems likely that you're a better talker than you might think you are. In one analysis of seven different experiments involving a total of 2,304 people, those who were asked to have a simple conversation with a stranger thought they would have more difficulty starting and stopping a conversation than they reported experiencing after the conversation was over. People found themselves to be more capable in conversation with a stranger than they expected. These talkers also thought they'd have more difficulty knowing how much to talk than they reported having after the conversation was over. These gaps between people's expectations and their experiences were especially big among those who reported they didn't normally talk to strangers. This makes sense, of course. If you think you're not a great conversationalist, then you're also not likely to try it often, and as a result miss chances to learn that your conversations might flow more easily than you'd expect.

Not only might a conversation go more smoothly than you'd expect it to; it might also leave a more positive impression on your conversation partner than you expect it will, leaving the other person learning more and even liking you more than you imagine beforehand. In the experiments I just described where people underestimated how much they would learn in conversation, we also found that people tended to believe that they learned more from their conversation partner than their partner learned from them. If conversation teaches, then the people in our experiments underestimated how good their own teaching was.[23]

Other researchers have documented a similar result in how much people think their partner likes them in conversation. In one experiment after another, with people ranging from age four to seventy, in contexts ranging from research laboratories to city parks to the office, people report liking their conversation partner more after talking with them than they think their partner likes them in return, an effect referred to as "the liking gap."[24]

I think Hume was right to recognize a willingness to be a "cheerful good-humour'd companion" in conversation as a moral virtue. What we can get wrong is assuming that being good in conversation is "a rare and precious gift." The data I've covered in this chapter provides encouragement that you probably have more of this gift than you'd guess, that your self-doubt is a bit misplaced, and that both you and others around you would be a little better off if you tried using the same superpower that Claire Feuer recognized in herself a little more often.

Reaching Out Pushes Back

If a lifeguard walked up to the edge of the ocean and declared it free from sharks by looking at it through a microscope, you'd have a right to be skeptical. Fine, you might think, you've looked at that spot right *there,* but what about over *there*? Or over *there*? Or *there*?

Studying social life using experiments is a bit like scanning a beach for sharks with a microscope. The experiments I've described can reveal what happens in a given time and place with a level of detail that our everyday lives rarely afford. Rarely do you write down how you think some event is going to unfold so that you can go back and compare it with your actual experience afterward. Even more rarely do you get a bunch of people to do this. Rarer still do you randomly assign a bunch of people to act differently in order to identify consistent tendencies across people in the hopes of identifying general rules or patterns. Experiments are the best microscopes we have to understand the details of our daily lives because they allow us to test hypotheses and observe results that we wouldn't get to see otherwise.

However, social life is a vast expanse of different people interacting in a dizzying variety of contexts that might seem poorly suited for surveying with a microscopic lens. You might be skeptical about whether the precise experiments researchers conduct apply beyond their narrow confines. Indeed, the most common reactions I hear when describing our experiments on buses and trains in Chicago is some version of "That's great, but that would never happen here," or "to me," or "today." There's some sense that if you look at other places, or at different people, or at different times, then reaching out to strangers might be just as bad as you expect it to be. I shared that wariness at the beginning of our research, but it has dulled over the years as we've continued to look through our microscopes. We just haven't found limits where my skepticism expected to find them.

For instance, we took our research microscope to a place where it might be easy to imagine a less positive outcome than what we observed on the trains and buses in Chicago: commuter trains going in and out of London. Londoners aren't typically held up as the world champions of chattiness. Even *The Independent*'s tongue-in-cheek article "7 Stereotypes About British People That Everyone Believes" had this in the No. 5 spot: "British people are rude."[25] In fact, when Jonathan Dunne, a frequent rider on the London Tube, started up a campaign called Tube Chat to try to encourage riders to talk with each other just as Claire Feuer did in New York, the response online was vitriolic opposition. After he set up his own "Tube Chat" Facebook page and handed out "Tube Chat?" buttons on the train, a rival "Shut Up Tube Chat!" Facebook group started handing out its own "Shut up!" buttons that came with instructions: "Want nothing less than a 'chat' with one of your fellow passengers? Wear this badge to let them know you'd rather drink a pint of bleach than talk with them!" We definitely thought we were taking our research into hostile territory.

Those fears, however, were again more prominent in people's imaginations than in their real experiences. When we partnered with the BBC to run another experiment on commuter trains going into London in the morning and out to the suburbs in the evening, we found that London commuters also reported having a more positive commute when we asked them to connect than when we asked them to keep to themselves or to do whatever they normally do.[26] Londoners, it turns out, are human beings, too, and as a result enjoy connecting with other people just as much as everyone else does.[27]

We also asked London commuters to tell us how they felt in their own words. Those in the solitude condition generally told us they weren't doing anything out of the ordinary. This isn't surprising, because only 14 percent told us they normally talk to people on their train ride. The experience was different for those in the connection condition. "It was nice! I enjoyed my conversation, and it made me think I should talk to strangers more," wrote one person. "Nervous but it was nice to talk to others while waiting for a very delayed train!" wrote another. "A little apprehensive but then I'm really glad I took part now as I have a new friend," wrote a third. Even talking about boring topics was nice: "Had a chat with an older woman on the train about the weather, was good to socialize and communicate instead of just sitting and listening to music." Many commented on feeling awkward while starting the conversation but having it go well once they started ("Felt good to talk to someone but a little bit uncomfortable at first"; "Slightly uncomfortable at first, but then ok"), with some even mentioning the experiment serving as the encouragement they needed to talk. "It gave me an excuse to talk to people," wrote one of our commuters, "in my case, two A-level art students who sat next to me and who, without the excuse of the study, it would have been weird to have talked to." Once you understand how positively reaching out to others actually tends to go, I don't think you'll need an excuse to try it more often.

Other limits have also been harder to find in our data than you might imagine. We don't find consistent differences in expectations or experiences of talking with strangers by gender, or even between genders, not only in laboratory experiments that you might think of as relatively risk-free, but also in our studies on trains and buses. This may stem from people's choice of conversation partners.

Participants on the buses in Chicago and trains in London might have chosen partners who seemed safe and nonthreatening, as Claire Feuer told me she does. Jessica Pan, the shy introvert from chapter 2, told me the same thing. "I choose who to talk to carefully," she said, noting that she talks to other women more often so she's not as likely to be misunderstood as potentially flirting (even though her first enjoyable test conversation was with a friendly Finnish man on the London Tube). We observed something similar in our London experiment, where people had some choice in whom they talked to based on where they sat down. Here we found the only gender difference we've ever observed, with women reporting talking to another woman most of the time (73 percent, to be exact), and men not showing any gender preference (speaking to a woman 51 percent of the time). This surely stems from the obvious and unfortunate difference in the potential risks that women and men face in their social lives, but even considering those risks, we still find across our experiments that women and men tend to underestimate how much they'll enjoy connecting with a stranger regardless of that person's gender.

We also don't find that extroversion matters as much as you might imagine, either for people's expectations or for their experiences connecting with strangers, echoing much of the research on extroversion we went through in chapter 2. If anything, across the wide range of experiments I've covered in this chapter, extroversion is generally more strongly related to people's beliefs about how positive they will feel in a social interaction than it is to their actual experiences, but even that result doesn't emerge consistently. The best we can conclude at this point is that the surprisingly positive experience of connecting with another person is not likely to vary a lot based on whatever "type" of person a personality test says you are.[28]

Instead, what matters more is the type of interaction you have. From learning new things, to liking your partner, to loving the interaction, the less of an interaction people had, the less positive they tended to report on almost any outcome we can measure. On buses and trains, in laboratories and public parks, the less people report talking, the less they report enjoying it, the less they report learning, and the less they feel connected to their partner. Nevertheless, when researchers asked people to predict how they would feel over the course of a roughly twenty-minute conversation, they generally thought it would start out well but then get less positive as time wore on and they ran out of things to talk about. But those same people didn't experience this decline. Rather, conversations remained good for longer than people expected they would.[29]

These results aren't much of a surprise to psychologists, who beginning in the 1950s started documenting how powerful physical proximity to others was for friendship. Analyses of friendships among families living in graduate student housing at MIT found that people tended to become friends with those who lived closest to them, even though apartment assignments were random. People were most likely to become friends with someone living next door, followed by someone on the same floor, followed by someone in the same building, and least likely to become friends with someone in a different building.[30] In a study of police cadets, the first letter of their last name was almost a perfect predictor of whom they would name as their best friend in the program because people sat next to each other in alphabetical order and overwhelmingly became friends with the people they spent the most time with.[31] When actually put under the microscope, becoming more familiar with another person tends to breed liking rather than contempt.[32] In fact, there's a name for strangers we've chosen to spend enough time with to know that we actually like them: friends.[33]

Reaching Out Changes You Back

If we can learn that our social expectations are often overly pessimistic by looking carefully through our experimental microscopes, then why don't we see this through our own eyes in our everyday lives?

Actually, I think we would, if our expectations didn't hold us back from reaching out and learning so often.

Not long after conducting our experiments on trains and buses, Juliana Schroeder and I took our experiment on the road again to another potentially "silent space": cabs. Cabs are chattier spaces where conversations between strangers are considerably more common. To put some more precise numbers to this, Juliana and I found that nobody in the control condition of our train experiment in Chicago reported usually talking to a stranger on their commute, and only 7 out of 112 people did so on the trains in London, whereas 49 percent of people in a survey we conducted said they'd be likely to talk to a stranger in a cab (most likely the driver). This context then provides an ideal place for measuring if people actually learn from their experience. Would those who typically talk to their drivers be both more optimistic and more realistic about how connecting with a stranger might go?

Yes, they were. In another experiment following the same structure we used on trains and buses, we asked cab riders to either do whatever they normally did on their ride (our control condition), keep to themselves (our solitude condition), or connect in conversation with the driver (our connection condition). We learned that those who reported routinely talking to their drivers—the "talkers," who were 65 percent of our sample—believed they would enjoy their cab ride more in the connection condition than in the solitude condition, while those who reported rarely talking to their drivers—the "loners"—thought exactly the opposite. However, when we actually put the people into cabs and asked them to try having a conversation with their driver or keep to themselves, both the talkers and the loners enjoyed their ride more when they talked than when they kept to themselves. These differences in expectations between talkers and loners are easy to understand if you think about what their expectations have allowed them to learn. If you actually believed that connecting with a cabdriver might be fun and interesting, you'd probably try it and over time learn what it's like compared with keeping to yourself. But if you believed that talking to the driver would be unpleasant, as the loners might have in this study, then your beliefs would keep you from having the very experiences you needed to learn from.[34]

You can see direct evidence for learning from experience even more clearly if you measure what people learn right after having a conversation with someone. In our train experiment in London commuters in the connection condition indicated they were more likely to consider talking to a stranger again, while those in the solitude and control condition didn't change their views.

However, a single experience rarely teaches us much. Just as your determination to exercise spikes immediately after visiting your doctor but then reverts to its typically low level in a day or two, my bet is that the good intentions you might have to be more social after having a nice conversation fade right along with the positive mood you experience from the conversation. Instead, we need meaningful and sustainable learning from our own experience, which comes from a change in our social habits.

In one especially fun experiment, Gillian Sandstrom and her colleagues created a social scavenger hunt involving twenty-nine different "missions."[35] In the talking condition, these missions required spotting someone of a particular description and then having a conversation with them for a few minutes. These missions included gems like "Artsy" (someone who looks artistic), "Bossy Pants" (someone who looks like a leader), and "Manscape" (someone who has a beard or goatee). Some missions required talking to someone with very specific features, like "Nailed it" (someone with funky nails), whereas others were general, like "Hands free" (someone not carrying anything) or "Inside" (someone inside). You get the idea. In the control condition, people played the same scavenger hunt game but only looked for these people rather than actually going up and having a conversation with them. Over the course of the week, people played the scavenger hunt, earning points in the app for each mission they completed, and also filling out surveys each day measuring their beliefs and experiences.

The results clearly show that we can learn from social experience as long as we have a meaningful amount of experience to learn from. In stark contrast to the bumper sticker on Alex Gregory's *New Yorker* cartoon that reads, "The more I talk to people the more I like my phone," what people learned from their social experiences was much more optimistic. Over the course of the week, those in the talking condition thought it was far less likely that they would be rejected if they tried to talk to someone, expected that conversations with strangers would be less awkward, and thought they would leave a more positive impression on the person they were talking to. These changes happened a little bit each day as people added more and more experiences to their personal data set. On day 1 of the experiment, for instance, these social scavenger hunters thought they'd be rejected about 70 percent of the time. By day 5, these same people were expecting they'd be rejected only about 30 percent of the time.

Perhaps more important, though, is that those in the talking condition also got more realistic as they got more experience approaching others. On day 1, when people expected to be rejected 70 percent of the time, they were actually rejected only 10 percent of the time, a figure that remained constant over the course of the week. By day 5, these talkers were still overly pessimistic, thinking they'd be rejected 30 percent of the time, but they were much more realistic.

Not surprisingly, just as people in the scavenger hunt were getting more realistically optimistic, they were also getting better at reaching out and engaging with others. Over the course of the week, their conversations felt less awkward, they thought their conversations had improved, and they believed they had left a better impression on the people they talked to. Over the course of the week, the talkers came to see themselves as better conversationalists. As with any skill, practice makes you better, if not perfect.

In contrast to those in the talking condition, people who simply watched other people showed no changes in their beliefs over the course of the week because they weren't having interactions to learn from. It's not surprising, then, that one week after the experiment was over, those in the talking condition had changed their behavior and continued to talk to more people than they had before the experiment started, whereas those who simply observed others did not.

This social scavenger hunt clearly shows that we can learn from social experiences when we have good data to learn from, and that this learning could make you more optimistic, more realistic, and more interested in reaching out. Instead of being afraid of strangers, those asked to be a little more social by talking in the social scavenger hunt came to see strangers as positive opportunities to learn new things, create new friendships, brighten both your own and others' days, and leave a positive impact in the minds of others. With a bit more experience and practice, I expect you'd find that you can be a surprisingly virtuous conversationalist, too.

It's one thing to learn that reaching out to connect with others is a surprisingly positive experience, but it's quite another to put that into practice. After finishing our very first experiments on the Metra commuter trains in Chicago, I called up our contact person in Metra's marketing department to share the results. She told me that she had ridden the train herself for many years and that her favorite trips were always the ones in which she talked to someone. "But," she continued, "you're not going to believe what we're about to do." Metra was introducing a new "Quiet Car" policy, in which one car on a line during rush hour would require riders to be silent. "This is what riders said they wanted when we asked them on a survey," she told me. I told her that the people in our experiments also said they would rather be quiet than talk to another person on the train, but that those preferences seemed to be mistaken for their own well-being and for the people they would talk to as well.

I asked if they had ever experimented with the opposite of the Quiet Car. Maybe something like the Chatty Car, where talking with new friends and neighbors might be encouraged rather than discouraged. "No," she chuckled, but they used to have something similar to that on the trains that went way out to the northwest suburbs: the bar cars. People would gather in those cars for a drink and to talk for the entire ride home, making new friends on the trains that sometimes lasted for years and occasionally turned into marriages.

They didn't have those cars anymore, though. I asked her why, imagining that she would tell me about the safety risks of people stumbling off the train drunk or fighting on the trains. "No, that wasn't it," she said. They didn't have the sociable bar cars anymore, *"because they were too crowded."*

Yes, exactly.

Learning that reaching out to others is surprisingly positive doesn't mean you should start doing this nonstop any more than hearing from a chef that putting salt onto a meal makes it taste better means that you back up the salt truck and bring out your shovel. Instead, I think the practice that our data suggests is to go ahead and reach out when you're on the fence between approaching and avoiding someone. Being a little more social would mean noticing the opportunities you have to connect with others more readily, taking advantage of the easy chances life gives you rather than forcing them. Your life is unique, and the opportunities you have to be a little more social are also unique. Once you start seeking them out, I think you'll find opportunities you're passing up fairly quickly.

One common theme in the comments people wrote about their experience with our experiments is that there are fewer opportunities for connecting with people in real life than there used to be, especially with strangers. Bar cars have been swapped for cell phones. Earbuds disconnect us from the world around us. The demand for these devices may actually come, at least partly, from misplaced anxiety about connecting with strangers, and they certainly create a less sociable world to live in. One of our London commuters said, "I see myself as a fairly gregarious person" but nevertheless struggled to connect when we asked them to. "I looked at everyone on their phones with their earplugs in," this person wrote with some lament, "and felt awkward thinking about striking up a conversation. So I chickened out."

I don't know how much times have changed in terms of our anxiety about reaching out. In the 1970s, for instance, the social psychologist Stanley Milgram tried to understand what increasing urbanization might do to our everyday social behavior. Milgram described what he thought were a variety of social norms in urban life that discouraged people from engaging with strangers, including on the subway. "Even though riders are often squeezed into very close proximity," he wrote in 1978, "they are rarely observed to converse."[36]

What has clearly changed due to technology, though, is that we now have to make a choice that most humans never had to make in the past:

not just *whether* to connect with another person, but *how* to connect. Talk or type? Call or text? Talk to one or broadcast to many? Choosing *how* to connect requires understanding how the media through which we choose to interact affects the outcomes of those interactions. Unfortunately, as I'll describe in the next chapter, some of the same psychological barriers that can make us overly reluctant to reach out and engage with others may also lead us to choose how to connect unwisely, choosing to interact over media that are less social, and thereby keep us more distant and disconnected than we could be.

5

The How of Connection

> The great pleasure of conversation and society . . . arises from a certain correspondence of sentiments and opinions, from a certain harmony of minds, which, like so many musical instruments, coincide and keep time with another.
>
> —ADAM SMITH, *The Theory of Moral Sentiments*, 1759[1]

In 1876, Alexander Graham Bell placed the first phone call (to his assistant; "Mr. Watson, come here, I want to see you"), enabling voices to carry beyond earshot ("without ever leaving your home," as Bell later boasted to his father).[2] Just under a century later, in 1971, Ray Tomlinson sent the first email (messages so forgettable that Tomlinson forgot them),[3] enabling text exchanges at a speed that shamed the postal service (also without needing to leave your home). Today, those options are quaint thanks to the iPhone arriving in 2007, which put new methods for connecting into our pockets, including instantaneously delivered text messages, real-time video calls, and an ever-changing landscape of social media like Facebook, Instagram, and X. For most of human history, *how* you connect with another person was never a choice. Now it's a choice you make many times every day.

At their best, these innovations provide a Swiss Army knife of options for choosing to connect with anyone, anywhere in the world, at any time. The challenge is that connecting at a distance requires different channels from connecting up close and personal. Some media come as close to face-to-face social interaction as possible by allowing us to hear, see, and interact with someone in real time, like video calls. Other options keep us more socially distant by taking the fire hose of information available in live social interaction and restricting it to a garden-hose trickle, like the text-based media of emailing and texting.

Sometimes these very different methods of connecting mistakenly get treated as similar in our minds. When my kids tell me that they just "talked" to their friends, I have to check whether they used their faces or their fingers to "talk" on their phones because they think of them as interchangeable. Shortly after an assassination attempt on Donald Trump, the chief executive of X, Linda Yaccarino, sent an internal memo to employees saying, "At moments like this, the world turns to X and we have a responsibility to protect the conversation happening on our platform." The *conversation* happening on X? Is it right to lump whatever kind of interaction is happening on social media with in-person conversation?

No. Research now makes it abundantly clear that how we connect—the medium we use for our interactions—matters a lot for how connected we actually feel to each other. However, research also makes it abundantly clear that it's easy to overlook these differences and therefore make choices about *how* to connect with someone unwisely. Our expectations are largely focused on the static features of our interactions that are easy to think about, such as *whom* we're talking to and *what* we're talking about. What our expectations can leave out are the dynamic and interactive features of the context we're interacting in, such as the back-and-forth responsiveness in conversation, or the variable sound and tone of our voices. But exactly what we say and who we're interacting with tend to matter less than we often expect, while the medium we use matters more than we'd expect. This often leaves us making the mistake of typing too often and talking too rarely for our happiness and social connection without realizing how big a difference it makes.

I've jumped to this conclusion quickly here, but it took me more than two decades and dozens of experiments to reach it myself. Let me walk you through my journey much faster by starting with someone else's journey to a similar discovery. The first glimmerings of misunderstanding the importance of *how* we communicate with each other came to light more than one hundred years ago, long before the existence of emailing or texting or snapchatting.

The Magic of Conversation

When the British anthropologist Bronislaw Malinowski traveled to the Trobriand Islands near Papua New Guinea in 1915 to study "the savage mind," he brought along many theories that he would come to learn were wrong. One was about the purpose of language, and hence the function of communication. "Language, in its developed literary and scientific functions," he wrote to emphasize this as a well-accepted fact, "is an instrument of thought and of the communication of thought." Language, in other words, is meant for transferring useful information from one mind to another.

This made sense for many of the interactions that Malinowski observed. When the islanders were hunting, fishing, or farming, they coordinated their efforts by talking with each other: "move forward," "fish here," "plant this." In these cases, "speech is . . . the one indispensable instrument for creating the ties of the moment without which unified social action is impossible."[4] When we need to get some activity done, our exact words matter.

This pragmatic function of language, however, made much less sense for other interactions that Malinowski saw. At the end of a long day, for instance, the islanders would get together around a fire and talk about . . . well, mostly nothing. Despite having little useful information to pass along, they still talked happily for hours. "Inquiries about health, comments on weather, affirmations of some supremely obvious state of things" were the dominant topics of conversation, including chitchat classics like "Nice weather today" and "Ah, there you are." Was this seemingly useless gum flapping meant to pass along useful thoughts or coordinate important actions? "Certainly not!" Malinowski realized. Instead, language was being used to fulfill "one of the bedrock aspects of man's nature in society": connecting with other people. In this case, language wasn't passing along useful information; it was passing along a handshake.

Somehow this social function of spoken conversation had been overlooked by social scientists of the day. Malinowski pronounced his discovery so profound that it required new terminology. "There can be no doubt that we have here a new type of linguistic use—*phatic communion* I am tempted to call it [derived from the Greek word *phatos*, or spoken]—a type of speech in which ties of union are created by a mere exchange of words." Something more was connecting people that had little to do with the exact words being used. Not knowing exactly what was creating connection made phatic communion seem almost magical.

What Malinowski had stumbled upon was the surprising power of spoken conversation to connect people, even when it's only small talk. Malinowski wisely understood that phatic communion wasn't unique to the islanders but was the same thing European socialites did while lounging over cocktails back home. "In pure sociabilities and gossip we use language exactly as savages do," he wrote, using the jarring language of the early twentieth century, "to establish bonds of personal union. . . . As long as there are words to exchange, phatic communion brings savage and civilised alike into the pleasant atmosphere of polite, social intercourse." As different as people around the world might seem, Malinowski believed he had spotted a human universal: Spoken conversation connects.

Why was this a discovery? Wasn't it obvious?

I think not. Even today, our research reveals that it's easy for us to overlook how the dynamic process of conversation connects us in our everyday lives. Our social interactions unfold like a movie over time, connecting us through moment-by-moment forces that pull us together over the course of the conversation. Our expectations about our social interactions, however, are more like a photograph, focused on the static features of an interaction, such as whom we might be interacting with or what topic we might be talking about. Because the static features of our interaction are obvious to us before the conversation begins while dynamic forces are complicated and unfold in ways that might be hard to imagine over time, our expectations tend to overestimate the impact of static features and overlook the impact of dynamic forces that are actually pulling us together. Two dynamic forces in particular—synchrony and sound—have a *surprisingly* strong tug because they rarely catch our notice. Choosing *how* to connect and forming accurate impressions based on *how* we're connecting require understanding both the obvious features that animate our interactions and the important but easily overlooked ones.

The Subtlety of Synchrony

Conversation seems like it should resemble a tennis match: One person speaks, the other responds, and so on, back and forth with each side taking turns ("walkie-talkie style," as the researchers Gus Cooney and Andrew Reece rightly describe it).[5] This is certainly how the gist of an interaction unfolds, and therefore how we remember our interactions: "I said this, and then she said that, and then I responded with this," and so on.

This type of volley is not, however, how a live conversation *actually* unfolds. When we put our interactions under a microscope, recording every audible sound as a single turn in the conversation, you see much more going on than just words passed back and forth.

Below is a completely ordinary snippet from an entirely typical conversation between a white woman in her fifties, who I'll refer to as Emily, and a Black man in his sixties, who I'll refer to as Dennis. These two people participated in the research study I described briefly in chapter 4 that video-recorded thousands of conversations between strangers.[6] The researchers transcribed every sound each person made, at the exact time they made it, and then placed it on its own line as a single turn in the conversation as if they were actually going back and forth in a volley. This bit is from the start of their conversation, establishing the not-so-thrilling details of where they're calling from at the moment:

Woman | Man

…I'm in Warren, Michigan right

Um

outside of Detroit, uh,

Nice.

somewhat of a suburban area tonight.
Where are you at?

I am, right at the moment, we are in Banner Elk, North Carolina, so it's uh near Boone um

Yeah,

kind of like about an hour and a half north of Asheville.

Okay. Never heard of

Okay,

it. But familiar with North Carolina. So you said momentarily, are you guys just doing this because of the Corona thing?

Well, we actually about a year and a half ago, we sold all our house and all our stuff and went full time RV'ing, so for

Oh,

the

wow.

last month we've been here

Okay,

Yeah,

wow.

it's been interesting, but with the coronavirus, you know, a lot of things have closed down,

Right.

You know,

Right.

and so that was a little

Right.

bit nerve wracking, but I know it's been probably good because right now there's hardly anyone at this campground, so it's

Right.

been uh

Right.

we're like in the mountains, nature, and

Oh,

that's good.

that's kind of cool. That's pretty nice. I'm

Yeah,

not that adventurous,

we would,

but that's beautiful

The conversation continues for another fifteen hundred lines, covering everything from their jobs to religion to whether they own too much stuff. Beyond this wide-ranging content, what really jumps out is the conversation dynamic. Neither Emily nor Dennis is actually going back and forth, sitting silently as the other person is speaking. They're both doing some sort of speaking almost constantly, more like musicians playing together in a rock band. When Emily takes the lead vocals, Dennis provides the rhythm that keeps the conversation flowing with a steady backbeat of affirmations—"right, right, right, okay, wow." When Dennis grabs the mic to take the lead in the next stretch of the conversation, Emily picks up the rhythm—"yeah, okay, uh huh, yeah, yeah." This isn't going back and forth; this is constant collaboration. Over this thirty-five-minute conversation, the average length of each person's turn before their partner makes a sound is only 5.3 words, rarely enough for a full sentence. There's nothing unusual about this particular conversation. The average length across all conversations in this study is only 6.4 words. In other words, really short.

This background rhythm doesn't stick in our memories, and barely even registers as an important part of a conversation as we're going through it. But as every musician knows, it's the rhythm section that keeps a song moving even if the flashy lead singer gets all of the attention. Those brief one- or two-word sounds—called back-channeling—don't interrupt a conversation; they push it along. Back-channeling is the sound that shows we care about what someone is saying and are paying attention. It's also the sound we use to provide instantaneous feedback, making it clear when we understand (uh-huh) or are confused (huh?), when we're impressed (wow) or are surprised (oh?), and when we agree (yeah) or disagree (hmmm). This feedback shapes the conversation so that we communicate clearly and avoid misunderstanding. It also allows our conversation partner to make it clear that they truly understand us. Back-channeling is an essential ingredient for creating social connection because it is what gives us a sense of mutual understanding.

Even nonwords, like laughter, infuse our live interactions with the tones that pull us together. One of the most interesting insights about how spoken conversation functions is the psychologist Robert Provine's discovery that laughter isn't so much our spontaneous reaction to something funny as it is a signal of warmth and affection. When Provine recorded what people actually laughed at over the course of their day, he found that it wasn't what was said that mattered but rather whom people were with. In particular, people tended to laugh when they were with other people they liked and cared about rather than when something funny was said. Laughing communicates liking. This is why, Provine discovered, we laugh roughly thirty times more often when we're with other people than when we're alone. "The necessary stimulus for laughter is not a joke, but another person," Provine concluded.[7]

When the researchers analyzed the thousands of strangers they recorded in conversation, they noted that back-channeling was used universally and frequently. Every single person back-channeled to some extent, at an average rate of roughly one "yeah" or "uh-huh" every four seconds (usually accompanied by a corresponding nonverbal cue like nodding or shaking one's head). Of course, some of us play a more active rhythm section in our conversations than others. The more people used back-channeling, the more positive they reported feeling about their partner after the conversation. As the authors write, "A single 'mhm' may appear eminently forgettable, but when well-timed and particularly in the aggregate, backchannels become essential conduits of understanding and affiliation."[8] Those forgettable sounds are the dynamic moment-by-moment forces that pull us together over the course of a conversation.

The other revelation from analyzing the precise details of conversation is how fast they unfold, going back and forth between speakers at lightning speed. When I call my dad on the phone to catch up and open with, "Hey, Dad, how's it going?" my dad knows instantly that it's his turn to step in and respond. There's no need for a "you're it" tap on the shoulder, no baton to pass, no "over and out" walkie-talkie lingo required for him to know that it's his turn to respond. Despite this, my dad has no trouble picking up the conversation the instant I stop speaking, if not even sooner. Although I think my dad's the best on many dimensions, I have to admit that he's perfectly ordinary in this regard. When researchers time-stamp the moment when one person stops talking and the other person starts, the typical gap is an astonishingly fast 200 milliseconds.[9] This is about as fast as an eyeblink, which takes roughly 150 milliseconds.

Responding at eyeblink speed requires paying attention to what someone is saying while also looking ahead and predicting what they're going to say before they even say it, anticipating how a turn will end so that we're ready to jump in the instant it's our turn (or even jumping in before our partner is finished). A great conversation goes back and forth without an eyeblink's delay because two people care so much about each other that they're almost perfectly in sync, their minds tightly connected.

It won't surprise you, then, that our brains are exceptionally sensitive to how quickly someone responds to us in conversation. Delays of even just fractions of a second can make it seem like the other person isn't paying attention or is struggling to find what to say, in the same way that you'd assume a neighbor who rushes over the instant you ask for help cares about you more than someone who saunters over at their leisure. In one series of conversation experiments, the longer it took a partner to respond, the less connected people felt to their partner and the less they enjoyed the conversation. The speed at which a conversation went back and forth was taken as a signal of their partner's interest.[10]

Interestingly, our own response times in conversation are not as closely tied to how connected we feel or how much we enjoy the conversation.[11] What really matters for how connected you feel in a conversation is how interested your conversation partner seems to be in you.[12] Live, synchronous interaction allows that responsiveness to shine through and therefore allows us to connect much better than asynchronous interactions like email, texting, or most not-so-social media.

Synchrony, Overlooked

As important as synchrony seems for our sense of connection after I've spent a few thousand words describing it, it's easy to overlook when choosing *how* to connect in our daily lives. To see an example of this, consider one experiment in which we asked pairs of people to have a short interaction with each other.[13] We gave them five topics they could use to introduce themselves, including where they'd like to visit in the future, what hobbies they enjoy, and what kind of music they like. We then varied how they would interact. In one case, people would have a dialogue with their partner (a live conversation). In another case, people would record a monologue for their partner in which they answered these questions, and then each person would watch their partner's video answering the same questions. Notice that the monologue condition contains none of the moment-by-moment cues to responsiveness that are present in live interaction, including back-channeling and turn taking, whereas the dialogue condition contains all of them.

The importance of *how* they get to know each other in this experiment is obvious to us right now because we've been shining a spotlight on it, but it wasn't obvious to the people moments before they were about to interact. As you can see in the figure below, people didn't think that how they were connecting would matter, expecting to feel similarly connected after a monologue or dialogue. However, after the interaction was over, those who had a dynamic dialogue with someone actually felt more connected to their conversation partner than those who just watched their partner's monologue. This meant that only those who had a live conversation with another person significantly underestimated how connected they would feel after their conversation. Although you'd be much happier getting to know someone by actually talking in conversation with them, not appreciating this beforehand might leave you choosing the ease of email or one-sided social media to connect with someone instead.

If we don't recognize the power of *how* we interact for determining how well our interactions go, then we run the risk of forming mistaken impressions about the person we're interacting *with*. Indeed, when we randomly assigned people in another experiment to have a monologue with one person and a dialogue with another person, people felt that their dialogue partner was friendlier than their monologue partner.[14] Objectively speaking, that simply can't be true because *how* they interacted was randomly determined by a coin flip. More than that, when we asked who they'd rather be friends with in real life, more than half

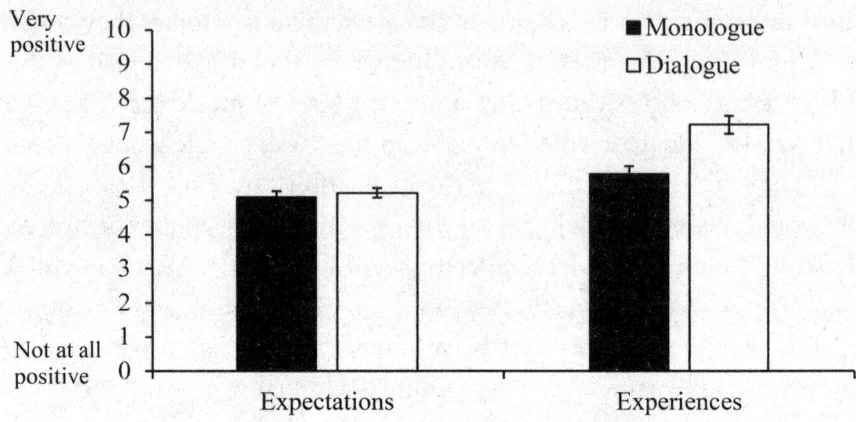

(54 percent) chose their dialogue partner while only a fifth (20 percent) chose their monologue partner (26 percent had no preference). Not appreciating that *how* they were interacting was responsible for how connected they felt rather than the person they talked to, people guessed that they wouldn't be friends with someone they met in a context that kept them from connecting better in a real conversation.

These mistakes matter because the technological tools that allow us to connect with each other at a distance often trade live, real-time interaction for easier asynchronous interaction. An email or text message can communicate ideas based purely on the words passed back and forth, but it lacks the rhythm that connects us. "The conversation happening" on X is not what happens when people have a real conversation with another person. Is it any wonder that social media can so often seem cold, cruel, and frankly antisocial? Online forums might be good places to find people to talk or have a dialogue with, but they're bad forums for actually connecting us with each other.

Even tools that come very close to live conversation still can contain surprising shortcomings. During the COVID-19 pandemic, many people turned to video-chatting software like Zoom to stay connected during the time when we were being encouraged to stay physically distant from each other. But we also learned that nonstop Zooming could be exhausting, leading to an entirely new concept in human life—Zoom fatigue—and even a new word in Yiddish for the exhausting experience, *oysgezoomt* (pronounced "OYS-geh-ZOOMT").[15] One reason is that Zoom isn't quite as synchronous as actual face-to-face interaction, and is more prone to transmission delays than even landline telephones. The delay isn't long enough to derail a conversation, but it's enough to turn what would be an otherwise pleasant interaction into an offbeat slog as you figure out when to talk and when your back-channeled "right" lands at precisely the wrong time.[16]

The point isn't that we should go back to the 1800s and only have face-to-face interactions any more than understanding the cost of car pollution means we should go back to the horse and buggy. The point is that being wise about how to use any technology requires understanding its costs and benefits. The ease of technology that allows us to respond to each other via text anytime at our leisure also comes with costs that are easy to overlook. Once you understand how dynamic forces are important for creating connection through conversation, then you can make decisions and form impressions more wisely. You might shoot off an email or text a little bit less often and pick up the phone and call someone a bit more. You might also recognize that your *oysgezoomt* is coming not from the person you're talking *with* but from the medium you're talking *in*.

The Sound of Connection

Another easy-to-overlook force creating connection is the dynamic sound of our voice. In a letter from 1910 declining an invitation to speak at a conference about the challenges of deafness in children, Helen Keller described how difficult it was to connect when you were unable to hear someone's voice. "I am just as deaf as I am blind," she wrote, but the "problems of deafness are deeper and more complex, if not more important, than those of blindness. Deafness is a much worse misfortune. For it means the loss of the most vital stimulus—the sound of the voice that brings language, sets thought astir and keeps us in the intellectual company of man." "To be cut off from hearing," she reiterated later in her life, "is to be isolated indeed."[17] Decades of research have now clarified the contours of Keller's experience. Our voice communicates much more than the very same words in the text of an email or a post on social media. What is it about our voice that connects?

Voice Clarifies. One obvious answer is what Malinowski assumed was the core purpose of language to begin with: to communicate thoughts from one mind to another.

But your voice conveys what's on your mind beyond the words that you're using. How quickly you speak reveals whether you're excited or bored, anxious or calm, frightened or fearless. Your volume communicates your emotions, your confidence, and your commitment to what you're saying. The tone of your voice, whether high-pitched and playful or low and weighty, tells whether you're teasing or being serious. The exact same word, "Daddy," from my youngest daughter, Lindsay, could communicate anything from being scared (Daddy!) to feeling happy to have me come home (Daddy!) to just identifying me to her friends (Daddy!). I couldn't know what Lindsay means just by reading the words she's using, but I know the instant I hear it. The more ambiguous our words are, the more the sound of our voice communicates the meaning of what we're saying.

You don't have to be deaf or blind to experience this. Just listen to the monotone flatness of text alone as you read the following iconic Hollywood movie lines: "I'm king of the world"; "Is he smart . . . or . . . or is he . . . ?"; "Good morning, Vietnam." From the words alone, you can't hear an ounce of Leonardo DiCaprio's exhilaration as he shouts from the bow in *Titanic*. You can't detect a teaspoon of Tom Hanks's heart-wrenching concern in his question about his newly discovered son in *Forrest Gump*. And you could scarcely imagine the kaleidoscope of emotions that Robin Williams reveals in his daily sign-on from the movie *Good Morning, Vietnam*. Your voice, in contrast, embeds that information within the words you're using.

Psychologists have learned just how much information a person's voice carries by doing the same thing I just did with movie lines, by comparing the sound of an interaction with the text of it. Researchers consistently find that we can guess what's on another's mind more accurately when we can hear what they're saying than when reading the exact same words in a text. In one such experiment, a group of roughly two hundred volunteers were asked to evaluate one of two dozen different conversations between two people. At random points, researchers paused the video and asked the volunteers to guess what the speaker was thinking and what the speaker was feeling. Researchers then compared the volunteers' guesses with what the actual speakers reported they were thinking or feeling at those same time points. Results indicated that the volunteers were notably more accurate at guessing what was going through a speaker's mind when they heard what the speaker was saying compared with when they read a transcript.[18]

In this same experiment, volunteers were no more accurate in judging a speaker's thoughts or feelings when they could see them in a video compared with only hearing their voice in audio, and they were the least accurate by far when the speaker's voice was removed and the volunteers could only see them in a silent video. The visual cues we get through another person's body language tend to be highly redundant with the cues we get through their voices (they nod along while saying "right, right," scrunch up their faces in a thinker pose while voicing "hmmm . . . ," or smile while their voice is lifting). Nonverbal behavior tends to be highly ambiguous on its own but can be clarified by the sound of someone's voice.[19]

When it comes to clarifying what's on our mind, your voice works so well because it's also so closely connected to our ongoing conscious experience. You're speaking as you're thinking and feeling. This fact highlights that it's not just our voice that conveys what's on our mind, but expressing our thoughts and feelings through real-time language as we're having the thoughts and feelings that really counts. Sign language, interestingly—which Helen Keller never fully learned herself—shows all of the same paralinguistic cues that the human voice does, but conveys them through bodily movement that contains many of the same dynamic attributes contained in our voice.[20]

Voice Reveals. There's something even deeper, though, that your voice can reveal beyond the thoughts and feelings that are on your mind. It can reveal that you actually have a mind that is capable of thinking and feeling, rather than being a relatively mindless animal or machine. That's a bit abstract, so let me explain.

The most fundamental divide in social life is between yourself and others. Others' minds, after all, are inherently invisible. You can experience yourself thinking and feeling, but you can't experience someone else thinking and feeling. Philosophically speaking, this is supposed to create a problem for you because you can't know for sure that any other mind exists in the world beyond your own.

I doubt, however, that you've ever lost even a second of sleep over this. Despite being unable to experience another person's mind, most adults have no trouble recognizing that other people can think and feel, too. Solving this philosophical version of the Other Minds Problem seems to be a problem only for philosophers.

Or is it?

Having direct experience with your own mind means that your own ability to think and feel shines brightly, while having to infer the minds of others makes their experience more abstract, less intense, and potentially a little dimmer. Your own ability to reason carefully, to think deeply, and to feel emotions intensely is clear. With others, you have to guess. When you have a headache, for instance, you feel your pain intensely. When another person has a headache, you feel nothing. Because you experience the intensity of your own pain but not others' pain, it's easy to think that your headache is more painful than someone else's headache. Is it any wonder that pain medicine is always advertised as "extra strength"?

The same goes for our emotions and even our thinking. Research indicates a reliable tendency to think that we feel emotions like joy, shame, guilt, and embarrassment more intensely than others do. And because you're aware of all the time you've spent ruminating about whom to vote for or what career to choose, it's easy to think that you're thinking a little more deeply and rationally than someone else is. In conflicts or disagreements, the consequence is a tragically misplaced tendency to think that one's own arguments are reasonable and rational while the other side's arguments are biased, illogical, or maybe even crazy. It's not just that we disagree with what's on their minds; it's that we think their minds don't work as well as ours do.

This tendency to think that other people have a less lively mind than we do ourselves is so widespread that we have dubbed it the Lesser Minds Problem.[21] However, the same cues of intonation, volume, and pacing in someone's voice that clarify what's on their mind can also reveal that they have a lively mind rather than being relatively mindless. You might not be able to "see" another person's mind, but—as Helen Keller implied—you can hear it. Notice, however, that none of the cues to a lively mind are available in text alone. When you read what someone has to say, the voice you hear in your head simply can't infuse the text with the same degree of mental life that you'd hear if the person was actually talking to you.

The upshot is that our lively minds, capable of intelligent thinking and intense feeling, are simply obscured in text compared with the mind revealed through our voices, making other people seem less mindful—less intelligent, less rational, less emotional, less *human*—when they're typing to each other than when they're talking to each other. We observed this directly in an experiment we conducted on the eve of the 2016 U.S. presidential election between Donald Trump and Hillary Clinton. The animosity then was intense. It wasn't just that Americans disagreed with what they believed people on the other side of the political divide thought or felt; it was that they weren't sure those people could think or feel at all.

"Democrats Prove to Be Delusional," read one op-ed headline I found around that time. "Donald Trump Is Crazy, but (Probably) Not Insane" was another. In this experiment, we asked Clinton and Trump supporters on the eve of the election to either listen to another voter explain why they were voting the way they were or read their explanation. Not surprisingly, the voters were rated by the supporters as being more mindful—more thoughtful, rational, and caring—when the supporter agreed with the voter than when they disagreed. More interestingly, regardless of agreement, the voter seemed more mindful when the volunteer could hear the voter's voice than when they just read their written statements.[22] In short, the written explanation made the voter seem relatively dead inside—less rational, less thoughtful, less caring. You can't see the mind of another person in the text they use to communicate, but you can hear it in their voice.

It's hard to escape the conclusion that text-based interactions are subtly dehumanizing. There are obvious consequences to this that you can easily bring to mind—the stoking of misconceptions, the fanning of prejudice, misplaced divides—but I have to admit there's a less obvious and more tragic consequence that haunts me as the father of a daughter with Down syndrome who struggles to speak as clearly as her peers do. In Helen Keller's letter that I quoted from earlier, she also described how she had "received letters from the parents of children who were either deaf or feeble-minded, the parents could not say which. The doctor did not know, or else he did not tell them the truth." Being unable to hear, and hence unable to speak without the aid of sign language, led at least some parents to mistakenly question their child's ability to think. I think it's no accident that being unable to hear and speak in Keller's day was referred to as being "deaf and dumb." Typers, beware.

Sound, Overlooked

In hindsight, I'm sure it was obvious to the PR manager Justine Sacco that typing was the wrong way to pass along what she thought was snarky sarcasm. For several days in December 2013, she had been sharing what she thought were sharp-witted observations to her 170 followers on Twitter and was now keeping up the shtick on a layover in Heathrow Airport on her way to South Africa. "Chili-cucumber sandwiches—bad teeth. Back in London!" she announced. Then, about half an hour before taking off on the last leg of her trip, an attempt to poke at the injustice of apartheid in a sarcastic joke: "Going to Africa. Hope I don't get AIDS. Just kidding. I'm white!" She kept an eye on Twitter, looking for some recognition of her humorous sarcasm but got nothing. She shut off her phone at the start of her eleven-hour flight and went to sleep.

They're just words: "Just kidding. I'm white!" No inflection. No change of pace. No uptick in volume to make Justine's sarcasm clear. No voice to reveal the mind behind her message. Words alone are a blank slate onto which we project our own preconceptions about what someone else is like. To those who just read the text online, the serious voice they heard in the text of someone they knew nothing about was that of a stone-cold bigot. When Justine landed, she turned on her phone and found it blowing up. "You need to call me immediately," her best friend texted. "You're the number-one worldwide trend on Twitter right now." Justine had just been identified online as the world's biggest racist, and the internet army was on the warpath. Some example reactions: "No words for that horribly disgusting, racist as fuck tweet from Justine Sacco"; "All I want for Christmas is to see @JustineSacco's face when her plane lands and she checks her inbox/voicemail"; and "How did @JustineSacco get a PR job?! Her level of racist ignorance belongs on Fox News. #AIDS can affect anyone!"

In his book *So You've Been Publicly Shamed*, Jon Ronson explains Justine's experience and its aftermath in surprisingly gripping detail.[23] For our purposes, I'll just say that Justine's joke landed with an earth-shattering thud. You might think it's unlikely for someone in a public relations position to not anticipate just how badly a joke sent through text alone could be misinterpreted. However, this episode reminded me of an experiment my colleagues and I had conducted more than a decade earlier.[24] This was a very public version of countless mistakes we had seen people make privately in our research.

Justine thought she was communicating what was on her mind perfectly clearly: It was a (bad) sarcastic joke. Those who read Justine's tweet also thought they had understood her mind clearly, when they had actually misunderstood her. We found the same pattern in our research. In one experiment, we showed one group of people a series of twenty statements, half of which were written to be sincere and the other half to be sarcastic. The people who wrote the statements were asked to pick the ten that they thought would be most easily recognized as sincere or sarcastic—and here's the catch—either by typing (as in an email) or by talking (as in a voicemail). After sending their message, the senders guessed how many out of ten a recipient would identify correctly. We then turned the tables and asked these senders to read someone else's messages and guess how many were meant to be sincere or sarcastic, and to estimate how many out of these ten they had actually identified correctly.

Again, for you and me who are thinking carefully about how the medium we use affects the message we communicate, it's obvious that it's easier to hear sarcasm or sincerity than read it. Indeed, as you can see in the figure below, recipients correctly identified the meaning of the messages 73 percent of the time when they heard the sender, but only 56 percent of the time when they read the sender's message. In fact, this 56 percent figure doesn't differ significantly from what we would expect by chance alone (50 percent), meaning that people were no better than a coin flip at guessing the true meaning over email. However, this difference was not obvious to the senders who were in the midst of communicating their messages, because they expected that recipients would get a similar number correct (around 78 percent) regardless of whether they were typing or talking to them. When you're communicating with someone, your intentions to be sincere or sarcastic are so clear that you can probably hear the tone of your own voice as you're typing out your snarky text—ha-ha clickety ha click—making it hard to realize that others aren't hearing the same voice as you're typing. Like Justine, people thought they were communicating clearly with their words alone. In fact, they weren't communicating clearly at all.

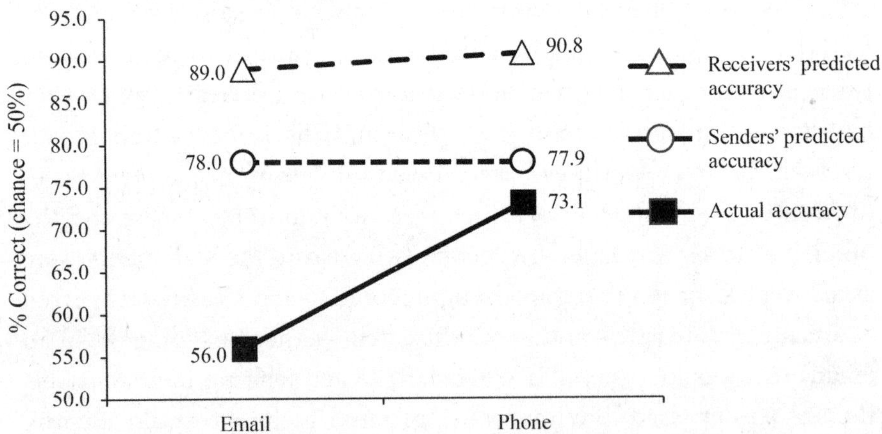

Even more troubling is that the recipients, like Justine's Twitter mob, were also unaware of how much the medium mattered for how well they understood the sender's mind. Recipients thought they had interpreted roughly 90 percent of the statements accurately, a figure that again was the same regardless of whether people were reading or hearing what someone else had to say. The left side of the figure explains almost all you need to know about the challenges of modern communication: Over text, people were no better than chance at communicating what was on their mind, but they thought they were communicating clearly, and recipients thought they were understanding with crystal clarity. The dynamic of Justine and her Twitter mob is dramatically more likely when you're typing to each other at a distance than when you're talking directly to each other.

It's not just that we're insensitive to how well voice clarifies what's on our mind—our thoughts and feelings. We're also insensitive to how well it reveals the existence of another's mind—that they are a thoughtful, intelligent, and emotional human being. In another series of experiments, we asked University of Chicago MBA students—among the brightest minds in the world—to give an elevator pitch to their favorite employer explaining why they should be offered their dream job.[25] They delivered their pitch both in writing and in a videotaped speech. The MBA students didn't think that *how* they delivered their pitch would matter for how mindful—how competent, thoughtful, intelligent, and likable—the employer would judge them to be. They expected the employer to form the same impressions of their mental capabilities regardless of whether they heard what they had to say or read it. As a result, they also didn't think they would seem any more or less hirable when their pitch was heard versus read.

In fact, when we presented these pitches both to volunteers who imagined being an employer in one experiment and to actual hiring managers from Fortune 500 firms in another experiment, our MBA students' genuinely bright minds were seen as even brighter—as more competent, thoughtful, intelligent, likable—when employers heard the pitch than when they merely read it. Both groups of potential employers were therefore more interested in hiring the MBA student when they heard their pitch than when they read it. And yet, when we asked a separate group of nearly a thousand people online how they would choose to express their thoughts to be seen as most intelligent, 70.6 percent said they would choose to write and only 29.4 percent said they would choose to speak. Believing that interactions are guided by the words we're using rather than the voice we're using to communicate them, as Malinowski did until he understood communication more deeply, could lead you to choose the wrong way to really impress someone.

Overlooking how our voices connect us to the minds of others can also lead to mistakes in how we might choose to connect to someone. Think about reaching out to an old friend you haven't talked to in a while. Would you want to reconnect by typing an email to them or by picking up the phone and talking to them? When Amit Kumar and I asked a group of people to imagine reconnecting with an old friend either by emailing them or by talking on the phone, directly contrasting these two modes against each other did make people recognize that how they connected would matter.[26] In particular, they thought they'd enjoy talking more than typing, thought they'd feel a stronger bond talking than typing, and thought they'd get to know the person again better talking than typing. However, they also thought it would be considerably more awkward to talk to an old friend than to type to them. Talking might be nicer, they seemed to think, but it'd also be more uncomfortable, creating a classic approach/avoidance conflict of the kind we discussed back in chapter 2. When we then asked them to choose how to connect, avoidance won: Most (67 percent) said they would rather type an email to their old friend than talk to them on the phone.

Like pulling a rabbit out of a hat, these would-be reconnectors then put their hands into a bag and blindly pulled out a slip of paper that said either "email" or "phone," which told them how to get in touch with their old friend. After they had actually done so, they told us how the reconnection went. Their experiences didn't differ based on what they had wanted to do; all that mattered was what they were assigned to do. As they had anticipated, those who reconnected by talking to their old friend did indeed have a more positive experience overall: Talkers enjoyed the experience more, felt a stronger bond, and felt like they got to know their old friend better. The fear that talking would be more awkward than typing, however, was mistaken: Those who called up their old friend reported feeling no more awkward than those who had typed an email to their old friend. This avoidance-oriented barrier would have led many people in this experiment to have unwisely chosen to type to their old friend, when picking up the phone and talking would have been better.

It's not just connecting with friends that we might fumble. Imagine you were about to have a conversation about politics with someone who disagrees with you. Would you want to talk to them or type to them? I understand that's a little like asking whether you'd rather have your colonoscopy while lying on your left side or your right side (it's unpleasant either way), but when researchers asked two hundred people in an online survey what they'd rather do, it was a landslide, with 83.9 percent saying they would choose to type rather than talk.[27] This choice to type about a conflict rather than talk about it, though, would be a mistake. In a series of nine experiments conducted everywhere from college campuses to online meetups, people who actually talked with someone they disagreed with ended up feeling that they understood their partner better, had less conflict in their conversation, and had a more positive impression of their partner than if they typed with someone they disagreed with. Your voice communicates your thoughts more clearly, reveals your mind more easily, and makes even difficult conversations run surprisingly smoothly.

Conflict, and the corrosion of civil society it produces, stems not only from the disagreements we have with each other but also from how we choose to interact over those disagreements. Your voice carries the sound of peace, as long as you choose to use it.

I sometimes wonder what Bronislaw Malinowski would think if he could watch a group of people sitting around a campfire with all the modern tools of connection available to them today. Would he even be able to see phatic communion in the same way he saw it in the Trobriand Islanders?

In many ways, he almost certainly would. Our idle chitchat surely sounds about as trivial as it did a hundred years ago, but it's also surely as nice as it's always been to pass the time connecting in conversation with friends, family, or even strangers. But then, at some point, the dynamics of a conversation today might change. Someone's pocket would buzz, and the synchrony of live interaction would be broken. Another might spot a seemingly urgent email from work. One of the two remaining would get bored for a split-second and check their text messages. Not wanting to be left staring at people staring at their phones, the last lonely person might have a quick look at the latest outrage online and get lost in the doomscroll. Before long, everyone would be sitting stone-faced around the campfire connecting in a mediocre fashion with others elsewhere, in silence. Would Malinowski count this as progress?

The technology that enables us to stay connected to anyone, anywhere, at any time can be a great blessing if we use our tools wisely, but it can degrade the quality of our connections if we use them unwisely. Beyond the obvious distractions of being constantly connected through our phones and the internet, the tools we use to stay constantly connected to others elsewhere can lack the rhythm of synchrony and sound of the human voice that makes interactions as enjoyable, informative, and connecting as they could be.

Sometimes the text-based, asynchronous media that are so suboptimal for connecting to each other suit our more pragmatic purposes perfectly well. If you're sending a spreadsheet, use email. And sometimes, when pragmatics dominate, time doesn't allow, or physical distance doesn't enable, second-best tools for connecting are still infinitely better than not being able to connect at all. I love being able to stay in touch over text with my kids while they're far away. But at other times, we make these choices mindlessly, choosing what's easy rather than what might be best without even realizing it. In those cases, if we understand the dynamics that draw us together in interaction, we can choose *how* to connect better.

The value of sitting down and talking directly with someone isn't a new remedy for strengthening our connections and increasing our happiness. In 1759, Adam Smith wrote, "Society and conversation, therefore, are the most powerful remedies for restoring the mind to its tranquility . . . as well as the best preservative of that equal and happy temper."[28] What's new is that in order to use this age-old remedy, you increasingly have to choose it.

What is not new, however, is that once you've made *the choice* to talk with someone in conversation, you have to decide what to talk about. Do you stick to the fond familiarity of phatic communion to talk about the weather or your work, or do you try to use the content of your conversation to go beyond small talk to have deeper and more meaningful conversation? Merely talking with someone connects, but talking deeply connects you even more. As I'll describe in the next chapter, the same mistaken fears that can lead you to avoid talking with someone in the first place, or to use more distant media to connect in the second place, can also lead you to spend more time stuck in shallow conversation than you should be.

6

Going Deeper

I am convinced that men hate each other because they fear
each other.
They fear each other because they don't know each other,
and
they don't know each other because they don't communicate
with each other, and
they don't communicate with each other because they are
separated from each other.
And God grant that something will happen to open
channels of communication.

—MARTIN LUTHER KING JR., lecture at Cornell College, Mount Vernon, Iowa, October 15, 1962

I was feeling far too nervous to believe that God was somehow using me to open channels of communication as I stood in front of a little more than fifty finance executives in the auditorium of a Connecticut-based hedge fund. These executives had flown in from around the country to spend several days at a financial decision-making conference. I assumed I was on the lineup as entertainment.

I wasn't there, though, just to entertain. I was there to run an experiment, and my audience had no idea what I was about to have them do. I didn't know exactly how it would turn out, either, because I had never run this exact experiment before.

After a few opening remarks, I revealed my plan. In a few minutes, I told them, I was going to pair them up randomly with another person in the room to have a conversation about the following four prompts:

1. For what in your life do you feel most grateful? Tell the other person about it.
2. If a crystal ball could tell you the truth about yourself, your life, your future, or anything else, what would you want to know?
3. If you were going to become a close friend with the other person, please share what would be important for him or her to know.
4. Can you describe the last time you cried in front of another person?

The response was not promising. A man in the front row immediately blurted out, "Oh, shit!" People groaned. A mutiny was brewing. I forged on, explaining that I first needed them to fill out a short survey before having their conversation. Using their phones or computers to access it online, my audibly pessimistic crowd reported how they expected the conversations would go: how awkward they would feel, how strong a bond they would feel with the other person, how much they would like the other person, and how happy they would feel about the conversation.

Put yourself in their shoes for a moment. How do you think you'd feel moments before a conversation like this with a stranger? The answer matters because just as you have to make *the choice* to reach out and approach or avoid someone, and choose how to interact with someone, you also have to choose how deep to go once you're interacting. Do you keep your conversations in the shallow end of the conversation pool, chitchatting about the weather and where you live, or do you invite a conversation that allows you to really open up and truly get to know another person? In the words of R.E.M., "Should we talk about the weather? / Should we talk about the government?"[1] If we're overly pessimistic about how deep and meaningful conversations will be, then we'll find ourselves sticking to the ankle-deep end of the conversation pool.

After they finished the survey, I paired everyone up and reminded them that they had about ten minutes to talk. Thankfully, nobody bolted. Once they were settled into their convresations, the feeling in the room changed dramatically. Their faces got brighter. The mood grew lighter. A pair in the front row was laughing. After talking for a while, one man in the back was tearing up. Now I was facing a different problem: How do I get them to *stop* talking? I eventually wrangled their conversations to an end after about twenty minutes by yelling a countdown from 5, a trick I learned from a kindergarten teacher. As people rose to return to their seats, the whole room seemed to be hand-shaking or back-patting. One pair was hugging. Even though I thought this could happen, I was still startled by what I saw. I had given countless lectures in my job as a professor. I had never seen anything like this.

I asked everyone to return to their survey, which asked the same questions as before their conversation, but this time telling me how their conversation actually went.

The surveys my audience completed showed that they were just as surprised as I was. Before their conversations, my audience generally thought their conversations would be pretty mediocre: fairly awkward, without leaving them feeling very connected or happy. After the conversation, they essentially said the conversation was great: not awkward at all, while feeling quite connected and really happy. These gaps between expectations and experiences were massive in statistical terms, but I didn't need the statistics to detect the difference right in front of me. Everyone could see it in the smiles on people's faces, and could hear it in the stories they told when I asked them to describe how their conversations had gone.

Despite entering their conversation with a twinge of dread, they left feeling delighted. Maybe the key to opening meaningful channels of communication in our daily lives is recalibrating our expectations?

Deep Talks

Looking back on it, maybe I shouldn't have been so surprised by how these conversations had gone. Decades of research have documented that engaging in deep conversations—conversations that go beyond surface-level pleasantries to share personally meaningful information—tends to be a really positive experience for at least three reasons.

First, most of us like sharing meaningful information about ourselves. According to one analysis, about 30–40 percent of what we talk about with other people and upward of 80 percent of social media posts involve our own thoughts and feelings. Neuroimaging research confirms that revealing meaningful information about yourself activates the same dopamine system that all rewarding activity does.[2] The first step to connecting positively with another person is letting someone truly know who you are so that they can understand and appreciate you better. Our brains reward us when we take that first step.

Second, learning meaningful things about other people is generally more interesting than learning mundane things. Do you really care what someone else thinks about the weather? Or would you rather know what they're most grateful for, most embarrassed about, or care the most about in their lives? It's not a close call. This is why the word "hate" so commonly precedes the words "small talk." When my collaborators and I showed research volunteers a list of twenty questions that ranged from really shallow ("What do you think about the weather today?") to really deep and intimate ("If you could undo one mistake you have made in your life, what would it be and why would you undo it?"), the questions they most wanted to ask another person were those that tilted toward the deeper end of the spectrum.[3]

Finally, the best social experiences involve both sharing meaningful information about yourself *and* learning meaningful things about someone else. My audience was in the perfect setting for that. Instead of texting each other or listening to someone monologuing online, my audience had the perfect medium for connecting: an actual live conversation. They had time to talk and encouragement to talk about meaningful topics. Being in dialogue with another person about things that really matter to both of you is about as good as social interactions get.

In fact, the questions I asked my audience to talk about were adapted from a method commonly used by psychologists known as the fast friends procedure. Designed by the social psychologists Art and Elaine Aron and made famous almost twenty years later by Mandy Len Catron in a *New York Times* article titled "To Fall in Love with Anyone, Do This," the method walks people through a conversation involving thirty-six questions.[4] Like slowly taking the stairs to see the great view at the top of a building, these questions start out a little deeper than typical small talk—"Before making a phone call, do you ever rehearse what you're going to say?"—and then gradually increase in intimacy until we reach some of the most deeply personal things you could ever talk about with someone: "If you were to die this evening with no opportunity to communicate with anyone, what would you most regret not having told someone? Why haven't you told them yet?"

Although the Arons didn't actually measure whether people fell in love, they did find that this procedure created a strong sense of friendship that dwarfed how close people felt after discussing a set of thirty-six fairly shallow questions (such as "When was the last time you walked for more than an hour?"). This result surprised the Arons, too, because they initially believed that at least three additional elements would be required to create strong connections: sharing similar beliefs, expecting to like the other person, and deliberately trying to connect during the conversation. However, none of these mattered for how close people ended up feeling after their conversation. The only thing that mattered was whether they were having a relatively deep conversation or a shallow one.

Despite knowing all of this—that people like sharing meaningful information about themselves, learning meaningful information about others, and reciprocally sharing meaningful information—I still couldn't shake the feeling that somehow *this* crowd would respond differently in *this* setting with *these* topics. I thought I was taking a big risk in this presentation. After all, *this* wasn't a group of female undergraduates as the Arons had studied. This crowd was mostly older wealthy white men hoping to learn how to maximize their fund returns. They hadn't come to talk about how much they loved their moms or about how they cried when their kid graduated from college. Plus, my crowd wasn't slowly easing their way into the deep end of the conversation pool over the course of an hour by asking increasingly personal questions; they were diving straight into the deep end of the conversation pool. And yet none of this mattered. When they sat down and opened themselves up to another person, their conversations were overwhelmingly positive experiences, just as the research I doubted in the heat of the moment suggested they would be.

These finance executives aren't unusual in how much they enjoyed these conversations. In the years since then, I have had more than 4,000 people go through these deep conversations (4,273 as I'm writing this, to be exact). More than once I've heard people say this was the best conversation they had ever had or that they had shared something they had never shared with anyone else. When I ask people in a survey to describe how their conversation made them feel, the overwhelming majority (88.3 percent) said it made them feel positive. One of our MBA students at the University of Chicago wrote, "The best conversation I've had meeting someone new at [school] . . . someone I NEVER would have approached (based on my own prejudices). Thank you for this." Another wrote, "Super positive, I feel like I have a lot of assumptions . . . about the people here but the more I get to know them the more I am completely and positively surprised that my assumptions were wrong." Less than 1 percent (0.26 percent, to be exact) wrote that they felt negative.

More important, these finance executives also aren't unusual in their misplaced pessimism about these conversations. I've now seen the same shift, from dreading beforehand to feeling delighted afterward, over and over again in people ranging from high-level managers to entry-level employees, from undergraduates to master's students to PhDs, among people representing more than eighty countries. The gaps between people's pessimistic expectations going into the conversation and the actual experience they report afterward are massive, as you can see in the figure below.

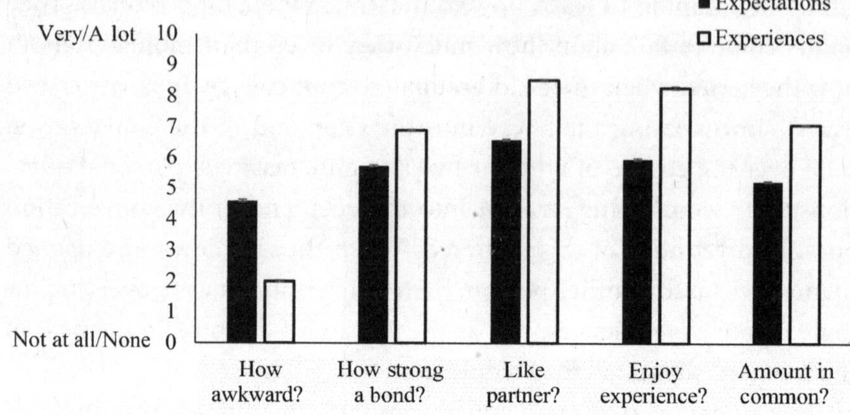

It's not that all of these deep talkers were clueless about how their conversations would turn out. Those who were most pessimistic did indeed feel somewhat less positive than those who were most optimistic before the conversation, but not by a lot. More important, as you can see in the figure below, this limited insight also exists alongside a more general tendency to be overly pessimistic. As you can see in the gap between how much people expected to enjoy their conversations in the gray line and how much people who gave each rating actually enjoyed their conversations in the black line, those with the most pessimistic expectations before their conversation were also the most pleasantly surprised by how much they enjoyed their conversation.[5]

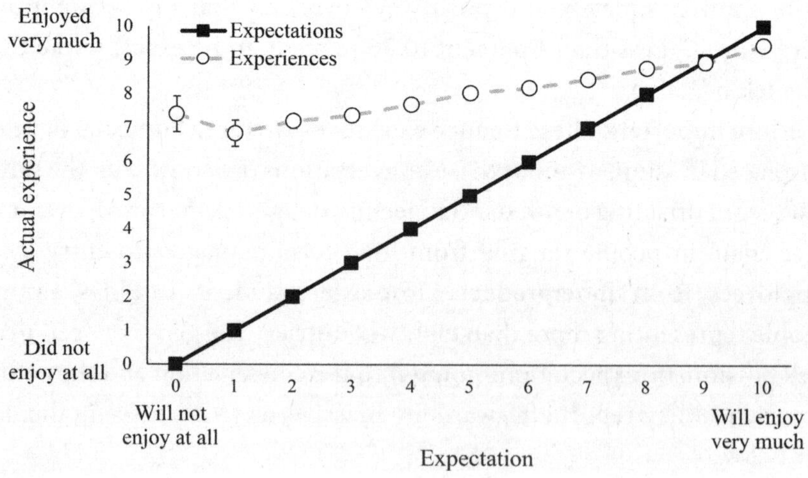

It's easy to imagine that we would see big differences in how different people would anticipate or actually experience these conversations—men versus women, older people versus younger people, those coming from one part of the world versus another—but any differences we observe in either expectations or experiences are dwarfed by the consistently massive gap between the pessimistic expectations people have going into these conversations and the positive experiences they report afterward. I've even changed up the deep topics I ask people to talk about, but it doesn't matter much. What matters is having a conversation that allows people to meaningfully open up.[6]

Overly Shallow?

When I've asked audiences how often they have such deep conversations, the answer is some version of "almost never." Isn't that interesting? If deep and meaningful conversations generally range from good to great, then why aren't we having them more often?

One possible reason is that we don't know how to have them. This is surely true sometimes, and it's also surely true that we could all become better conversationalists with more practice. However, I don't think this is the main problem, because research suggests that you probably have perfectly solid conversation skills that you're instead choosing to use less often than you could. The experiments I've described in this chapter so far make deep conversations easier by giving away a cheat sheet of meaningful topics to discuss, but I doubt it was horribly surprising to see the kinds of deep topics you *could* talk about if you tried. They are the kinds of topics you'd probably come up with on your own if you really tried to get to know someone.

In fact, when we stopped people in public parks around the city of Chicago and asked them to write down two questions they would typically discuss when meeting someone new, and two questions that are deeper than they'd typically discuss, they had little trouble generating deeper topics they *could* discuss if they chose to. You can see this in some examples of the topics people generated below:

Typical Topics	Deeper Topics
Where are you from?	What do you want people to remember you for?
What brings you here today?	Where do you see yourself in twenty years?
How do you like this park?	What is something you're really grateful for?
What do you do for a living?	Are you happy with where you are in your life?
How are you today?	What is your biggest regret in life?
What do you like to do?	What brings you joy?
How do you like the weather today?	What was the best day of your life?
How long have you lived here?	What is something that you want to accomplish?
Do you have children?	What are you passionate about?

In addition, when we asked people to have a conversation with a stranger about either the typical or the deeper topics they had just generated, these very same people enjoyed discussing their deeper questions more than their typical questions. I'm betting you *could* come up with deeper and more meaningful things to talk about in most of your conversations, if you chose to try.

Another obvious reason we might not be having deeper conversations more often is that we don't actually *want* to, perhaps especially with strangers. This again is surely true sometimes, and surely true for some of us more than others, but it doesn't seem to be overwhelmingly true for the more than four thousand people in the studies I described earlier. When I asked these people to rate how deep the conversation they just had was, how deep their typical conversations were, and how deep they *wanted* their conversations in daily life to be, their answers showed a crystal-clear pattern: The conversation I just asked them to have was deeper than they normally have, and they also wished they were having deeper conversations more often than they normally do. Note that they also didn't necessarily want their conversations to be quite as deep as the one they just had—maybe hold off on discussing the last time you cried in front of another person in your first conversation with someone—but they overwhelmingly wanted to be having deeper conversations more often than they were currently. This preference seems wise, because researchers consistently find that deep conversations tend to be more positive experiences than shallow conversations.[7] If you fall into this category of wanting more deep conversations than you're currently having, then you're in good company.

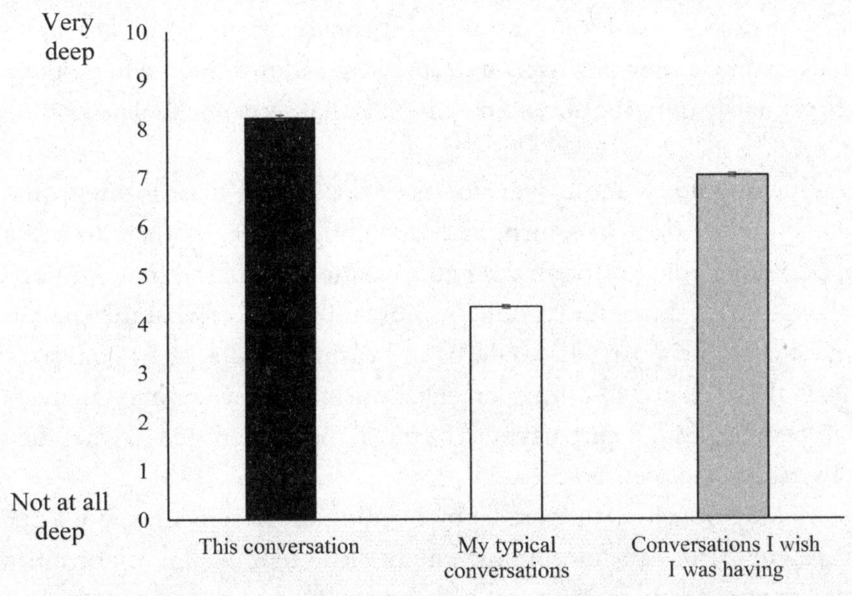

If we're capable of having deeper conversations and want to have them more often, then why aren't we? What's holding us back? Part of the reason comes from the same overly pessimistic expectations that nudge us to avoid engaging with strangers or picking up the phone and calling someone we haven't talked with in a while. This pessimism stems not from thinking we won't enjoy the conversations but rather from a long potential list of fears about how someone else will respond to us. Maybe the other person won't care about what I have to say? Maybe they won't open up to me once I open up to them? Maybe they'll get offended or think I'm weird if I ask overly sensitive questions? With fears like these, it's easy to see why we might play it safe and get stuck in the small talk we'd rather avoid.

These pessimistic fears, however, tend to be mistaken for the same reasons we've already covered. Opening up to someone in a genuine and authentic way is a sign of warmth toward another person that is typically interpreted positively. Opening up and taking a genuine interest in another person isn't demanding something from them; it's inviting them to open up with you. Nevertheless, it's easy for us to be focused on our own competence before a conversation and therefore wonder whether we'll be able to manage it effectively. Worrying about how well we'll be able to carry on a meaningful conversation is a good way to underestimate how positively a deep conversation will go when others are primarily thinking about how nice it is that someone took a genuine interest in them.

Opening up to another person is also a sign of trust in them that tends to elicit trust in return, just as smiling can lead others to smile back. Before going through their conversation, we found that our deep talkers expected that they would be more interested in what they had to reveal than their partner would be in hearing it. After their conversations, they learned that this perceived mismatch was wrong: On average, people found their partner to be much more interested in what they had to say than they expected.[8]

Making ourselves vulnerable by opening up to someone about our fears, concerns, or shortcomings might also seem like an opportunity for someone to judge you negatively, but those we're opening up to tend to see it differently. Not as something negative, but rather as a positive sign of honesty and courage, a perspective gap between how we expect to be seen when revealing our shortcomings and how we're actually seen that researchers refer to as "the beautiful mess effect."[9] Describing how their deep conversation made them feel, one person wrote, "I felt good. I felt heard, understood, seen. I also felt that my vulnerability was appreciated and reciprocated." That sentiment is a common thread throughout the comments people write after their deep conversations: "We literally cried together over one of the stories she was kind enough to share with me; positive." Another person who felt "very positive" also highlighted their surprise at how positively their partner responded to his openness: "I thought it will be super awkward to have a deep conversation with a stranger. But it turns out that the more I disclose myself, the deeper the conversation can go." However, failing to appreciate the power of reciprocity and responsiveness when talking with someone you don't already know can make that reciprocity seem more uncertain or unlikely than it actually is. As the *New York Times* columnist David Brooks remarked on his own efforts to engage in deep conversations more often, "If I respectfully ask somebody about their life story, how often do they say, 'None of your damn business'? Zero. Zero times in my life. People are dying to tell you their story."[10]

It's easy to see how these gaps between our expectations and our actual experiences can matter. Mistakenly thinking we'll offend, be uninteresting, or share too much is exactly what can keep you from having more meaningful conversations.

"I probably think about your research every day, to be honest," Jessica Pan, the "shintrovert" I introduced you to in chapter 2, told me after trying to put this research on deep conversations into practice. In her year of living intentionally as an extrovert, she said, "I found the deep talk thing to be one of the biggest things. I hate making shallow talk for ages with people," and yet small was the only kind of talk she was ever having. As a new parent, for instance, Jessica said she found it was "easy to talk with other parents about the boring stuff like naps and feeding, but you're also going through this really, really, really hard thing and you're not actually talking about the hard thing." So, she started asking parents how they were *really* doing, and how they were *really* feeling, and how they were *really* handling the job of being a parent. "Do you find they're open to it?" I asked her. "Yeah, yeah. I think they're a little bit taken aback by it, but then they just go with it. I think they're probably relieved that I did it."

Jessica's conversations have gotten better because she's not as pessimistic about deep conversations as she once was, and so she's more willing to open up and discuss the meaningful topics she'd actually like to talk about when the moment affords it. I can resonate. Although small talk certainly has its place, and can be notably more enjoyable at times than no talk, I've learned how receptive people can be when you genuinely take an interest in them and invite them into a meaningful conversation when you have a little time to talk privately.

The trajectory from a shallow conversation to a deeper one can be steep, not taking thirty-six questions as in the fast friends procedure, but often getting there in just two. I might ask someone where they live and then follow up by asking if it's the place they had always wanted to live. After someone tells me what they do for a living, I might ask what they love most about their job. On a recent train ride, I sat next to someone who was sharply dressed in a bow tie and a nice suit whom I had seen (and said hello to) once before. After sharing our names, I asked him how he had gotten to this point in his life where he needed to look so darned fantastic for his job. He smirked and said, "That's a long story." "I'd love to hear it," I said, and off we went on an adventure through the South Side of Chicago that sounded more like a Hollywood movie script than someone's real life. In this case, it only took me one question to get deep.

Everyone's got an interesting story to tell you if only you're willing to ask them about it when the opportunity affords it. After seeing thousands of data points and having countless experiences of my own, that psychological barrier of undue pessimism has been worn down to what I think is a more calibrated—and more optimistic—assessment of how these conversations are likely to turn out.

My conversations have gotten dramatically better thanks to this research because I'm more willing to take opportunities for meaningful conversation whenever I have a little time to talk with someone. To be clear, I'm not suggesting going overboard, living your life as a constant source of TMI (too much information), or becoming the World's Most Intrusive Stranger. Instead, our research suggests keeping an eye out for opportunities in a conversation to make it more meaningful than you might otherwise.

How many more meaningful conversations would you find yourself in if you were more optimistic about how they would turn out and therefore more willing to open up and try?

Tough Talks

I was once again fully aware of all of this wisdom while standing at the end of my driveway one morning feeling quite nervous about having yet another different kind of deep conversation from the ones I had been studying so far. *This* deep conversation wasn't about what you'd need to know to be my friend or the last time I cried in front of another person. *This* conversation was about one of the ostensibly divisive topics you're never supposed to talk about in the polite company of strangers: politics. And *this* deep conversation was being invited by a man carrying a loaded gun in a bulletproof vest.

"So what is it about Donald Trump you don't like?" he asked.

It was a morning in August 2020, right in the midst of the run-up to the presidential election between Donald Trump and Joe Biden. Americans were fracturing. Along the road in front of our home, I had placed two completely mundane campaign signs for Joe Biden. The day before, a car drove into the ditch to run them over. Earlier that morning, someone had stopped and stolen them. I mentioned all of this in a "just thought you'd want to know" phone call to our local sheriff, who happened to be driving nearby when I called and asked to stop by. When he arrived, he told me he was surprised because the only signs he had seen vandalized so far were for Trump (which surprised me). I introduced myself and mentioned that I worked as a university professor, and then he popped the Trump question.

I immediately recognized the same wall of anxiety and pessimism rise up that I felt with the red-hatted stranger that morning years before on the train. But by this time, I knew a little better. Although talking about something as potentially divisive as politics might seem about as wise as playing with fire in a match factory, we were actually in the perfect context for having a meaningful conversation, more like playing with fire next to a fire truck. It was, after all, just the two of us. We had no audience to present to, no cell phone held out to record this as a confrontation for our "followers." We were just two guys talking to each other, using our own voices, with time to talk, going back and forth in an actual dialogue.

Nearly a century's worth of research has now documented that when you bring people who are otherwise divided into ideal conditions like this—on equal footing and with time to have a one-on-one conversation using our actual voices—the social forces at play tend to pull people together rather than push them apart. Social scientists in the 1940s learned that white sailors in the merchant marines had more positive attitudes about their Black counterparts the more time they spent together at sea.[11] White and Black housewives in government-assisted housing liked each other more when they were randomly assigned to live in desegregated buildings because they actually got a chance to talk to each other.[12] When the Harvard psychologist Gordon Allport first articulated what came to be known as intergroup contact theory in 1954, specifying that prejudice between groups would actually decrease by bringing group members into meaningful interactions, he didn't know that he would inspire at least 515 different studies, involving 1,383 unique tests of his hypothesis with more than a quarter of a million people from thirty-eight different countries. He did, though, correctly anticipate the results. Analyzing this mountain of data, the researchers Tom Pettigrew and Linda Tropp found that 94 percent of these studies observed that increased contact between otherwise divided groups reduced prejudice. Most important, this is especially true under the optimal conditions that included having informal conversations with each other, like the conversation I was about to have. It wasn't much of a gamble that the seemingly tough conversation at the end of the driveway would not actually be that tough after all.

And yet, if you haven't seen data from a quarter of a million people, or had many of these conversations yourself, then it's easy to imagine that these conversations about your deepest disagreements might quickly devolve into a scene from Monty Python's Argument Clinic, where John Cleese relentlessly contradicts anything that Michael Palin says ("This isn't an argument." "Yes it is." "No it isn't, it's just contradiction." "Yes it is." "No it isn't."). To see this unwarranted pessimism in action, consider an experiment in which we asked a group of Americans to tell us the extent to which they supported or opposed a series of divisive issues in the United States at the time—issues like abortion rights, separating families to deter illegal immigration, strict separation of church and state, legalized same-sex marriage, and stricter gun control. We then told them they would soon be having a conversation about one of these topics with someone who either agreed or disagreed with their position.[13]

If you think you'd rather light your hair on fire than talk with someone you disagree with about such potentially divisive topics, then you'd fit right in with the intuitions we observed as well. When we asked a separate group to tell us how positive they thought it would be to discuss one of these topics with another person, they thought talking with someone they agreed with would be a pretty mediocre conversation, but that talking with someone they disagreed with would be a terrible conversation that they'd choose to avoid.[14] Not surprisingly, when we then told people in another experiment that they would soon be having an actual conversation with someone who either agreed or disagreed with them on one of these topics, they expected a much more positive conversation when their partner agreed than when they disagreed (with a third group that was uncertain of their partner's position falling in between). What *was* surprising, at least to the people who were having these conversations, is that whether they agreed or disagreed with their conversation partner didn't actually matter for how positive their experience was.[15] This means that the people who were most positively surprised were those who were having a conversation with someone they knew disagreed with them. One person left us a note that captured the overall results perfectly: "I did not think I would enjoy this; I was wrong."

Our expectations in cases of disagreement like this can be overly pessimistic for two reasons. First, those who we think differ from us tend not to be as different as we imagine them to be. Although liberals and conservatives in the United States, for instance, differ in their beliefs in predictable ways, those differences are not as big as liberals and conservatives think they are. Perceived polarization is bigger than actual polarization.[16] Part of this misunderstanding is stoked by the people we see most often talking about these divisive issues, because politicians tend to use more polarizing speech that doesn't reflect the actual beliefs of the citizens they represent.[17] One analysis of nearly four thousand Americans found that they tended to exaggerate how much people on the other side of the aisle disliked them by anywhere from 50 to 300 percent.[18] Learning that you have more common ground with someone on the other side of an issue is one surprisingly nice outcome from actually talking with them.

Second, the moment-by-moment dynamic forces of reciprocity and responsiveness that pull people together in one-on-one conversations continue to operate even when we disagree with someone. Not anticipating the power of these social forces in conversation is once again a reason we're surprised by the outcome.

You can see both of the effects of overestimating divisiveness and underestimating conversation in an experiment in which we varied not only the type of person our participants were talking to—whether they agreed or disagreed on a divisive political topic—but also the type of interaction they were having: an actual dialogue about their beliefs or watching a monologue of their partner alone explaining their beliefs. As you can see in the black bars of the figure below, the only thing our participants thought would matter before having their actual interaction was whether they agreed or disagreed with the person they were talking to. They didn't think the type of interaction they were having—a dialogue or a monologue—would matter at all.

In fact, as you can see in the white bars, the only instance when the beliefs of the person they were talking to actually mattered was when they weren't having a conversation at all. Just hearing someone you disagree with explain their views in a monologue is indeed a worse experience than having an actual conversation with someone you agree with. One-sided monologues are what we see in speeches, in media interviews, and often on social media, but simply listening to someone speaking lacks the magnetic forces that pull us together in actual conversations. Still, learning about the beliefs of someone with opposing views was more positive than people expected, largely because they learned that the person they disagreed with had more reasonable and more moderate beliefs than they expected beforehand.[19] More interesting, I think, is that the experience of having an actual conversation with someone they disagreed with was just as positive as having a conversation with someone they agreed with.[20]

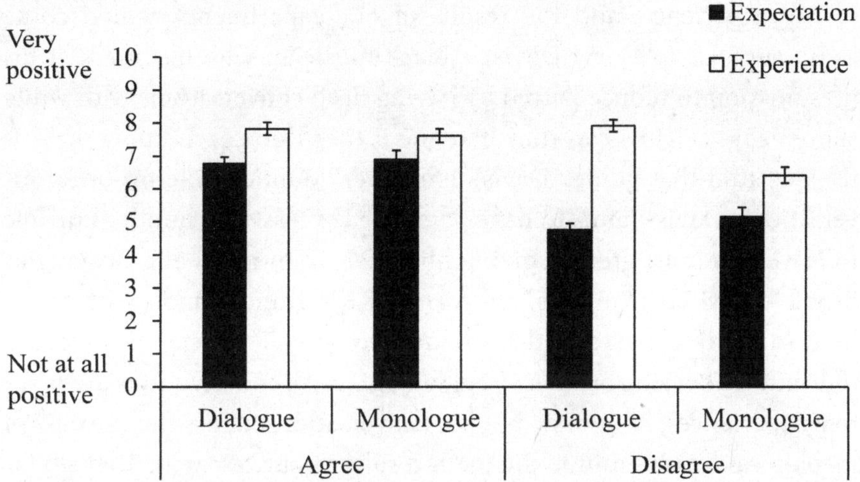

I didn't have time to think about all of this when the sheriff invited me into a deep conversation about politics at the end of my driveway. Maybe this was for the better? Had I stopped to think about it beforehand, I might have made *the choice* to avoid it. But this sheriff seemed to think otherwise and leaned in. He didn't come with a lecture. He came with a question spoken with a tone of genuine curiosity. If we approached other people the way this sheriff did more often, what would we learn about each other? I think we'd learn exactly what people in our experiments learned: I didn't think I'd enjoy this, but I was wrong.

The conversation with that officer was one of the better conversations I've ever had about politics. We spoke for more than an hour, long enough for Jen (my wife) to get worried about where I had gone. We asked about each other's experiences and background, how we had come to a belief and why, what we hoped and feared for the future, and how all of this made us feel. The magnetic forces of conversation led us to areas of commonality. I shared, for instance, that I had relatives who worked in law enforcement and had seen the stress it creates. He shared with me new challenges—fears of being hated rather than appreciated by some in the community, anxiety about how to enforce laws without being perceived as biased, a sense of being under attack for trying to do the job he had always wanted to do—with nuances I didn't fully appreciate until I heard it through his own voice.

My experience, and the results of our experiments, would come as no surprise to Daryl Davis, a Black musician who has made it his life's mission to reduce hatred by having deep conversations with white supremacists. "How can they hate me if they don't even know me?" is the question that guides Davis's life. Over countless one-on-one conversations, Davis claims to have persuaded at least two hundred people to leave extremist groups, giving him their Klan robes after leaving as proof. "Daryl saved my life," the former KKK grand dragon Scott Shepherd said. "Daryl extended his hand and actually extended his heart, too, and we became brothers." Not all of Davis's conversations are positive experiences, of course, but his conversations across the greatest of ideological divides mimic the main results of our research: They go far better than you might ever expect. What makes Davis different is his willingness to have a respectful conversation that many would find too offensive to even consider having. Most people "would not even tolerate the time," he explained on Joe Rogan's podcast, "but I will sit and listen . . . because in order for me to speak my mind, I have to listen to somebody else's." The implication is clear to Daryl. "If I can sit down and talk to K.K.K. members and neo-Nazis and get them to give me their robes and hoods and swastika flags and all that kind of crazy stuff, there's no reason why somebody can't sit down at a dinner table and talk to their family member."[21]

Overestimating how badly a conversation with someone you disagree with will go is one clear reason why we might avoid having these conversations at all. How many more seemingly tough conversations would you have if you really knew they'd turn out better than you feared?

Tough Love

Being overly pessimistic about the surprising power of deep conversations doesn't stop with strangers. Conflict, after all, is inevitable in every relationship. At some point you'll need to open up and have a tough conversation about whatever's bothering you. Maybe your roommate's a slob who leaves dishes all over the kitchen? Or your co-worker isn't pulling their weight? Or perhaps you don't see eye to eye with your partner about politics or religion or—what therapists sometimes refer to as the hardest thing to talk about in any relationship—how often you'd like to be having sex. These conflicts vary in countless ways, but they often have one thing in common: We'd rather avoid talking about it. And yet avoiding these conversations is precisely what keeps you from working through them, making both you and your relationship worse off.

What we're afraid of when opening up with the people we love or are connected to, of course, is also what we're afraid of when opening up to a stranger: that they'll be defensive, angry, or possibly indifferent, thereby making the interaction unpleasant. When we asked people in a survey to imagine confronting someone in their life they have an unresolved issue with, how negatively they thought the person would respond was the strongest predictor of people's interest in actually confronting that person about the issue. Also important was their own sense of how effectively they could communicate their concerns.[22] Beyond the immediate reaction, there's also the long-term concern that having this difficult conversation will actually ruin the relationship. This creates an obvious approach/avoidance conflict that almost anyone can relate to: The conversation you need to have to help your relationship is also the conversation you want to avoid because you don't want to hurt your relationship.

Once again, our fears in these cases aren't completely off the mark, but they are exaggerated in ways that encourage us to be overly avoidant. We've observed this in several different ways. First, when we asked people to imagine having a tough conversation they needed to have in a relationship they're currently in, they generally thought it would be a more negative experience than a separate group of people actually remembered a tough conversation in the past to be.[23] Second, when we asked people to imagine having one of the thirty-two most common types of confrontations that people report having with co-workers, friends, family members, or romantic partners, those who imagined confronting someone thought the person they were confronting would respond more negatively—be angrier, more hostile, more defensive—than those who imagined being confronted thought they would feel.

Third, when we actually ask people to confront someone in their relationship in a real conversation, it tends to be a more positive experience than they expected it would be beforehand. We've done this now with both roommates and romantic couples, enrolling these pairs into an experiment and asking them to fight for the sake of science.

Well, okay, we didn't actually ask them to do *that*. What we actually asked them to do was to think about an unresolved issue in their relationship that was bothering them.[24] The roommates raised issues that are common when you're living with strangers, from minor things like "Sometimes my roommate keeps things in the fridge for 500 years and it scares me," to more moderate things like "Sometimes it's hard to tell how she's feeling and it often seems like she's being passive aggressive," or the soul-crushing unfairness of "Sometimes I wish you would also buy beer." The romantic couples raised more serious issues, such as challenges opening up and communicating ("It feels like he won't 'let me in' "; "I wish she would be more honest with me about things that bother her"), differences in values ("My partner and I have remarkably different stances when it comes to dealing with money"), issues about control ("Often times I feel that my girlfriend tries to impose her thoughts and beliefs on me"), or incompatibilities ("You don't like to go to the gym, it bothers me"). We then asked each pair to have a private conversation about the issue. Before leaving, the person who was about to confront the other reported how they expected the conversation would go. When they got back, we put each person in a private space, and both the confronter and the person being confronted told us how the conversation actually went.

You might imagine that couples know each other well enough to have a pretty good sense of how these confrontations will go, but we again see the same pattern of overly pessimistic expectations that we saw in conversations with strangers. The roommates and romantic couples expected their conversations to be angrier and more hostile than they actually were. They also expected that the conversation would be more likely to harm their relationship than they actually found it to be.

We observed some new findings as well. For instance, we imagined that people might be playing nice as part of the experiment, saying they were less upset than they actually were, even though we didn't record these interactions and everyone had them in private. However, it wasn't just the confronters who thought the conversations went pretty well: The people who were confronted by their partner rated the conversation as similarly positive.

We also imagined that our couples could have been playing nice as part of the experiment, but then dropped the act after leaving the lab and had a *real* fight when they got home and were on their own. We didn't find any evidence for this. Two weeks after the experiment, we reached out to the romantic partners to find out how things had been going since. No one we heard back from was upset with us for ending their relationship or even angry for harming their relationship. When we asked how much regret they felt for having their difficult conversation, nearly everyone (85 percent) gave the lowest rating, corresponding to "none." Consistent with mountains of research on the importance of open and honest communication in relationships, the couples reported being generally happy to have had the conversation, reported that it led to positive changes with the issue they discussed, said they felt closer to each other after the conversation, and indicated that they'd be more willing to have deep conversations like these in the future.

What were these couples missing before their conversation that made them so reluctant to bring the issue up? Again it was the power of having an open, honest, meaningful conversation with another person. When we asked another group of people just to exchange their beliefs about an issue in a recorded monologue, the interactions went about as poorly as the couples expected. Only having a real conversation was surprisingly positive.

If you knew that having the tough conversation you've been avoiding would turn out better than you feared, how much longer would you let your relationship suffer while you avoided having it?

Dave Fleischer is no stranger to deep conversations. As a community organizer working to reduce the hatred and prejudice that can sometimes divide us, Dave doesn't avoid deep talk; he comes knocking at your door on the hunt for it. Dave's experiences started in 2009 after Californians voted to ban gay marriage, an outcome that shocked him and his friends in the LGBTQ+ community who couldn't understand how it could happen. He had the idea that in order to find out what had happened, he had to go "into the neighborhoods where we had been crushed and seek out the people who had voted against us . . . and ask them why they did that." Just as we've observed in our research, he was overly pessimistic when he started this more than fifteen years ago: "I didn't know if those voters would want to talk to us, but they did."[25]

Now in his early seventies, Dave and his teams have been responsible for creating more than twenty thousand deep conversations between people who are supposed to be deeply divided. He's watched people go from dreading the experience to being pleasantly surprised by it even more times than I have. Practicing a method known as deep canvassing, Dave attempts to connect so meaningfully with people in conversation that it melts some of the prejudice and fear that divides us. To get there, he told me one day, he tries to move past small talk within the first one or two minutes, ideally by talking about someone in their lives who they love. Dave might be knocking on your door to talk about the importance of voting in an upcoming election and sharing a story about someone he cares about who also hasn't voted. He might visit you before a referendum on gay marriage to share his experiences as a gay man and to learn about someone you love who might also be gay. Or he might stop by to talk with you about transgender rights with a transgender friend of his who wants to share their experience and learn about your own. Instead of reading from a canned script like a walking robocall, Dave actually tries to have a deep conversation with someone while standing in their doorway and invites them to share a story of someone they love in return.

Presuming that a nontrivial number of these conversations must have gone badly, I asked Dave the first time I talked with him to tell me if he'd ever had a really bad conversation while deep canvassing. I'm imagining that someone must have screamed at him, threatened him, or let the attack dogs out after him. After scrunching up his eyes to think for a minute, he said, "Yeah, I remember one, but not about the really divisive stuff." The only bad conversation he could remember was about a relatively innocuous issue—having to pay a fee to use plastic bags at the grocery story—that made someone get angry with him. The guy walked out and started shouting to the neighborhood that "this guy's here to raise your taxes on plastic bags!" Certainly people don't always want to talk or they shut the door when they hear his pitch, but once he actually gets into an open, honest, and deep conversation with someone he's genuinely interested in, he doesn't see the hostility you might find so easy to imagine.[26]

Let this experience sink in for a minute. Dave goes knocking door-to-door looking to talk about the most meaningful issues that divide us, and he couldn't think of a deep conversation about these divisive issues that had gone really badly.

In his Substack newsletter titled *Dave's Substack*, Dave reveals that "almost all of my writing describes what it's like connecting with someone who, in some noticeable way, is not just like us. The differences are real. Yet repeatedly—in thousands of voter conversations—I've learned that these differences do not rule out connection, even if they sometimes complicate it."[27] A gay Black man named John Newsome, who goes door-to-door deep canvassing with Dave, describes how he learned to have more optimistic—and more realistic—beliefs through his own experience. "The first few doors are scary. What's going to happen? How are people going to receive me? . . . Then someone opens a door and they're usually lovely, and I can't detect any sort of hostility towards me as a black man. . . . They want to have a conversation." When you open up to someone, they tend to open up in return. Speaking of his experience deep canvassing, John wrote, "I always leave feeling better about people, about my community, about our democracy, wishing that we did these engagements all the time." If John had followed his pessimistic expectations and avoided these conversations, what would his view of humanity be?

How do you overcome this pessimism and learn to have the conversations you actually want to be having? Jessica Pan, Daryl Davis, Dave Fleischer, John Newsome, and the thousands of people we've led through deep conversations in our experiments show the way. You start by taking a genuine interest in getting to know other people and then test the fears that might be holding you back by opening up and asking them the questions that allow them to open up in return. The results are likely to be surprising, and the lessons you learn are empowering. The barriers that are keeping you from having meaningful conversations more often may be figments of your imagination rather than facts of life.

PART III

What If?

Making *the choice* to reach out and connect with others versus avoid them goes far beyond deciding whether, how, and how deeply to engage in conversation. It is also at the core of three basic human virtues: thankfulness, kindness, and honesty. What if we recognized the psychological barriers that were keeping us from being good to others, and chose to test those barriers a little more often?

7

Choosing Thankfulness

Gratitude is not only the best, but the parent of all other virtues.

—CICERO, 54 BCE

You might think that after writing nearly fourteen hundred pages of a book titled *The Principles of Psychology,* William James—one of the founding figures of psychology in America—might have run out of principles to discover. And yet, after receiving a glowing letter of gratitude from his students at Radcliffe College, James had a revelation: "I now perceive one immense omission in my Psychology—the deepest principle of Human Nature is the *craving to be appreciated*."[1] James even diagnosed the cause: "I left it out from the book, because I had never had it gratified till now."

Receiving an expression of gratitude might seem minor for a celebrated professor, but it hit James *surprisingly* hard. "I am deeply touched by your remembrance," he opens his response. "It is the first time anyone ever treated me so kindly." He predicted that he would feel uplifted for longer than his students would remember the course content. I'd bet on that, too.

In fact, one compliment I received decades ago while in college still stands out with crystal clarity. I was on the football team of the small college I attended in southern Minnesota (St. Olaf College—Go, Oles!), playing a nearby rival (Bethel College). Our quarterback called a running play that had me, an offensive lineman, lumbering downfield to block one of the much faster defensive backs. Never one identified as "light on his feet," I usually missed these shifty targets. This time, however, I hit the cornerback squarely in his chest and drove him flat on his back. We called this rare feat a "pancake." For lumbering linemen who never touch the football during the game, this is as much glory as we ever get. As I was pulling my helmet up from his chest, the player I pancaked grabbed my face mask with both hands and shouted, "That was an awesome play—great job!" I couldn't believe it. I have indeed remembered that compliment longer than almost anything else I learned from my professors at St. Olaf, many of whom I thought were every bit as great as William James.

James and I aren't alone: The power of appreciation also came as a surprise to Celine McGee.[2] A telecommunications director in Philadelphia, Celine created a habit of helping the City of Brotherly Love live up to its nickname by deliberately doling out compliments to random strangers. While doing so, she encourages others to do the same by handing out a card asking them to join her as part of "the Compliment Squad," an informal group dedicated to sharing kind thoughts rather than keeping them private. The spark for Celine's appreciation habit came from a revelation she had during a garage sale years earlier. To advertise her sale, Celine and her sister made what she hoped would be attention-grabbing signs, such as "Someone's Trash Is Someone Else's Treasure" and "Stop By for a Compliment." At the sale, nobody mentioned coming to turn Celine's trash into treasure, but multiple visitors asked for a compliment. She discovered it was surprisingly easy to find genuine compliments to share once she started looking for them. She also remembers that just a few small words left her customers feeling terrific. It made Celine feel terrific, too.

That revelation led her to take on the role of "complimenter" with her family and friends, but it took some time before she was prompted to extend her habit to strangers. "Fast-forward and my life happened," Celine explained to me, "and I moved to Philly." She started walking with a friend after work—"healthy socializing," she called it—and noticed that she would often appreciate what someone was doing or wearing but wouldn't say anything. As most of us might do, she kept her appreciation to herself, until "one day, I think I just got brave."

Take note of that word: "brave." Celine felt that bravery was needed to reach out and express her appreciation. I'll come back to that.

With her garage sale experience in the back of her mind and her courage up, Celine saw a woman in an outfit she thought looked great and she made *the choice* to tell her so. She doesn't remember exactly what she said, but she remembered that the person lit up like a streetlight. "Oh, here's a data point, super positive," she remembered thinking. "Why don't I do this more often?"

Take note of that question, too. I'll focus this chapter on it.

Celine had noticed what it felt like to be what the journalist David Brooks calls an "Illuminator": a person who notices and appreciates others, shining a positive light on them that leaves them feeling better as a result.[3] "Wouldn't it be cool," she thought, "if I could pass along something with my compliment to remind them to pay it forward?"

And that's where the cards came from. "Pretty ugly business cards," as she described the first versions. They have evolved into professional-looking cards with "Compliment Squad" on one side and encouragement to "help spread smiles, kindness, & human connection" on the other.[4] She thought of her habit as the opposite of what happens when someone infects your day with negativity. "So," she tells me, "imagine that you're in a car and someone cuts you off and they scream at you, and unfortunately you sometimes carry that unhappiness into your next interaction and spread bad vibes. . . . I'm trying to give the person something positive so that their next interaction is positive."

Celine now had a mission. When she's in her "compliment mode," she'll head out and spread good vibes for an hour or two, but more often she sprinkles in her compliments as a routine part of her day, while walking to work or getting groceries or when out for a weekend stroll. She maintains a few guardrails, mostly complimenting other women because she doesn't want anyone to misunderstand her intentions, and always gives authentic compliments because it only feels good when the kindness is genuine. But even with these guardrails, she tells me that she finds many opportunities "to spread a little love" that she never would have noticed if she wasn't on the lookout for them. Celine thinks of this as her hobby and treats it like routine exercise for her happiness. I'd call this being wisely social.

When I talked to Celine, I asked her the same question I asked Dave Fleischer, the deep canvassing guy from chapter 6: What happens when it goes poorly? "It's never gone really poorly," she said, echoing Dave's experience. I must admit that I was again a little surprised. It's hard to shake off even my own pessimism completely. Of course, not everyone lights up like a streetlight after she gives them a compliment, but the worst she experiences is that sometimes someone won't respond or will seem suspicious. In those cases, "I just move on," she says. Celine shows that she's genuine by dropping a compliment and then continuing on her way, knowing that she's leaving happiness in her wake. Often, though, her warm words will be the spark that gets a nice conversation going.

"Are you ever exhausted?" I asked her, sharing the common intuition that socializing is tiring. "I did it once when I was in a bad mood and then I was exhausted, but mostly I feel energized and happy," she said.

Exhausted only once. Mostly energized and happy. I feel the same way when I pass along appreciation. I bet you do, too. Why, then, *don't* we do this more often?

Happiness, with a Gas Pedal

Research makes it clear that Celine's experiences aren't unusual. If there's one surefire thing you could do on any given day to feel both happier and more energized, it's to think of someone you feel grateful to and then share your feeling with them. From something as small as passing along a genuine compliment to a stranger to something more substantial like writing a letter to someone you feel really grateful to, the positive outcomes of expressing gratitude are both wide-ranging and widely documented. Scientists have learned that feeling grateful increases positive mood, happiness, and life satisfaction while decreasing stress, anxiety, and depression.[5]

Focusing on what you have to be grateful for also makes the future look brighter, increasing your sense of hope and inspiration. Of course, the emotional uplift of a single moment of gratitude is just as fleeting as the health benefits of a single visit to the gym. If you want consistently better mental health, you'll need to turn it into a habit, as Celine has done. Those who express their appreciation routinely are less stressed, better rested, and therefore in better health than those who express it rarely.[6]

As good as appreciation might feel, it feels even better—as William James experienced—to *be* appreciated. Celine told me that she counted the success of her effort by the size of the smile on someone's face, which tended to be even bigger than her own smile. This experience isn't unusual. When I ask my MBA students at the University of Chicago to express their appreciation to someone they're grateful to in a letter, my students report feeling positive afterward, but their letter recipients report feeling even more positive. It's no wonder. Being appreciated by someone else satisfies our most basic human needs of competency and relational connection.

The British philosopher G. K. Chesterton once defined the experience of gratitude as "happiness doubled by wonder." I think an even better definition is "happiness with a gas pedal," because appreciation also energizes action.[7] Appreciation can remind us of something someone else did for us, making us feel happier while also inspiring us to reciprocate not just to the person we feel grateful to but to others as well. In psychologists' terms, appreciation triggers both direct reciprocity to the person who benefited us *and* indirect reciprocity to people completely unrelated to our gratitude. Celine's compliments won't only prompt their recipients to be kind to Celine in return, but will prompt them to be kind toward someone else, too. The sociologist Georg Simmel even speculated in 1908 that "if every grateful action, which lingers on from good turns received in the past, were suddenly eliminated, society (at least as we know it) would break apart."[8]

Thankfully, no researcher has ever eliminated gratitude in order to measure society breaking, but many researchers have consistently confirmed that appreciation encourages us to both feel and act better. In one experiment, for instance, those who felt grateful because another person in the experiment helped them were also more likely to help a third person when asked.[9] Other research finds that appreciation decreases cheating, encourages sharing, increases donations to charity, and makes us more likely to uphold moral norms by punishing people who behave unethically.[10] In short, appreciation makes us better versions of ourselves.[11] Even the scientist who conducted the original groundbreaking studies on the power of gratitude, Bob Emmons, was surprised by how much feeling grateful spread across people's social lives. "An unexpected benefit from gratitude journaling—one that I did not predict in advance," Emmons wrote about one of his earliest experiments on appreciation, "was that people who kept gratitude journals reported feeling closer and more connected to others, were more likely to help others, and were actually seen as more helpful by significant others in their social networks." It shouldn't be surprising, then, that feeling grateful also makes you a more likable person. "The family, friends, partners, and others that surround them consistently reported that those who practiced gratitude seemed measurably happier and were more pleasant to be around."[12]

The prosocial inspiration that comes from gratitude resonates with me. One of the teachers I feel most grateful to, who inspires me to be a better person for my own students, was my band teacher at Cedar Rapids Prairie High School, Craig Aune. Mr. Aune cared for us with a level of intensity that routinely had him tearing up in our practices when we'd finally play a song just right or nail a routine at a marching band competition. His voice was so loud that every one of us could hear him cheering from the top of the bleachers when we were marching on a football field. When one of our classmates was killed in a car accident, Mr. Aune commissioned a song in his honor (titled "I Am") that we performed in a concert through tears. For years now, I have channeled the deep sense of appreciation I feel toward Mr. Aune to make me a more positive influence on my own students. Focusing on that gratitude is now one of my regular warm-up routines to get in the right state of mind before I go into class, encouraging me to be more open, kind, and enthusiastic than I'd be otherwise. My experience is common. When the psychologist Sonja Lyubomirsky and her colleagues mapped out the full range of emotions prompted by gratitude, the strongest feelings were not just the hedonic hits like happiness and positive mood but also the energizing force of inspiration.[13] Appreciation is happiness, with a gas pedal.

Despite this, William James claimed not to have felt so deeply appreciated until late in his life, and Celine McGee felt that she needed bravery to pass along a compliment. And even though I felt grateful to Mr. Aune my entire adult life, for decades I avoided reaching out to tell him so. Even though giving a compliment can make another person feel great, people we asked in a survey reported withholding compliments that came to their mind roughly a third of the time (36.4 percent, to be exact).[14] In other surveys we conducted, "give compliments" and "express gratitude" were the two social activities that people felt most deficient in, believing they did both significantly less often than they felt they should or wanted to.[15] William James's experience of not being appreciated until late in life may not be just an experience from a bygone era.

If gratitude feels great, and expressing it feels even better, then what's holding us back from both feeling grateful and expressing our gratitude more often? In this case, it's not just one misplaced psychological barrier that's keeping us from feeling better, but at least two. The first is not feeling appreciation to begin with, and the second is not sharing our appreciation once we do feel it. Overcoming the second barrier of not sharing appreciation by making it a routine habit, I think, will also help you overcome the first barrier to help you feel appreciation a little more often. Let me explain.

Not Feeling It: Enemies of Gratitude

There's a profound, but somewhat hidden, truth in the experiments I just described about the benefits of gratitude. In all of those experiments, people were prompted to feel appreciation for something that had already happened to them by writing a gratitude letter, thinking about what they're grateful for, or counting their blessings. Notice that these prompts don't provide anything new to appreciate—a new friend or a new job or a new bar of gold—but rather remind people of something they could feel grateful for if only they had thought of it. These reminders work, then, because the things we have to be grateful for are also things we get used to, and are therefore easy to overlook. "I've got a perfect body / But sometimes I forget," Regina Spektor sings in one particularly insightful example. "I've got a perfect body / 'Cause my eyelashes catch my sweat."[16]

Whether you're overlooking your perfectly shaped eyelashes or something else, overlooking what you have to appreciate is not a new human experience. "Reflect upon your present blessings—of which every man has many—not on your past misfortunes, of which all men have some," advised Charles Dickens in 1835, clearly believing that most people living in even those hard times needed to be reminded of what aided their lives.[17] Dickens even considered it a profound character flaw if "a jovial feeling is not roused" at Christmastime: "That man must be a misanthrope indeed." Writing even earlier, in 1739, the Scottish philosopher David Hume went beyond character flaw to criminal: "Of all crimes that human creatures are capable of committing, the most horrid and unnatural is ingratitude."[18]

Although overlooking appreciation might seem like a hideous character flaw, psychologists in more recent decades have identified several perfectly ordinary features that make appreciation surprisingly easy for anyone to overlook. The Cornell psychologist Tom Gilovich, one of the people I'm most grateful to for serving as my PhD adviser and longtime collaborator, identifies at least three psychological barriers that keep our minds from noticing things we could appreciate. Tom refers to this triad as "enemies of gratitude."[19] Their names are adaptation, comparison, and adversity.

Enemy No. 1: Adaptation. Typically, adapting to our circumstances is considered a good thing. When it comes to feeling grateful, however, adaptation is a formidable foe.

Regardless of whether it's something awful like being laid off at work or wonderful like earning your dream job, our pains and pleasures fade over time. The dream job you're so grateful to have, with all the people you have to thank for helping you get it, eventually becomes your regular job and your warmth toward your supporters fades. What's surprising is how quickly your warmth can fade. Sports fans in one experiment, for instance, expected that they would be notably happier the day after their favored team's win, and less happy the day after a loss. But when the day after actually came, both the thrill of the previous day's victory and the agony of its defeat had faded almost completely.[20]

In my own job as a professor, receiving tenure is a goal every young academic strives for, but it takes surprisingly little time for either the great feeling of receiving tenure or the great pain of being denied it to fade. In another experiment, professors who had not yet reached the tenure promotion process thought they would be notably happier in the five years after being awarded tenure than if they were denied tenure, but actually being granted versus denied tenure in the last five years did not have any measurable effect on how happy a separate group of professors who were actually granted or denied tenure were with their lives.[21] Our appreciation for other people also seems to fade as quickly as our emotions do. Research finds that we appreciate others the most while they're helping us do something, but appreciate them less as soon as that thing is done.[22] Our emotions return surprisingly quickly to baseline after something happens to us, and so does our appreciation for the people who helped us get there.

It's not a moral failing that makes our appreciation fade, but rather the typically helpful feature of adaptation that keeps us from being chronically overwhelmed by the emotions of the past. Adaptation is normally a desirable feature, but you have to actively fight against it if you want to maintain your sense of appreciation. Even the greatest human minds have struggled to do this. Albert Einstein, hardly a crime-addled misanthrope, wrote, "A hundred times every day I remind myself that my inner and outer life depend on the labours of other men, living and dead, and that I must exert myself in order to give in the same measure as I have received and am still receiving." I'm no Einstein, but we share the same need for reminders, which is why pictures and mementos of my family and friends are prominently displayed in my office, and why I keep the letter I received awarding me tenure in my desk drawer. I want easy reminders of what I have to be grateful for in plain sight and close at hand.

Enemy No. 2: Comparison. It's not just our emotions that change over time. Our standards of comparison also change in ways that create barriers to feeling appreciation. No matter how well you're doing in life, there's almost always someone, somewhere, on some dimension who's doing better. You might get a raise, but someone else's is bigger. You move into a nicer neighborhood, but your neighbor has a nicer house. You might be one of the greatest athletes in the world, but you won the silver medal while someone else won the gold.

How we compare ourselves with others matters a great deal for our well-being. In fact, bronze medalists at the Olympics actually look happier than silver medalists both immediately after their events and on the medal stand because they're making different comparisons.[23] A silver medalist tends to be looking up the medal stand and thinking they just missed winning a gold, while the bronze medalist is looking down and thinking they could have missed a medal entirely. When your comparisons change, doing objectively better can sometimes mean feeling subjectively worse, leaving you feeling less grateful when you might actually have more to be grateful for.

The gratitude-killing tendency to compare ourselves with others isn't, however, inevitable. When researchers studied what differentiates happy from not-so-happy people, they found that unhappy people tended to compare themselves with other people (and generally focus on those who were doing better rather than those doing worse), whereas happy people tended to compare themselves with their past (and therefore focus on ways they've been improving over time).[24] Teddy Roosevelt claimed that "comparison is the thief of joy," but he was only half right. Comparing where you are today with where you were in the past can actually highlight progress and brighten your sense of appreciation rather than dim it. This is why reflective exercises like counting your blessings or writing a gratitude letter can be so powerful—because you have to pause and look back on where you've been, highlighting what you have to be grateful for.

Enemy No. 3: Adversity. Both adaptation and social comparison highlight how our thoughts and emotions are heavily determined by our attention. Feeling appreciation requires paying attention to the blessings we've received at any given moment, rather than focusing on the burdens in our way. Unfortunately for our sense of gratitude, the blessings that help us don't capture our attention nearly as readily as the burdens that hinder us.

As Shai Davidai and Tom Gilovich note, every bike rider has experienced this.[25] When you're riding with a tailwind pushing you along, you barely notice it. But when you turn around to ride back home, the only thing you're focused on is fighting against the headwind. This is because the burdens that get in our way necessarily require our attention in order to overcome them, while our blessings help us without needing any attention whatsoever. The canceled flight on your holiday trip requires you to make alternate plans, but the flight that takes off and lands without incident requires only that you sit back and enjoy it. Our attention, therefore, has an adversity bias. When our burdens scream in our face but our blessings blow quietly at our backs, it's no wonder that we have to actively remind ourselves of what we have to appreciate.

Not Sharing It, Part 1: Undervaluing Gratitude

Not feeling appreciation is one thing, but feeling it yet hesitating to express it is quite different. Remember that Celine McGee said she needed to be brave to pass along her compliments, and that people in our survey reported withholding about a third of their kind thoughts from others. It also took me more than thirty years to reach out and express my deepest appreciation to Mr. Aune. Why? Maybe it's hard to know exactly what to say? Or it's never quite the right time? Or it'll be awkward to express something so meaningful out of the blue?

These are common psychological barriers that our research suggests may be holding you back more often than is warranted. Just as with reaching out to talk with a stranger or having deeper conversations with loved ones, it's easy to underestimate how positively people will respond when you express your appreciation. Our research on appreciation started small, with a mere seventeen alumni from the University of Chicago in a class I was teaching. This was a successful group who had plenty to be grateful for. Every one of them, however, had someone they felt very grateful to, but had never told. This included friends, college roommates, neighbors, bosses, spouses, and parents. To find out what would happen if this group expressed their appreciation, and to better understand why they hadn't done so already, we asked each person to write a letter explaining why they felt so grateful to this person and then to send it to them. After sending their letters, our students indicated in a survey how the experience made them feel, and also how they expected their recipient to feel when they received it.[26] We then reached out to the recipients to find out how they *actually felt* when they received their letter. The result was so crystal clear, and the response so powerful, that I've now done this exercise with more than eighteen hundred people and counting. Of those, about twelve hundred have allowed me to reach out to their recipient, and roughly a thousand recipients have responded to tell us how the experience made them feel. Thousands of pages of gratitude letters taught us three things.

First, expressing appreciation feels good and being appreciated feels even better. About 94 percent of people who wrote gratitude letters and 99 percent of those who received the letters and responded to our survey report feeling more positive than they normally do. Eighteen percent of letter writers and 55 percent of recipients gave the most positive response on the survey possible, indicating that they felt *much* happier than usual.[27]

Second, we learned that our letter writers knew that their recipients would feel good, but they still underestimated how positive they would feel. Specifically, letter writers underestimated how surprised their recipient would be, how surprised they would be by the letter's content, and how positive their recipient would feel, while *overestimating* how awkward their recipient would feel.[28] Although 55 percent of recipients gave the most positive response possible when asked how they felt compared with normal, only 19 percent of the letter writers expected their recipients to feel that good.[29] People thought that expressing gratitude would make their recipients feel *good*. In fact, it made their recipients feel *great*.

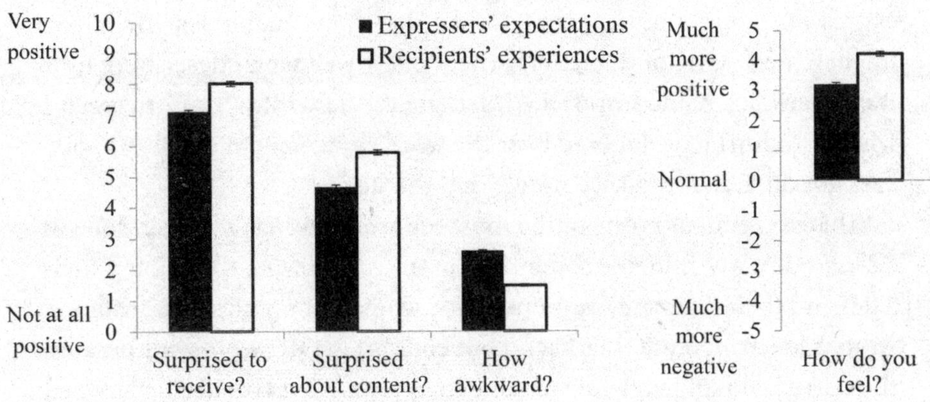

Finally, we learned that one reason we underestimate how positively our appreciation will be received comes from the perspective gap in attention to competence and warmth that we covered in chapter 3. Think about sitting down to actually write a letter of appreciation to someone to whom you feel really grateful. What pops into your mind as you're putting your pen to paper or your fingers to keys? It almost certainly has to be about the task at hand. "How on earth am I going to say this?" "Will I get the words just right?" "Won't it be weird getting a letter out of the blue?" But remember that others evaluate us more in terms of our warmth. You might be worried about how competently you're expressing yourself, but the person you're appreciating is likely to be thinking about how kind you are. After all, think about the last time someone expressed their appreciation to you. Did you wordsmith their grammar? Would it *really* have mattered that it took someone a decade to say how much they mean to you, if you didn't know of their feelings in the first place? Doubtful. In fact, when we asked our letter writers to predict how their recipients would evaluate their letter in terms of its competence (the extent to which they got the words "just right," and how articulate it was) and in terms of its warmth (how warm and sincere the letter would seem), they thought their letter would be seen as less competent than it was warm. However, the letter recipients actually rated them very positively on both dimensions, meaning that our letter writers' concerns about how effectively they conveyed their appreciation were misplaced.

It's not that the precise words you use are irrelevant when you're expressing your gratitude, but rather that they matter less than you might expect. One of the letter writers put it well when describing how the experience made him feel. "It felt great!" he wrote. "In retrospect, I wish I wouldn't have labored over the word choice in the email. Nobody ever got offended by a nice note." That is true.

This experiment is one of the most rewarding things I've ever done in a classroom. My students sometimes even tear up when describing their letter and their recipient's response. One woman in my class, for instance, wrote a lovely poem to her friend but couldn't get the words out because she started choking up while reading them. Her friend beside her stepped up to read them instead. The whole class broke out in applause. It was beautiful. The many notes I get from the letter recipients are beautiful, too. One wrote, "Reading [this] letter made me fill with pride, gratitude and fulfillment of being a mother. I had tears of happiness and was totally caught off guard." Another wrote, "For what it's worth, I started crying at my desk when I saw [this] email. It meant so much to me—I love him, and I'm very proud of what he's accomplished, and the impact I know he will have on our world. You never know what someone is going through, or how such a small gesture can have such enormous impact, but needless to say I don't even think I knew how much I needed to hear those words until I saw them. Things like that make all the bad days worth it." One time during a break in class, a tough-looking male student who usually sat quietly in the back pulled me aside and showed me a text he had gotten from his buddy after sending his letter: "Dude, you can't send me this stuff at work. I can't be crying at my desk like this." I could go on and on with these examples.

The positive experience also comes through in the answers both letter writers and recipients give when asked how the exercise made them feel. "So happy I could cry," one gratitude expresser wrote. "Overwhelmed with thankfulness," wrote another. "Amazing; I was reluctant to do it at first, but it was very emotional and really increased the love and admiration I have for [the recipient]," wrote a third.

How did the gratitude recipients feel? "Like a Giant, a Superhero, super humane individual," "tears of love, joy, and respect," "overwhelmed," and "blown away" are just a few typical examples. "I felt wonderful," one person wrote, "because it means that I was successful in doing what was and is the most important accomplishment in my life." Many get inspired: "The side effect was I decided to send some appreciation letters myself." A few even had the same kind of experience that William James did: "I can never describe, adequately, the feelings. I was totally overwhelmed with so many emotions. It made me feel loved and appreciated more than I have in my entire life. I have never been touched in quite this way."[30]

This experiment has changed the way I live my life. Not thinking it would matter that much, and that it would be pretty weird to contact him out of the blue, is what kept me from reaching out to Mr. Aune, my high school band teacher, for so many years, despite feeling grateful to him routinely. I wasn't expecting that to change when I started writing this chapter, but then it became obvious that I was committing the same mistakes that my students were making. I therefore reached out to a well-connected high school buddy (thanks, Todd Jones!) who got me Mr. Aune's phone number.[31] I sent a text to double-check the number and explain why I wanted to talk. "Wow, what a great surprise to hear from you today!" Mr. Aune texted back when I reached out. "Full disclosure," he then wrote, "I had tears running down my cheeks as I read your note!" My phone call a few days later was as wonderful as phone calls get. We talked for nearly an hour. A few days after our call I got another text message: "You need to know that this entire experience over the past couple of days has been an incredible blessing to me—there is no way you can ever truly know how much it means to me." Mr. Aune didn't need to fill out a survey after our conversation for me to know that I had left him feeling wonderful, and that the worries that kept me from reaching out to him for so long were misplaced.

Not Sharing It, Part 2: Insufficiently Complimentary?

Appreciation doesn't always come in supersized proportions that you'd put into a heartfelt gratitude letter. More common are countless small things you might notice, appreciate, and compliment someone on, "sprinkling a little love" around, as Celine McGee would call it. Opportunities for sprinkling compliments might be all around once you start looking for them. Just yesterday as I was writing this, for instance, I noticed someone on my train wearing an awesome brown suit, saw a janitor named Keith when I arrived at my office building who has one of the most contagious smiles in the building, and then had an early meeting with my terrific lab manager, Janice Im, who had solved a tricky logistical issue for a class I was teaching. On my way home, I passed someone working on their beautiful front yard, saw a train conductor who is unusually friendly, and made it home just in time for the great dinner Jen had made at the end of her long day.

Each of those are little moments where I could brighten someone's mood, and through that moment of connection brighten my mood as well. But as Celine mentioned, even a simple act like giving someone a compliment when you have one to pass along can create anxiety. If I tell Keith that his smile is contagious, or the woman that her front yard looks great, or Janice for what seems like the millionth time how wonderfully helpful she is, might it be weird or misinterpreted or simply too minor to be worth the bother? Just as with more elaborate expressions of gratitude, that uncertainty about how someone might respond is what can hold us back from sharing kind words when we have them to share, and why even a little bravery might seem needed to start passing along your compliments more routinely.

Those barriers are again a bit misplaced. Consider an experiment we conducted at the Garfield Park Conservatory in Chicago, where we thought people might have a little time on their hands to participate in our experiment. We set up our table, invited pairs of people visiting together to participate, and then sent one person off to another part of the garden while the other person stayed with us. The person who stayed became "the complimenter," who we asked to think of authentic compliments that they could write about the person we had just sent away, but that they hadn't already given to the person for whatever reason. After writing them, the complimenters then predicted in a survey how they expected their recipient would feel when they came back and read them.

These friends, family members, and romantic partners were hardly strangers to each other, having known each other for an average of nearly eleven years, ranging from two weeks to seventy-six years. Nevertheless, it was still easy to think of compliments that they had not yet expressed. "I love how dependable and reliable you are," one complimenter wrote. "It makes me feel really safe and really loved." "You have an incredibly big heart and your kindness brings light into the lives of others," wrote another. One husband wrote to his wife, "I love how drop-dead-gorgeous you are, even when you are not giving any effort whatsoever."

It's easy to imagine that these compliments would make their recipients feel pretty darned good, but even these pairs underestimated how great their kind words would make their recipient feel. In fact, they didn't seem to think their compliments would matter much at all. Those who had just complimented their partner expected them to feel no more positive than people in the control condition who were simply having a pleasant day in the park. Those passing along compliments also thought their recipient would feel a little more awkward than they actually did. Passing along a compliment may not require much bravery at all.

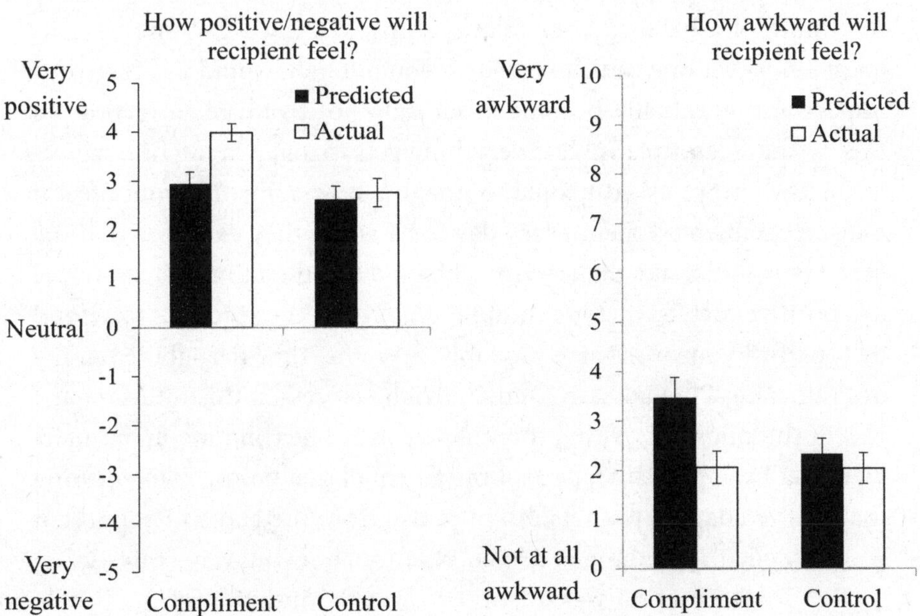

These mistakes extend to compliments we could give to strangers as well. As we were conducting our experiments in Chicago, another research team was having students give a simple compliment to a complete stranger (of the same gender, following the same rules as Celine McGee), saying that they liked their shirt (or jacket or dress, if a shirt wasn't visible). Just as we found with those who had known each other for a long time, on average, these complimenters underestimated how positive their kind words would make their recipient feel.[32]

Our research teams have now replicated these results many times. We learned during the COVID-19 pandemic that giving people compliments over Zoom produced the same effect as doing it in person, that people underestimate how much someone will appreciate a compliment given when first meeting them, and that people with more pessimistic expectations are also more likely to mistakenly keep their compliments to themselves rather than sharing them. We all learned that people with more optimistic (and also more accurate) expectations are also more willing to give someone a compliment.

It might be easy to accept that hearing a single compliment out of the blue is surprisingly good, but what if you turned this one-off experience into more of a habit in your relationships, sharing a genuine compliment whenever one came to mind? If you did that, would you lose your impact and eventually become a boringly positive broken record? In theory, that seems plausible. Everything gets tiring, you might imagine. In fact, when we asked people to imagine how someone would feel if they complimented them every day for a week, they expected that the first day would make them feel really good but then they'd steadily feel less positive each day.[33] One compliment is nice, the second is okay, and by the third your words are probably tiresome, they thought. Even my own amazing PhD adviser, Tom Gilovich, expressed this intuition as I was in the midst of writing this chapter. After hearing me in an interview that he appreciated, he sent me an email that began, "I'm guessing that you've adapted to this kind of praise from me and so I suppose it will only elicit something of a 'meh' reaction, but you were fantastic."

But Tom's intuition was off, and so was the intuition of the people considering repeated compliments in our experiment. When we asked people to write five different—but still genuine—compliments to someone they appreciate, recipients who got one each day showed no decline in how positive each compliment made them feel. We adapt to things that are the same, but each new compliment was unique. Tom's email ended with, "I'm proud to call you a former student and friend." Although I could have guessed that Tom felt this way because he's shared similar sentiments before (and I feel the same), hearing it this way felt beyond terrific. There is surely some point at which kind words become tiresome. Our data, however, suggests that this point is further off than you're likely to guess, and a point that I suspect most people are unlikely to reach in practice. I think it's safe to act as if your kind words never become tired words.

Underestimating how positive even seemingly small compliments can make someone feel stems partly from being overly focused on our competence. Even the great wordsmith Mark Twain might have experienced this gap when he wrote, "And I will remark here that the happy phrasing of a compliment is one of the rarest of human gifts, and the happy delivery of it another," while also writing in a letter that "I can live on a good compliment for two weeks with nothing else to eat." Our experiments suggest that the happy phrasing of a compliment isn't that rare at all, but the happy delivery of it is rarer than it should be.

It was late in the COVID-19 pandemic with Christmas fast approaching. My family needed something uplifting. As good midwesterners raised in the Christian tradition, we usually turn to chocolate as our preferred source of uplift at this time of year. Specifically, we turn to Advent calendars, those cardboard boxes of magic that have twenty-four little tabs with a small piece of molded chocolate behind them. But this year, after all the data I had seen on compliments, I proposed that we try a "compliment calendar" instead.

I revealed my plan at the tail end of November as I passed out paper to everyone in my family (except our youngest, Lindsay, whom we helped with the task). The paper included four prompts—things like "I love you because . . ." or "You are . . ."—that they were to complete for each family member. The math worked out such that we could cut up each compliment, bend it into a ring, and staple it to another compliment until we had a chain of twenty-four compliments for each family member. We would then open one every day. With three high-school-age sons at home at the time, you can imagine the lack of enthusiasm for this plan. "Do we have to?" was heard multiple times.

The tune changed, though, once we started. It was easy for all of us to come up with compliments we could share and fun to write them down. Most of all, it was wonderful opening a different one each morning. The kids would mostly open theirs in private and hide them away for safekeeping. It wasn't just a positive experience, but a *surprisingly positive* experience, just as our data would suggest. I still have several sitting under the computer monitor in my home office as a little bit of uplift when I need it.

So, why wouldn't I do this more often?

I try to keep this question on the top of my mind, like Celine McGee, so that expressing appreciation when I feel it is an automatic habit rather than something I have to think about. I notice someone dressed especially nicely, I tell them and move on, confident that the risk of misunderstanding is small compared with the high probability that I'll be leaving someone feeling great in my wake. When I see someone doing a great job at work, I grab one of the thank-you notes I keep stocked under my desk, and pass the note along, knowing that I have more power to uplift someone than I used to think. When I hear a kind word shared about someone I know, I'm quick to pass that bit of kind gossip on to its target (not sharing who said it), telling them that I heard someone loving them behind their back. And when I'm connected to someone I appreciate every day, I try to remember that kind words don't become tired words, but that each unique bit of kindness is more like a new verse in a lovely song rather than a broken record.

Maybe you could do this a little more often, too?

8

Choosing Kindness

And anytime you feel the pain, hey Jude, refrain,
Don't carry the world upon your shoulders.
For well you know that it's a fool who plays it cool
By making his world a little colder.

—THE BEATLES, "Hey Jude"

It's impossible to start a business when you're terrified of rejection and therefore refuse to ask for help, so Jia Jiang, an aspiring entrepreneur, decided to dull his fear by getting rejected relentlessly. Jia had learned that some psychotherapists effectively treat anxiety by exposing people to whatever they're afraid of every day for roughly a month (known as exposure therapy), but Jia thought his fear was particularly intense so he needed more. His plan, detailed in his book, *Rejection Proof*,[1] was to make an outlandish (but not impossible) request for help a hundred days in a row, assuming he'd get rejected every day and thereby develop the thick skin he needed.

Jia's first attempt was a success. He walked up to a security guard, asked if he could borrow $100, and was instantly rejected. The tone of the guard's rejection, though, was kinder than Jia expected. "I thought he might pull out a gun or yell at me or something," he said in the moments afterward, "but he just said no. That's not so bad."

Jia's second attempt was also a success. He walked into a Five Guys fast-food restaurant, ordered and ate a burger, and then walked back to the counter to ask if he could get a second burger for free—a "burger refill," he called it. The guy behind the counter chuckled, asked, "A what?" and eventually said, "We don't do that." Fair enough. "It was kind of cool," he later said about the employee's humorous reaction—with a second surprisingly not so bad experience in his data set.

On day 3, Jia started failing. This time he went to a Krispy Kreme doughnut shop and asked the employee working behind the counter—Jackie Braun—if she could make him a set of doughnuts in the interlocking shape and colors of the Olympic rings. In Jia's video of the interaction, you can see Jackie dropping into Rodin's *Thinker* pose, with her hand on her chin in serious consideration. "When do you want them?" she asks. Jia wasn't prepared for this. "Uh . . . the next fifteen minutes?" he stammers back. Jackie keeps considering. "I didn't even pay attention to the Olympics this year," she says, questioning what the rings look like and then drawing them with Jia's equally confused help on the back of a receipt. "I'll see what I can do," she eventually tells him. Roughly fifteen minutes later, Jackie's back with a box—almost apologetic because she thought she could have done better—containing a beautifully colored set of five doughnuts.

Jia is nearly speechless in the video. "What do I owe you?" he stammers. "Oh, don't worry about it, those are on me," Jackie says. Jia commented afterward, "With people like Jackie, mankind is worth saving after all." In the end, Jia walked away "failing miserably" in his quest for rejection, but also having learned an unforgettable lesson about kindness. "Wow, sometimes you make a crazy request and you get an awesome answer."[2]

In one request after another over the next ninety-seven days, Jia continues having a surprisingly hard time getting rejected. Walk up to a stranger's house and ask the owner to take a picture of Jia playing soccer in the guy's backyard (day 6)? "I guess so," Steve, the homeowner, says. Ask to make an announcement on a Southwest Airlines flight (day 19)? Jeff, who takes Jia's ticket at the gate, responds without flinching, "You can't do the safety thing, because you have to be in your seat for that, but you can do the welcome." Minutes later, Jia's on the mic with an airplane audience: "Hello, everyone, welcome on board." Ask random people to give him compliments (day 21)? Challenge a stranger at a track to a hundred-meter dash (day 39)? Ask to sit in the driver's seat of a police car (day 41)? Ask to plant a pink rose in a random person's front yard (day 61)? Ask to take a nap in a mattress store (day 65)? Go to a private airport and ask to copilot a small plane without having flown anything ever before (day 92)? "Yes" is the answer to all of these, and many more.

In fact, when we evaluated all of the 105 purposefully outlandish requests Jia ended up making, including a few days where he got carried away with multiple requests, we found that he was rejected *less often* than he was accepted (forty-eight rejections to fifty-one acceptances, to be precise, with six of those rejections being a more mixed reaction of not agreeing to the specific request but agreeing to something else).[3]

Jia had been living in a confusing learning environment, where his fear of being rejected when he asked someone for help kept him from even trying, and thereby kept him from learning that his fear might be exaggerated. When Jia made *the choice* differently, by approaching rather than avoiding, he got the chance to learn how others actually react. He thought the tone of the interactions would be harsh. In fact, people were overwhelmingly kind, even when rejecting his request. When we watched all of Jia's videos, 65 percent of his requests received a clearly positive reception, including 43 percent of his rejections. Only 7 of the 105 requests were received with any hint of negativity in them, and even these rare cases were mild.[4] He wasn't yelled at even once.

"I started out with this idea of desensitization, that if I get enough 'nos,' I will be tough," Jia told me. "But when I got started, the first day I found that this is not as bad as I thought." Jia's mind was full of overly pessimistic expectations. "Just before heading into [a request], I felt really bad, like I was going to die, you know, but then when it happened, it wasn't that bad," he explained. As he kept doing it, Jia found it to be fun, uplifting, and most of all, empowering. Actually testing his pessimistic expectations and learning that they were off the mark expanded what he thinks is possible. "We reject ourselves way more than we're rejected by others," he told me. "I see the world as a much kinder place than I thought it was."

To be clear, Jia always asked for help that others could provide without too much difficulty. He wasn't asking anyone for a million dollars on the street or for a spare kidney. As the stakes rise, so would the likelihood of being rejected. The point of Jia's experience isn't that other people were willing to do anything he asked. The point is that Jia made his requests expecting he would be rejected every single time, but other people were considerably more willing to help than Jia ever imagined they would be. As a result, Jia lost his fear of rejection, not because he developed thicker skin, but because he learned that his pessimistic fears were exaggerated.

Underasking?

Jia's experience was mind altering for him, but maybe there's something unusual about Jia, about the unusual requests he made, or about the people he happened to ask for help? To test whether Jia's experiences are common, and therefore might apply to you, we need a different kind of experiment with many different people asking for more typical requests for help.

In fact, behavioral scientists have already done this. Years before Jia set out to get a hundred rejections, researchers measured people's beliefs about how likely others were to help if asked, and then compared those beliefs with how likely others actually were to help when asked. In one experiment, researchers gave undergraduates in New York City the challenge of getting three strangers to let them borrow their cell phones (calling the lab from the stranger's phone to confirm the acceptance). Before going out and asking strangers on the streets to hand over their phones, the students predicted how many people they would need to ask in order to get three to agree. In essence, this method puts precise numbers on our fears of rejection, measuring how often these students *thought* they would be rejected when they asked compared with how often they were *actually* rejected. Like Jia, these students thought they'd be rejected more often than they actually were, expecting they would need to ask an average of 10.1 people when they actually needed to ask only 6.2. Again, it's not that everyone helps when asked, but rather that others agreed to help more often than expected.

This experiment is permanently etched in my memory. On the very day I first read about this result, I found myself on the train platform needing to let my wife know that I was running late but—you guessed it—didn't have my cell phone with me. At the time, I never would have thought to ask someone for help because I'd have feared being on the receiving end of a cold shoulder, but I was feeling empowered by this finding and so put it to the test. The first person I asked immediately said, "Of course!" as if he'd been waiting to be asked. The bonus was that with both of our moods uplifted, we then kept talking and I had a nicer commute home than I would have had otherwise. I now have the title of the paper reporting these results stamped into my brain like a mantra: "If You Need Help, Just Ask."[5]

Other experiments produced similar results. In one, volunteers estimated they would need to ask, on average, 20.5 people on the streets of New York in order to get 5 to fill out a survey for them. In fact, they only had to ask roughly half that (10.5, to be exact). In another, volunteers estimated they'd need to ask 7.2 people, on average, to get someone to escort them across Columbia's campus. In fact, they only had to ask 2.3. In a third, new workers at a nonprofit raising money for cancer thought they'd have to call 210 people, on average, to achieve the fundraising goal they had set. In fact, they only had to call half that many (122 people, on average).

A former PhD student in my department at the University of Chicago—Claire Tsai, now a tenured professor in the University of Toronto's Marketing Department—has told me multiple times how walking into the business school building and asking our MBA students to fill out surveys for research changed her outlook on life because people were so much kinder when she asked them for help than she thought they'd be. Had Claire not asked for help, she never would have found out how helpful others could be if you made *the choice* to reach out and ask.

Not only do we underestimate how likely others are to help, but we also seem likely—as Jia did—to underestimate how positively someone might feel to be asked for help. At the core of this gap between our expectations and our experiences is the age-old tension between the debating Thomases—Hobbes and Jefferson—about whether human nature is fundamentally selfish or prosocial. Do we care only about ourselves, or do we also genuinely care about others?

Team Hobbes is our inner cynic: "Of the voluntary acts of every man, the object is some good to himself." Team Jefferson is our inner idealist: "I believe, on the contrary, that the moral sense is as much a part of our constitution as that of feeling, seeing, or hearing; . . . that every human mind feels pleasure in doing good to another." Both Jia's expectations and my own when asking to borrow a cell phone tilted in the direction of Team Hobbes, assuming that others wouldn't want to help when asked. Our experience, though, aligned more with Team Jefferson, finding that others seemed not just willing to help when asked but also surprisingly happy to help.

Again, this pattern of overly pessimistic expectations seems to be more of a general rule than a rare exception. Consider an experiment, for instance, that took my collaborators and me back to the Garfield Park Conservatory in Chicago, the site of the compliment-giving experiment from chapter 7. Instead of giving compliments, this time people were asking for help. Specifically, we gave people an instant camera that would print out a physical photograph of them, and asked them to find another visitor to ask if they'd be able to help by taking their picture with the camera. Before asking for this help, we asked the requesters to tell us how they thought the person they asked for help would feel. We then stopped each helper after they were done taking their picture to ask how being asked to help actually made them feel.

Our results aligned with both Jia's pessimistic expectations and his more positive experiences. The requesters were almost never rejected; 94 percent of those approached agreed, with all requesters getting a "yes" by their second request. The requesters were also met with a kinder reaction than they expected. Specifically, they underestimated how happy the helpers would feel after being asked for help and overestimated how inconvenienced and coerced the helpers would feel. Before asking for help, our requesters tended to share Hobbes's view that they would be forcing another person into helping them. The people they asked for help, however, aligned with Jefferson's sentiments and were happier to have helped someone. Putting Hobbes's expectations up against Jefferson's experiences means that other people were not just happy to help but *surprisingly* happy to help. Requesters left with fun pictures and helpers left feeling happier after being asked for help.

I find myself thinking about this experiment almost every time I'm out in a public place. Walking around my hometown of Chicago, I routinely see people in lovely tourist areas who want their pictures taken. Instead of reaching out and asking for help from someone nearby and creating a moment of connection, many instead reach their arm out to take a selfie. Or worse, use an ungainly selfie stick. I avoid this when the opportunity allows and go straight to asking for help with a smile because I'm optimistic that the moment will be a pleasant exchange that leaves the person I ask for help feeling better afterward. In fact, I now think of not asking for help when I need it as being unkind because I'm not doing something that I'm confident will make someone feel a little happier than they would have otherwise.

I can't think of a single time when someone has said no, or a single time when it's been anything other than a pleasant experience. There was the moment when I was with my friend Leaf on the Chicago lakefront and two people visiting from France agreed with big smiles to help take our picture, and we talked for a little while about where they should visit in the United States. Or the time my family and I were in Wisconsin and the person who took our picture happened to have grown up in the very small suburb we live in. Or the time I was in New York City with my daughter Tsion in front of Rockefeller Center with a delightful woman who insisted on getting just the right photo of us together. My photo album is filled with nicer pictures, and nicer memories, because of this research. To me, the selfie stick is a product designed to satisfy a social misunderstanding.

These surprisingly positive experiences of being asked for help aren't restricted to the world of photography. Agreeing to help when asked directly seems to be the norm rather than the exception all around the world. One study surveying people from eight different cultures across five continents found that 88 percent of direct requests for help were accepted (with only tiny differences between cultures). If you need help, just ask, wherever you happen to be. The good feeling we get when we're able to help someone who asks also doesn't seem to be unusual. Both economists and psychologists note that helping tends to leave people with a "warm glow," generally feeling more positive after we successfully help someone, and even more positive than when we do something kind for ourselves.[6]

This doesn't mean, of course, that every request is met with happy acceptance. Far from it, in fact, as I'm sure you've experienced in your own life. There is one key ingredient in the requests I've described so far that explains our misplaced pessimism, and also identifies when our requests are more likely to get the cold shoulder that we expect. Every request I've described involves one person directly asking another person for help, usually face-to-face (or over the phone with one's voice). If you ask for help over a more socially distant communication medium like email, where the social forces of responsiveness and reciprocity are much weaker, and where your warmth and authenticity aren't as obvious, then you're likely to get a notably less positive response.[7] Leave an anonymous note on someone's door asking for help when they can't see you or hear the warmth in your request, and people are more likely to dodge you.[8] Ask a group of people rather than a single individual, where the connection between you and any person in the group is likely to be weaker, and you're likely to be met with a less positive response. What's likely to be surprisingly positive is reaching out to another person directly for help.

Only experience can free us from the misplaced fears that are holding us back. Steve Jobs learned this lesson early in his life when, at age twelve, he found the phone number for Bill Hewlett, co-founder of Hewlett-Packard, in the phone book and called him up out of the blue. Hewlett picked up the phone himself. Jobs said he introduced himself and asked Hewlett if he could have some spare parts for a piece of equipment he was building. Hewlett gave him the spare parts, and also offered him a summer job. "Most people don't get those experiences because they'd never ask," Jobs said, recalling it later. "I've never found anyone that didn't want to help me if I asked him for help." What I think separates Jobs from many of us isn't the positive reaction he received when he reached out, but rather his lack of hesitation in the first place. "Most people never pick up the phone and call, most people never ask, and that's what separates sometimes the people who do things from the people who just dream about them."[9]

Underhelping?

Our reluctance to reach out in the realm of kindness isn't limited to asking for help. It can also extend to being reluctant to be kind by offering help. When Jen and I lost our daughter six months into Jen's pregnancy, we experienced tremendous support from some of our friends, but others seemed to be avoiding us. Jen found other parents steering clear of her when she dropped our older children off at school. A few of my colleagues came by my office more often to offer their support, but many who knew what happened seemed to come by less. This avoidance surely came not from indifference to our pain but rather from concerns about their own competence.

Sheryl Sandberg, former senior executive at Facebook and author of the bestselling business book *Lean In,* can relate. After she lost her forty-seven-year-old husband to heart failure on a family vacation, her normal social routines with friends and acquaintances "just stopped and people kind of looked at me like I was a ghost. And I think they were so afraid of saying the wrong thing that they hardly said anything at all."[10] It's not just death we're reluctant to reach out about. "You want to silence a room?" Sandberg observes. "Get diagnosed with cancer . . . have someone in your family go to prison. Lose a job. Sexual assault." Wanting to help but worried that we might say or do the wrong thing, especially to someone we don't know well, we hold back and end up leaving someone in need alone. And here we are again: *the choice*.

Indeed, when we asked a sample of people online to think about reaching out to express support to someone, they generally reported feeling an approach/avoidance conflict: simultaneously feeling a strong desire to help *and* a strong concern about doing the wrong thing and hurting the person's feelings. In this survey, the more people reported having these avoidance concerns, the more dissatisfied they were with the amount of support they gave to others. In another study, we found that people's beliefs about how positive and supported the other person would feel if they reached out had a bigger effect on their willingness to express support than did the perceived need of the person they were reaching out to.[11] Our decisions about reaching out and expressing support seem driven more by how we think another person will respond to us than by how much we think the other person needs us.

To test whether these expectations were on the mark, we invited people in one experiment to think of someone they know who was going through a difficult time and could use some support, but whom they haven't yet reached out to. We then asked these volunteers to write a letter to this person, trying to support them in whatever way they chose to. They expressed support for many reasons: "they just lost a family member," "a break-up," "financial trouble," "depression," "school troubles," "[an] upcoming medical test." They also wrote to a wide range of people: family members, best friends, roommates, mentors, neighbors, and casual acquaintances. Before sending their letter, they also told us how they expected their letter would make the recipient feel. We then reached out to the recipients to find out how it actually made them feel (emphasizing confidentiality to everyone involved every step of the way).[12]

We learned two things in this experiment. First, we learned that our letter writers were, on average, overly pessimistic (or maybe insufficiently optimistic) about how their recipients would feel. Letter writers thought that recipients would feel more awkward, and less well supported, than the recipients actually did.

Second, we learned that our misplaced pessimism gets larger as the person we're reaching out to is more distant from us. Recall that our letter writers reached out to a wide variety of people to express their support, from close family members to casual acquaintances and neighbors. Our letter writers *thought* that how close they were would matter, expecting more positive reactions from people they were closer to and less positive reactions—more awkwardness, less sense of sincerity, and a less positive mood—from people they felt more distant to. This closeness, however, did not matter at all to the recipients, who felt equally positive (and not awkward) regardless of whether the letter came from someone close or more distant. This means that the letter writers were most mistaken when they were expressing support to someone who was more distant from them. Our letter writers knew that they had the power to effectively support those they knew well and were close to. What they didn't know was that their power to uplift someone extended far beyond their close circle of friends and family.

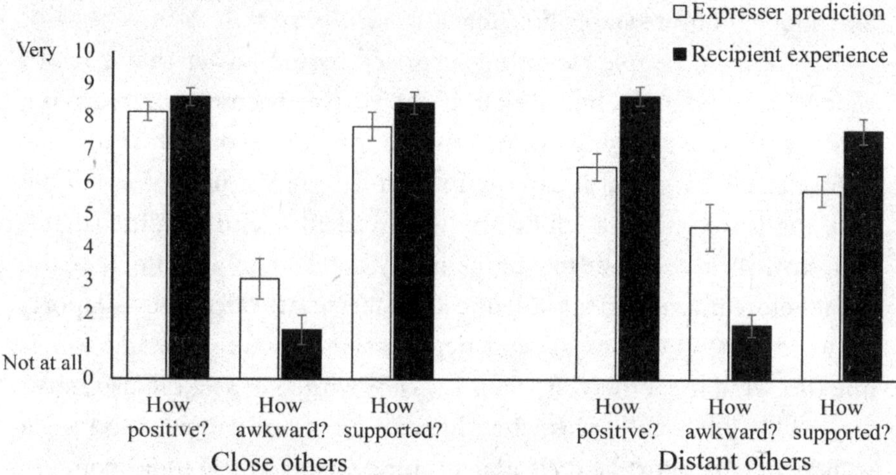

In fact, our research suggests that your ability to be supportive extends to complete strangers. In this experiment, we paired up random strangers and asked one person to describe a challenge they could use some help with and support for, and then asked their partner in the experiment to do their best to offer support in whatever way possible. The issues people sought support for ranged from fairly minor, such as figuring out how to balance time between work and friends, to major, such as a fifty-five-year-old who needed hip replacements but couldn't find a doctor, or another person who was occasionally homeless and in desperate need of a job.

Those we randomly assigned to offer their support weren't very optimistic about how well they'd be able to do it, expecting their recipient would feel pretty uncomfortable and unsupported. In fact, the supporters were more capable of helping the recipients than they imagined they would be. The kind of support offered in this brief interaction varied widely depending on what the issue was. The person who tried to support the fifty-five-year-old who needed hip replacements shared that her mother had encountered similar problems in her life and had simply started waiting in her doctor's office, refusing to leave until she was seen ("I'll try that," the fifty-five-year-old said). The person who expressed support to the unemployed person offered to continue talking after the experiment to search through their social network to help the person find a job and more stable housing.

Again, most people might be surprised by the power they have to support other people, but not all. If you've ever been on the receiving end of someone reaching out to you in a time of need, then you know full well how powerful it can be. In my own life, I'll never forget how uplifting it was when a fellow graduate student friend of mine (thank you, Justin) reached out to call me in my hotel room at ten o'clock the night before my very first academic job interview to offer some supportive words when I was an absolute nervous wreck. His call felt like someone throwing me a life vest when I was drowning at sea. I'll also never forget how powerful it was when Jen and I lost our daughter to have a wonderfully supportive colleague of mine (thank you, Linda) come to my office day after day with a hug, knowing that there was nothing she could say to take our pain away but showing up for me anyway. And Sheryl Sandberg won't forget the people who were there for her after her husband died, not to say something magical or do anything extraordinary, but to keep her from feeling alone. And yet, what can keep many of us from reaching out to express support at times like these is the same fallacy that can keep us from starting a nice conversation with a stranger or expressing gratitude when we feel it: being too focused on our competence when what someone in need values is our kindness and warmth.[13]

This gap in how we evaluate ourselves versus how we're evaluated by those we're reaching out to explains not only why we might be overly reluctant to do so but also why our efforts to express support can sometimes go wrong. Sheryl Sandberg recalled that before she lost her husband, she used to ask people going through a hard time, "Is there anything I can do?" which was a request she offered in kindness but came from a focus on her competence to try to make the person feel better. The problem is that this request puts the responsibility on the person in need to come up with something to ask for (which is hard enough on its own), when the recipient primarily values anything kind and supportive that might be done for them that expresses warmth and concern. Sandberg now advises us to just show up for someone and do *anything* that would be kind. "Say," she recommends, " 'I know you're going through something terrible. I'm coming over with dinner tonight. Is that okay?' " When you stop holding yourself back due to concerns about doing the wrong thing and instead focus on doing a kind thing for someone who you know needs it, you'll be surprised by how much good your kindness can do.

A Little Good Goes a Surprisingly Long Way

Opportunities for kindness in sizes both big and small exist around us but are easy to miss if we don't think our actions will make much of a difference. A compliment can be passed along anytime one comes to your mind, whether you think your recipient needs to be uplifted by your kind words or not. A letter of gratitude can be shared anytime you genuinely feel it, whether it's precisely timed for a moment when you think your recipient really needs it or not.

Every year I ask my MBA students to go out into the world and do a random act of kindness for someone—random in the sense of being unexpected or not obligated—so that we can analyze how it made them feel. They go all over the place and do all sorts of kind things. They help a stranger get to where they're going by walking with them, take an extra shift with their early-rising kids so their partner can sleep in, buy coffee for the person standing behind them in a coffee shop, send their friend a bouquet of flowers just for fun, drive an acquaintance where they need to go, leave a box of chocolates at the front desk of their apartment building as a gift to their neighbors, and cook a dinner and take it over to their friend's house as a surprise. Their acts of kindness range from small to large, for friends or strangers, with some planned but most being spontaneous. One student found that his planned act of kindness turned into a spontaneous one when he picked up a bouquet of flowers to surprise his fiancée, only to enter into a conversation with an elderly woman on the way home who said his flowers looked beautiful but that she didn't get flowers from people anymore. Hesitating for a second, he altered his original plan and gave the elderly woman his flowers with a smile and a hope that she loved them. Not to overlook his fiancée, my student ran back and happily bought a second bouquet for her, too, getting two acts of kindness from one kind intention.

The 2,178 (and counting) acts of kindness that my students have unleashed on the world vary widely, but their impact on my students' experience varies less. Although sometimes these acts of kindness leave people feeling worse when their effort to make someone happy fails, those outcomes are rare. By far the most common outcome is that these acts leave both the recipients and my students feeling great. When asked, 90 percent indicated that their act of kindness left them feeling more positive than they normally feel. Only 2 percent said it left them feeling more negative than normal.

My students aren't unusual. Being kind typically feels good because it satisfies basic human motivations of competency and social connection.[14] The acts of kindness that feel best are easy to do, make the person you're being kind to feel great in some way, and make you feel a personal connection to them. The rare cases where being kind leaves people feeling a little worse come when our attempt doesn't "work" because the recipient doesn't view it as kind, such as when one of my students tried to give someone living on the street a sandwich and they refused because they had already eaten and didn't want it. Because these failures are rare (being nice usually works), it's not much of a gamble that being kind will leave at least two people feeling good.[15]

You might imagine that something that feels this consistently good might also be something we do too often, like overeating junk food. Overdoing it does not, however, seem to be a problem for kindness. When I asked my students how often they perform acts of kindness compared with how often they would like to, 67 percent said they do them *less often* than they would like to and only 10 percent said they do them more often than they'd like to. Kindness is more like exercise, recognized in the abstract as something we should try more often but are reluctant to choose in the moment.

One obvious reason we might be reluctant to be kind to someone in the moment is that we don't *want* to. Doing something kind for another person can require time, effort, and money that we might not want to bother spending on someone else. Although this can certainly happen, many of the acts of kindness that you can do on a daily basis, and that my students typically did when I asked, were small things that cost them almost nothing. In addition to not wanting to help someone, underestimating how much good you'd do for another person if you actually did something kind for them could also keep you from being kind more often.

Testing the extent to which people might underestimate the positive impact their kindness can have on others led to one of the nicer experiments I've ever been involved with.[16] One year we encouraged my students (106 in all) to do their act of kindness for someone they knew whose email they could pass along to us. I then reached out to the recipients and asked how the act made them feel (just as we did with the gratitude letter recipients I described in chapter 7). As usual, people had some sense of how their kindness would make their recipient feel. They knew that their recipients would feel much more positive than they would feel uncomfortable, but their expectations also weren't perfectly calibrated. The recipients reported not only feeling more positive than my students thought they would; they also said they valued the act of kindness more than my students did. When asked "how big" their act of kindness was, my students mostly said, "Not very." But the recipients consistently said these apparently small acts of kindness actually seemed much bigger to them. When asked how much my students had invested in their act of kindness—how much effort, time, and money—the recipients consistently thought the act required much more than my students said it did. If you knew of an investment that would be valued by others at more than double what you put into it, you'd invest everything you had. A little bit of kindness goes a surprisingly long way.

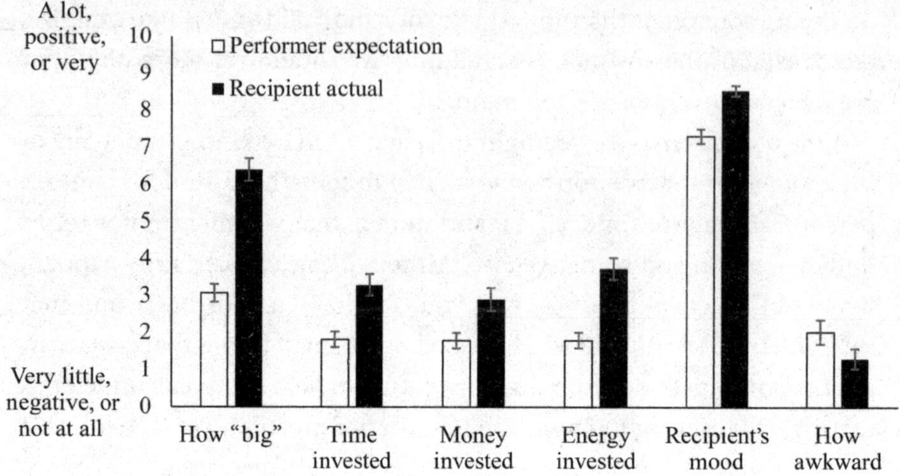

Over many more experiments, we've continued to see the same results, including sending a friend or family member a card out of the blue, giving away a cupcake or a cup of hot chocolate in Chicago's Millennium Park, and giving away a gift to someone in a lab experiment. We've also learned that in addition to underestimating the positive impact that our kindness can have on our recipients, we may underestimate how our kindness will get passed on, leading the recipient of our kindness to "pay it forward" by being kinder to someone else down the line. This indirect reciprocity, where a good deed is repaid not to the original benefactor but rather paid forward to someone else, wasn't expected at all by those who performed the initial kind act. When we fail to appreciate how powerful reaching out with kindness to another person can be, most of us may also fail to appreciate how far the impact of our kindness can go.

Once again, most of us, but not all of us. Bill Hewlett, who agreed to Steve Jobs's request for spare parts, reportedly lived his life and built his company around an often-repeated mantra: "Never stifle a generous impulse."[17] And yet stifle we often do. How much brighter would your days be if you realized the power you have to lift people up and make their day, rather than thinking that your kindness is weak? How much better would your life be if you acted on your generous impulses instead of letting mistaken beliefs hold you back? How much better would your days be if you kept an eye out for opportunities to make someone else's day a little better?

I wasn't planning to stifle a generous impulse when I was standing in line at Chick-fil-A with my family on our annual trip to get my wife's favorite holiday dessert, a peppermint shake, but there I was stifling anyway. The seven of us were quite a sight, with four older children in high school and college, while I was holding our youngest, Lindsay, who was not happy to be waiting any longer. As I was fumbling around for my wallet to pay, I got a gentle tap on my shoulder. A man who was roughly sixty years old, of slight build with his adult son standing beside him, was smiling and holding out a $100 bill. "Here, please, let me get this," he said.

I wasn't prepared for this. Here someone was trying to do a random act of kindness for me and my first thought was to resist. I didn't want him to think I was in need when I wasn't, and I didn't want to feel indebted to someone. So I tried to decline: "Oh, thank you so much, but I really couldn't accept that." He persisted, "Oh, no, I'd really like to." I continued to stifle his generosity, "No, no, really, we're doing okay."

And then he offered a revelation: "Can you not accept a blessing when it's offered to you?"

Those words hit me so hard that it felt like being punched in the face. In that moment, all of the research I've described in this chapter about the surprising power of kindness came back to me all at once. Here was this man reaching out in kindness to me, and there I was, in the lyrics of "Hey Jude" from the Beatles, being a fool by making the world a little colder. I was embarrassed by how unkind I was being to him by resisting his kindness to me.

I paused for a moment, letting this all run through my mind while trying not to cry in front of him. It didn't quite work. I reached out to hug him and told him that he had just made me a better person by pointing out a mistake in me. "Oh no, it's nothing," he said, not realizing how deeply his kindness affected me. At that moment I realized that I was in one of my own experiments, feeling overwhelmed by how positive he had made me feel while he was thinking he had done only a small thing for me. I haven't been the same since.

Jia Jiang also told me that he hasn't been the same since learning about the power of kindness in others. "I'll be honest," he said, "it changed my personality. I've become someone who's much more inquisitive. I'm more assertive." What Jia is saying is that he's changed how he makes *the choice,* making it a habit to reach out and try to connect a little more often than he did before his experience changed his mind. It's not that Jia lives in a saccharine world where kindness rules every day, but rather that he's more optimistic about other people and hence more likely to reach out. "I feel I have this superpower," he told me, because of what he learned about other people when he stopped holding himself back. He approaches people more often now, "without any dread. It just made a huge difference."

When it comes to reaching out with kindness, what psychological barriers are standing in your way to being a little more social? Fred Rogers, patron saint of kindness and host of *Mister Rogers' Neighborhood* for thirty-three years, once encouraged us to wonder what a world without those barriers would be like. "Imagine what our neighborhoods would be like," he said, "if each of us offered, as a matter of course, just one kind word to another person?" My suggestion isn't to wonder, but to try a little more often to find out. I think you'll discover that when it comes to kindness, you also have a superpower to improve both your own and especially others' well-being, if you choose to use it.

9

Choosing Honesty

Honesty is such a lonely word.
Everyone is so untrue.
Honesty is hardly ever heard.
And mostly what I need from you.

—BILLY JOEL, "Honesty"

It's hard to think of a trait we feel more conflicted about in our relationships than honesty. We want, appreciate, and need honesty in order to be truly and deeply connected to others in our relationships. And yet it's often hard actually *being* honest in our relationships. Why is honesty something we so often want in our relationships, but so often choose not to give?

When articulating what we want in relationships, we're on Ben Franklin's side: "Honesty is the best policy."[1] There's good wisdom there. Everything I've covered in this book relies on honesty and authenticity at its core. Feigning interest in a conversation, whether it's shallow or deep, is miserable. Giving insincere compliments or hollow gratitude leaves you feeling like a fake. Trying to be supportive without honestly wanting to help another person is an imposition. Honesty helps us connect with others because it shows that you trust someone, which allows them to trust you in return. And when honesty is used to help someone, such as by providing honest feedback, then it's also seen as kind. This is why honesty is considered part of the very definition of interpersonal warmth that other people value in us so much and that connects us to others so quickly.[2] Dishonesty, in contrast, distances us from others because it creates distrust. This means that honesty isn't just something we want in our relationships. It's the critical ingredient that we need for them to thrive.

And yet, when actually making *the choice* to be honest, we can seem more aligned with Jack Nicholson's snarling character in *A Few Good Men:* "You want answers? . . . You can't handle the truth!" It's easy, after all, to be pessimistic about how well others will handle the truth when you offer it. So, we post pictures online that make our families look more perfect than they are, tell our colleagues we love their work more than we do, keep secrets that allow other people to hold a more positive image of us than they otherwise would, and put off difficult but necessary conversations in relationships more than we should. Our moments of misdirection come in many different shapes and sizes, from actively lying to more passively concealing facts, on matters ranging from massive to minor.

Honesty might be the best policy for connecting better with other people, but it's also a policy we're often reluctant to choose because we fear how others will react to it. In fact, there are two truths that we fear others can't handle.

One Virtue, Two Barriers

One truth we fear others can't handle is about *ourselves*. We deceive others either by actively lying or by passively concealing in order to protect our image in the eyes of others. This is why a politician misleads about an affair, or a spouse hides a secret that they fear their relationship couldn't bear. We might be worried that someone would think poorly of us if we were completely honest and authentic, so we evade topics that might make us look bad.

These fears create secrecy. When researchers showed more than a thousand people a list of thirty-eight common types of secrets (such as about a romantic desire, a family detail, a financial matter, a mental health issue, telling a lie), they reported currently holding a secret in thirteen of these categories, on average.[3] In another survey, 31 percent of people who possessed at least one marginalized identity (such as being a racial or ethnic minority) felt like they couldn't be fully open and authentic in a conversation they had in just the past week.[4] Honesty can seem like personal vulnerability. If we reveal our imperfect selves, other people might think less of us, so we hold back the truth. We'll call these self-protective lies, because they're driven by a desire to keep other people thinking well of us.

The second truth we fear others can't handle is about *themselves*. The truth, after all, isn't always nice to hear, so we're tempted to distort the facts in order to be kind to another person. This is why we tell our dinner host that we love the food when we really don't, or why we say we'll come to someone's party when we probably won't. We'll call these prosocial lies because they're motivated by the moral virtue of kindness. Just as self-protective lies can lead others to hold mistakenly positive impressions of us, prosocial lies can lead people to hold mistakenly positive impressions of themselves. Because they are driven by kindness, they tend not to be judged negatively by other people. In fact, people who are kinder and more compassionate are the ones who tell prosocial lies more often.[5] Deception comes both from the most narcissistic among us and from the nicest among us.

As with the virtues of appreciation and kindness, our choices about honesty are fundamentally social. This explains why dishonesty is something we grow into rather than something we're born with. Psychologists find that children under four to five years old rarely lie because they haven't yet developed the capacity to recognize that other people have minds of their own that can perceive the world differently than they do.[6] If Mom caught you when you were three years old eating a cookie before dinner, you just stated the facts: "But I was hungry!" As you got older and more socially sophisticated, you came to realize that you could influence what other people believed. Six-year-old you realized that if Mom didn't *think* you had eaten the cookie, then you could keep her from being angry. Your first attempts at dishonesty were probably clumsy, like claiming you hadn't eaten the cookie with crumbs on your chin. But by the time you were a teenager, you had grown into one of the most socially sophisticated beings on the planet. Now you're rearranging the plate while cleaning off your face and implying that your insatiable dog was to blame. However, as socially sophisticated as we might become, it's still very hard to accurately understand what's really going on in the mind of another person, which creates the opportunity to misunderstand how another person might actually react to the truth if you offered it. Mom might have handled the truth better than you had feared.

After all, when we make *the choice* to be honest or not, our perspective typically differs from that of the person we're being honest or dishonest with. If we underestimate how positively others will respond to our honesty, then we might end up being less honest than is ideal for our relationships, and for our own well-being.

Secrecy Is Lonely

"Secrets usually hurt their holder most," argues Michael Slepian, a psychologist at Columbia University and the world's leading expert on both the causes and the consequences of secrecy in everyday life.[7] By the time Slepian started studying secrecy as a graduate student in 2010, psychologists had already identified a long list of miseries that result from keeping secrets. Shame, guilt, and uncertainty top the list, leading to unhappiness, depression, and isolation. What is it about secrecy that actually hurts us so much?

As Slepian describes in his book, *The Secret Life of Secrets*,[8] it's not for the reasons that psychologists long believed. It's not, for instance, about possessing information about yourself that others don't know. After all, we all know a library's worth of irrelevant details about ourselves that we don't share with others; that doesn't bother us one bit. When I was in second grade, for instance, I had green-and-yellow Adidas shoes that I loved, had my first crush on a girl, and was a pretty mediocre point guard on our local YMCA basketball team (go, Trailblazers!). That's just the tiniest tip of my totally irrelevant iceberg. Jen, my wife of nearly thirty years as I write this, learned those facts just as you did, by reading them here. She also cared almost as little about them as you did just now. Most details of our lives never pop into our minds as something worth sharing, and hence don't cause us any angst, because we've never decided to keep these things secret. Even important aspects of our lives, such as the entirety of our dating histories, aren't discussed if we don't think they're relevant to a given relationship we're in.

It's also not the evasive act of keeping something secret that hurts. When Slepian asked people how many times they had to actively conceal their secret in normal conversation, those who had to conceal more often didn't feel any worse than those who had to conceal more rarely. Most of us have no trouble changing the subject, or avoiding topics in conversation. In fact, Slepian found that even secrets people said they *never* had to conceal in conversation could still hurt.

Instead, Slepian discovered that what really hurts is how often you *think about* a negative secret. The more it pops into your mind, the heavier the burden. Slepian discovered that people tend to think about their secrets about twice as often as they actually conceal their secrets in conversation.[9] "The hard part of having a secret," he wrote, "is not that we have to hide it in conversation, but that we have to live with it alone." Keeping secrets hurts *because it's isolating.*

Slepian's insight clarifies our otherwise fuzzy understanding of secrecy and also clarifies how you overcome the isolation that secrecy creates: You share your secret with someone you trust.[10] Sometimes, though, the barrier to revealing our secret is so big that we can't bring ourselves to share it with an actual person, so we instead reveal it in a journal or post it on an anonymous website. In the ancient Greek myth of King Midas and the Donkey Ears, the king with the golden touch insults the god Apollo, who then punishes him by transforming his ears into donkey ears. Ashamed, Midas hides his ears under a turban and tells only his barber, who he commands to keep it secret. Burdened by this secret, Midas's barber eventually runs to the top of a distant mountain, digs a hole, and whispers his secret into the ground. A king's wrath is no longer what keeps most of us from sharing our secrets openly and honestly with others, but it's still the same palpable fear that someone else will judge us harshly that keeps us isolated with our secrets, both big and small.

If our fears are on the mark, as they might have been for Midas's barber, then we're likely getting the balance between revealing and concealing just right. But if we're off the mark, thinking that others might judge us more negatively than they actually would, then our fears might be keeping us overly lonely.

Let It Go?

Testing whether we're isolating ourselves in secrecy wisely requires having people do something they clearly think is unwise: to open up and share a negative secret in a relationship.

On average, the 150 couples who signed up to be in our experiment had been together for roughly two years, ranging from one month to forty-one years.[11] They did not know beforehand that one person in the experiment was going to be asked to reveal a secret to the other. One member of each couple quickly learned that they were randomly assigned to the role of revealer, and would be getting a chance to do something they had never done before. If they agreed, they would have a conversation in which they revealed a negative secret that they had been keeping from their partner.

"We would like you to think of a negative secret," we told the revealer, "that you have not shared with your partner but would be willing to share with him or her." We further explained that "this could be a secret that has been weighing on you and that you would like to get off your chest, or it could just be an aspect of your life that you have not shared yet." To make sure it was a secret they felt they could share if they chose to, we further explained that "this should be something which you have meant to reveal to your partner but which, for whatever reason, you haven't had the opportunity to share with him or her yet."

This turned out not to be a very hard assignment. Nearly all of our revealers—94 percent, to be exact—could think of something they were concealing in their relationship:

"I want to spend more time together but want you to put in effort to spend time with me as well."

"My anxiety is getting worse."

"I still talk with my ex from time to time."

"I have fantasies about other women sometimes."

"I'm going to try to see if I can get a job in Antarctica this winter."

"I feel like I'm not a good daughter because I am pretty disrespectful to my parents."

"I have been meaning to reach out to a therapist for my mental health."

"I'm worried about how much I drink."

"I sometimes regret not having kids."

Our couples thought of a wide range of issues, from the pretty minor ("I eat chocolate at night after she goes to bed") to the extremely serious ("I regret not leaving the U.S. permanently [when] I had the chance"). Some said their secret didn't feel like much of a burden to carry ("I've thought about entering relationships with other people during our bad times"), whereas others said their secret felt very heavy ("I have cheated in my previous relationships"). Perhaps more important, it was quite clear why they were concealing these secrets: because they thought their partner would think less of them or be hurt, if they knew. More specifically, when we asked them to guess what their partner would think, they expected that their partner would have a less positive impression of them overall and would be in a less positive mood after hearing their secret than they were beforehand.

These pessimistic expectations, though, were consistently off the mark. Despite generally knowing each other very well, most people still expected that their partner would respond more negatively than they actually did (this was especially true for those with the most pessimistic expectations to begin with). If anything, revealing their secret was a somewhat positive experience for both people in the relationship. On average, the recipients' impressions did not change, and the recipient of the secret actually left the conversation feeling more *positive* than they did before the conversation. The recipients also didn't have more negative impressions, or feel in a less positive mood, than those in a control condition who simply had a conversation with their partners. Revealing something negative didn't make their partner think better of them in some way, but it also didn't have the negative impact that the revealers expected. Their partner, it turned out, handled their truth better than they had expected.

Just as important, letting go of their secret actually had a positive impact on the revealer, leaving them in a more positive mood and feeling less burdened. Two weeks later, we reached back out to these couples (none of whom had broken up by then), and found that their thoughts and feelings hadn't changed. Those who heard their partner's secret still had a more positive impression of their partner, and felt more positive about their relationship, than the revealers had expected right before revealing their secret two weeks earlier.

In another experiment, revealers were even more pessimistic about how a stranger would evaluate them, compared with a friend, after revealing a secret they had never shared with another person. Those revealing their secret generally expected to be judged as less honest, less trustworthy, and less positively overall by a stranger than a friend, but strangers and friends actually judged the revealers more similarly (and positively) after their conversation. This meant that people were the most overly pessimistic about a stranger's reaction to the truth. Being honest about ourselves to others doesn't seem to leave us as vulnerable to harsh judgment as we might imagine.

As important as I think these results are, it's just as important to keep them in perspective. These results do not indicate that we're completely wrong about how others will evaluate us. In all the experiments we've conducted, we consistently observed modest correlations between how people expect to be evaluated and how they were actually evaluated (correlations around 0.3, if you're statistically inclined). If you think some secret about yourself is particularly negative while other secrets aren't so bad, then you probably have some reasonable sense about this. Across this spectrum, though, our evaluations of precisely how bad revealing something negative about ourselves will be for us looks to be consistently off the mark, and those who were the most pessimistic are also furthest from the mark.

What are our expectations about honesty missing?

What Honesty Reveals

When Johannes Haushofer, then a psychology professor at Princeton University, decided in 2016 to post a résumé (or CV—curriculum vitae—in academese) revealing all of his failures as an academic, he never imagined his list of career lowlights would become a viral sensation. After all, "if there's one thing you'd never do," one article on *Science Alert* noted, "it's list your failures on your CV, right?"[12] Journalists referred to Haushofer's decision to post his CV of Failures online as an act of bravery, but he didn't actually suffer slings or arrows from anyone. The reaction was overwhelmingly positive. "Strangely inspiring," "a beautiful thing," "refreshing," "thank you thank you thank you" were just some of the many positive reactions his apparent act of bravery garnered.[13] All of the positive attention caught Haushofer off guard, leading to a final entry, a failure about failures: "This darn CV of Failures has received way more attention than my entire body of academic work."[14]

When we're open and honest about ourselves, we're actually revealing two things: content and character. Misunderstanding either, or more often both, can keep us more isolated in secrecy than we need to be.

First, honesty reveals the specific information we've been concealing. Typically, we tend to conceal negative information about ourselves. One common misunderstanding is assuming this information influences another person's impression of us more than it actually does. When we're making *the choice* about whether to reveal something, our attention tends to be laser focused on whatever we're revealing, making it easy to miss that someone's impression of us is based on a broader perspective, including what we're revealing plus whatever else they happen to know about us (which is usually more positive than the negative secret).[15] Who among us, though, can't create their own list of life's failures, thereby allowing us to empathize with someone else's failure? And yet, if we're all concealing negative information about ourselves to some extent, then it can be easy for us to underestimate how much others will be able to empathize with us if we open up.[16]

Second, and perhaps more important, by releasing his CV of Failures, Haushofer revealed part of his character, suggesting that he is open, honest, and therefore trustworthy. Those signs of warmth are what we appreciate most in another person.

These two aspects about what honesty reveals—both information and moral character—can help explain why we might be overly pessimistic about how others will handle the honest truth about us. When people revealed their secret, we found that they were heavily focused on its negative content. In contrast, we found that the recipients were primarily evaluating the person's character, and therefore evaluated the act of revealing more positively as a result.[17] If we think that only the content of what we're revealing is going to matter when the recipient actually cares about the positive character that our honesty is revealing, then this gap in perspectives will likely leave us being overly pessimistic about how well someone will handle our truth.

Honesty, Surprisingly Appreciated

Our tendency to be overly pessimistic about how others handle the truth about us isn't restricted to revealing secrets.

For instance, it also emerges in misunderstanding the benefits of apologizing. Researchers find that apologizing isn't as aversive as people expect it will be, because those who receive an apology generally react more positively to the moment of honesty than apologizers expect.[18] In one landmark study reported in 2010 at the University of Michigan hospital, researchers found that a medical error–disclosure program that encouraged doctors to go directly to their patients and apologize when they made mistakes led to surprisingly positive outcomes for all involved.[19] In contrast to the obvious fears of the hospital's lawyers and administrators, malpractice lawsuits did not go up. Instead, they went down, from thirty-nine per year to seventeen per year. The time to reach a resolution also dropped by roughly 30 percent (from 1.36 years to 0.95 years). The program reduced overall liability by 60 percent.

Apologizing works, according to the hospital's chief risk officer at the time, Richard Boothman, because it "gives permission to doctors and other caregivers to do what's important and what they want to do—take care of the patients and make sure the same error doesn't ever happen again. . . . When you break that paradigm of litigation and give patients the chance to understand the human element of the other side—of the doctor and what they are struggling with—you find that people are far more forgiving and understanding than has been typically assumed."[20] Most states in the United States (thirty-nine as of 2024) have now tried encouraging doctors to apologize by passing laws that forbid their admissions to be used as evidence in court. The outcome of these laws, compared with states without them, has been to reduce malpractice lawsuits, settlement times, and therefore legal costs.[21] Doctors get a chance to explain what happened, patients no longer have to sue to get the honest information they really want, and patients forgive faster after they're apologized to than after they're avoided.

Our misunderstanding of the value of honesty not only leads us to mismanage the delivery of bad news but also leads us to mismanage the delivery of good news about ourselves. Nervous about being seen as a braggart, you might be tempted to keep some of your successes to yourself. Researchers, however, find that this strategy of hiding success can actually lead others to feel more distant from us than if we shared our good news openly and honestly with them.[22]

If you do decide to share some good news about yourself, your misplaced fears might even tempt you into an ineffective strategy known as humblebragging: concealing a boast within a note of false humility ("I'm tired of people mistaking me for a model!") or false complaint ("I work so fast that I am bored the rest of the day"). This strategy is driven by a belief that the concealed boast will evoke sympathy or yield a more positive impression, but it tends to backfire. When researchers investigated how people respond to others' good news, they found that humblebragging is less positive than straight-up bragging about yourself because humblebragging appears dishonest. If you're going to toot your own horn, you're better off tooting it authentically than putting an insincere mute on it.[23]

Finally, misunderstanding the value of honesty can lead us into another suboptimal social strategy known as paltering: concealing a truth you'd rather not share by revealing one you're okay sharing. In other words, telling part of the truth, rather than the whole truth. "There is not a sexual relationship—that is accurate," said Bill Clinton when the *PBS NewsHour* host Jim Lehrer asked about his relationship with Monica Lewinsky. Here, Clinton was paltering—trying to conceal one truth (that he had a sexual relationship with Lewinsky in the past) by revealing another (he wasn't having a sexual relationship at that precise moment).

The danger of paltering, much like the danger with white lies, is that it makes us feel okay about being dishonest. When Todd Rogers and his colleagues at the Harvard Kennedy School of Government gave people opportunities to palter in a negotiation, those who did evaluated the action more favorably because they were focused on the exact content of what they did (which was technically not lying), while those who learned they were paltered to evaluated it just as negatively as a lie. Paltering was seen as dishonestly concealing the truth, and therefore damaged the concealer's reputation.[24]

What we really seem to miss is that others will appreciate our honesty and authenticity above and beyond the content of whatever secret we fear would be damaging to reveal.[25] It's hard to learn these lessons, though, if our anxiety keeps us from actually being open and honest. Writing months before the U.S. presidential election in 2024, the journalist Thomas Friedman sounded a note of warning about the guarded answers that Kamala Harris was giving in interviews when asked very pointed questions: "Politicians always underestimate how much voters (and the news media) respect a leader who can say, 'We didn't get this quite right the first time, and I'm going to fix it.'" The veteran Democratic strategist James Carville concurred on the value of unvarnished truth: "A leader who can openly admit a change in her understanding would feel like a breath of spring air for a lot of voters." We'll never be able to test Friedman's and Carville's claims about the impact of openness and authenticity on actual presidential elections, but those claims are well aligned with the impact researchers observe from openness and honesty in our personal relationships.

Trusting other people with the truth about ourselves will always be a delicate balancing act. Sometimes knowing that your expectations about being honest are overly pessimistic isn't going to be enough to have you open up. These gaps matter when you're on the fence in an approach/avoidance conflict, such as when you'd like to get a secret off your chest but are worried about how your friend might respond to it. In these cases where you're conflicted, failing to appreciate how much others will value your honesty and authenticity can leave you isolated in secrecy.

Handling Their Own Truth

We conceal the truth about ourselves out of fear that others won't be kind to us, but we tell prosocial lies about others because we fear being unkind to them. After all, sometimes the truth can be hard to hear: Your boss isn't as impressed with your work as you hoped, a friend doesn't value your relationship as much as you thought, or the person you had a great first date with doesn't want to see you for a second. Although giving someone good news is joyfully easy, giving someone bad news can be painfully hard. As Emma Levine, my colleague at the University of Chicago, points out, delivering a negative truth is hard because it creates tension between the competing virtues of honesty and kindness.[26] Wanting to be both honest *and* kind puts us in a mental bind.

The typical way we manage tension is by trying to reduce it. When it comes to the tension between honesty and kindness, we have many options. The easiest is to avoid delivering the bad news altogether: cancel that tough performance review you're supposed to deliver, ghost the person you'd rather not see again, or don't mention that the meal your spouse cooked was mediocre. If you don't have anything nice to say, the common wisdom goes, then don't say anything at all.

Another approach is to pick one virtue or the other. You might lean into kindness by telling partial truths or sugarcoating bad news, being dishonestly kind. Or you could lean into honesty by telling the truth no matter how unkind it seems, being brutally honest. You could also try balancing your virtues, sandwiching your painful truth in between a few nice words, using the age-old feedback technique of the shit sandwich. Of course, the most optimal way to deal with this tension is to align truth with kindness, communicating in ways that are both honest and helpful. Although this isn't always possible, the optimal solution might be easier to hit than you imagine.

Take, for example, company layoffs. I think most people would agree that telling someone that they're laid off is a very hard truth. This is certainly the experience a senior executive shared in a class I was teaching. He'd been referred to as the hatchet man because his specialty was in trying to lift companies out of bankruptcy, usually requiring layoffs. Early in his career, he told the class, there was a strong temptation to soft-pedal the facts to spare people's feelings and avoid anger. That approach usually failed. People could often tell when he was hiding something, which bred distrust while leaving people unprepared to lose their jobs or have their salaries cut. Although holding back on the truth seemed like a way of being kind to those on the receiving end, concealing honest news was actually cruel. While in my class, the executive had just gone through the most extreme bankruptcy he had ever experienced, with a company needing to lay off roughly 90 percent of its staff all at once. This time, though, it tried being both honest and kind by being as open and transparent as it possibly could. He told me this ended up being both the hardest and the best of experiences he had ever gone through. Employees trusted the company to help them find new jobs (which it did), and roughly 50 percent came back to work for the company once it was back on its feet.

In his book, *Reputation Rules,* the organizational psychologist Daniel Diermeier confirms this executive's experience. When managing crises, Diermeier writes, "trust is the magic word." Diermeier finds that maintaining trust through open and honest communication is what distinguishes good corporate responses from bad ones, "and it is the first issue which companies should focus on." Diermeier had to write his book highlighting the critical importance of delivering hard truths, of course, because the trustworthiness revealed through honesty is typically *not* what we focus on when we have hard but potentially helpful truths to share.

Instead, we focus too much on the content of the hard truth we're revealing. But hard truths about ourselves or our relationships are often the most helpful things to hear in the long run. The tension between honesty and kindness is typically strongest in the very moment that we're delivering bad news, but diminishes or disappears in the long run. Focusing too much on the negative content of what we're revealing can also lead us to overlook the character that our honesty reveals. It's a good friend, after all, who's honest even when the truth is hard to hear.

I can painfully remember in college watching a keynote speaker at an undergraduate psychology conference give an hour-long presentation with his fly unzipped. This was glaringly obvious because he was wearing jet-black pants and blindingly white underwear. I imagine someone could easily have said something before he walked out onstage, but nobody wants to embarrass someone by calling out their blunder, even at the very moment it's needed. Objectively speaking, not telling the speaker the truth was unkind because it meant that he gave an overly revealing keynote address.

One experiment shows precisely how common this experience might be. In this setup, it wasn't a wardrobe malfunction that needed feedback but rather something even more obvious: a blemish on someone's face.[27] Over the course of a few days, researchers at the University of California at Berkeley sent three female undergraduate assistants around campus asking their fellow students if they would complete a short survey. But the survey was only one part of the experiment. Each assistant also had an obvious problem on her face: smeared hot-pink lipstick in one case, a chocolate brownie smudge on her mouth in the second case, and a red marker streak on the bridge of her nose in the third case. In each case, the problem on the assistant's face was both obvious—literally staring them right in the face—and easily remedied.

Think about this for a moment. If you were walking around with something smudged on your face, wouldn't you want someone to tell you so you could clean it up? Wouldn't honesty be kind, and saying nothing be cruel? Of course it would, and yet, out of the 155 people who both agreed to fill out the survey and reported noticing the blemish on the assistant's face (when asked about it on the survey that they agreed to complete), only 4 (an anemic 2.6 percent) told the assistant the truth, while the remaining 151 people (97.4 percent) said absolutely nothing. When asked why they chose not to say anything, the vast majority (77 percent) mentioned not wanting to be rude or to embarrass the assistant. The researchers wrote that the number of people who told the awkward truth was even lower than they expected it would be.

Although this experiment didn't measure the obvious fact that the smudge-faced research assistant would have been happier knowing the truth, additional experiments from this research group asked about it directly. Across a variety of contexts where constructive feedback could be given, from small things, such as mispronouncing someone's name, to more consequential things, such as interrupting colleagues too much, those who imagined giving any type of constructive feedback thought the recipient would not be especially interested in receiving it. In fact, those who imagined receiving this constructive feedback indicated being more interested in receiving it than the givers expected.[28]

In the most compelling experiment, pairs of friends, roommates, and romantic partners were assigned either to give constructive feedback about something their partner could change for the better or to receive the feedback.[29] Those giving feedback thought of issues ranging from fairly small (not putting away your laundry or getting to bed earlier) to larger (driving recklessly, working less, being on your phone too much), and generally thought they were bringing up issues that their partner didn't really want to hear about. When asked if they would rather give the feedback or avoid it, only about half (48 percent) said they wanted to give the feedback. The recipients, however, reported being more interested in hearing their partner's feedback than the givers expected; 86 percent of the receivers said they wanted to hear the feedback. After their conversation, the givers and receivers did not differ in how negative they rated the feedback itself. What they differed in was how helpful the feedback was, with receivers reporting that the constructive feedback was more helpful than the givers thought it would be.[30]

The gap in our beliefs about how honesty will be received doesn't seem to come from how the content might make someone feel. Instead, the gap comes from how kind and helpful the feedback seemed to the person hearing it. Only by learning the truth about ourselves can we learn how to make both ourselves and our relationships better. When bad news is delivered with the twin virtues of honesty and kindness, it's likely to be *surprisingly* well received.[31]

Habitually Honest

What if you took the lessons from this chapter to heart and tried putting them into practice in your everyday conversations? When someone asks how you feel, you wouldn't just say "fine" but would actually share how you're feeling. When someone asks for your opinion, you wouldn't mislead out of kindness but would express it honestly in order to be helpful (and in the long run, kind). When you didn't know something, you would say so. When you made a mistake, you would admit it. When something was troubling you, you would share it. How would your days go? Do you think you would feel closer to the people you were being honest with, or drive them further away?

Until this point, we have covered how surprisingly positively others handle bits and pieces of honesty, but what if you strung them together as a more regular part of your character? What if you made honesty a habit?

If you recoiled a bit at the thought of being completely honest all the time, then you're not alone. In fact, Emma Levine and her collaborator Taya Cohen asked a little over two hundred people to imagine how spending three days being completely honest in every conversation would turn out. The general consensus was, "not well."[32] In contrast to imagining spending three days being completely kind in all of your interactions, or paying closer attention by being more mindful in your interactions (the control condition), people expected that being completely honest would lead them to enjoy their days less and make them feel less connected to others. Honesty, compared with kindness and mindfulness, was expected to feel bad and hurt others.

There were also fears that the harm from being honest would linger. Those who imagined being completely honest also thought their relationships would be less positive two weeks after the experiment was over. Given this pessimism about honesty, it's also no surprise that when asked to select which approach they would choose if they had the option, only 21 percent chose honesty while 37 percent chose kindness and 42 percent chose being more mindful in their conversations. If you thought being completely honest would be a relatively negative experience, then you'd probably avoid it, too.

These pessimistic expectations about honesty, though, did not match the experiences of a separate group of people who went out and actually practiced it for three days. Although people imagined that being completely honest would leave them feeling less connected to others than being kind or mindful, those who practiced honesty ended up feeling just as connected as those who were completely kind and more connected than those who were just conscious of their conversations. People also imagined that the relatively unpleasant impact of honesty would sting for several weeks, leaving them feeling worse about the experience and harming their relationships, but those who were actually honest generally felt the same positive impact as being kind. In fact, those who were completely honest for three days felt just as positive about the experience overall. Two weeks after the experience, those who were completely honest reported that they enjoyed it more, were happier with their experience, felt their honesty had a more positive impact on their relationships, and appreciated their experience more than those in the control condition who paid closer attention to their interactions. These patterns meant that being completely honest, when put into actual practice, had similar effects on their well-being and relationships as being completely kind. This fact—that honesty is often experienced as kindness—is one thing our expectations about honesty tend to miss.[33]

Honesty wasn't without its challenges, which you can hear echoed in the words people used to describe their experiences. In fact, 11 percent of people in the honesty condition wrote about conflict, while nobody did so in the kindness or control conditions. The conflict, though, wasn't necessarily negative. "[Being honest] wasn't easy every time," one person wrote, looking back on it, "but it always made me feel a lot better afterward because I was able to say what I felt needed to be said, regardless of how it would be taken." Another person remembered lashing out at a co-worker, creating some tension that lingered. "Nonetheless, I felt it was worth it," this person wrote. "What's the point of pretending when someone asks how you are feeling? . . . Being honest allows for better relationships and more trust."

What jumps out the most in the words people used to describe the experience of honesty was the positive contrast with their typical routine. One person said, "During the study, I did not really find being completely honest to be difficult. I actually found it to be rather refreshing." Another mentioned, "Communicating honestly was refreshing for me since it allowed me to express my feelings with no consideration of having to 'hide' my feelings." Indeed, significantly more people mentioned that their interactions were unexpectedly positive in the honesty condition (19 percent) than in the control condition, where nobody mentioned it. Some talked about the surprisingly positive effect that honesty had on how others viewed them: "I was particularly surprised when being honest got me further in my position in an organization because voicing my honest opinion made others think about the situation more and come to the conclusion that I was thinking as well." Others mentioned that honesty was received positively rather than negatively: "People reacted differently than what I thought. They liked and appreciated the honesty and honestly I did not believe that would happen. It was refreshing. . . . I was happy to talk about what was on my mind and not worry about what was said."

Analyzing these written responses confirmed what their surveys had said was the source of this surprise: how positively others handled the truth. Wisdom lies in identifying this gap between how we expect honesty will be received and how it's actually received.

Remember Michael Slepian, the psychologist who literally wrote the book on the psychology of secrecy? Past midnight on the day of his interview at Columbia University (where he has now taught since 2016), Michael found himself on the receiving end of a secret when his father called: "I need to share something with you; can you sit down?" That night, he learned that his father had been biologically unable to have children and that both of his sons had been conceived through artificial insemination. Michael and his brother were not biologically related to their father.

Michael told me that he and his brother didn't ask very many questions after his father first called to reveal the secret, and it was only writing his book about secrecy that really nudged him to ask more. When he did, he learned that his parents, in coordination with his grandparents and other relatives, had decided they would keep this secret because they didn't want Michael and his brother to ever think they weren't fully part of the family. Michael's father thought it was an unimportant medical detail. His mother thought they probably wouldn't understand as young children. So, the truth was set aside without much bother or burden until Michael and his brother got older and started to ask normal questions about what traits they might have inherited from their parents. Michael's mother started feeling that they needed to reveal what they had been concealing, and got into an argument about it with Michael's grandfather, who was more reluctant to reveal the secret. In a phone call afterward, Michael's brother asked his mother what had caused the argument. "Something we decided that we would never tell you two boys," his mother said.

That conversation between Michael's mother and his brother is what sparked his father's phone call on the day of his interview. Interestingly, Michael learned from talking to his mother that it was his research on the burdens of secrecy that caused her to start questioning their decision. The dishonesty started out of concern that Michael and his brother would react negatively, possibly feeling that they weren't fully part of the family. And yet, when Michael learned the news, he didn't respond negatively. "My immediate reaction was, 'Who cares about genetics?'" he told me. "This doesn't change anything for me." The only thing that bothered him was that they weren't honest with him sooner. Even that, though, faded as he learned that his parents had concealed this truth with good intentions, and that his grandparents, in particular, loved him and his brother so much that they'd been especially concerned that the truth would be hard for them to handle.

I asked if learning the truth about what their parents had been concealing had pulled their family closer together or pushed them apart. "It definitely pulled us together," he responded instantly, noting that what pulled them together wasn't the factual content but rather talking about why it was so important to his parents and grandparents that Michael and his brother would always feel unquestionably loved. Michael's only regret was that his parents hadn't felt comfortable telling him the truth earlier, because he was never able to talk to his grandmother before she died about her misplaced concern.[34] The truth, he told me, wouldn't have made an ounce of difference in how much he loved her, or in how loved he felt.

PART IV

What Now?

Recognizing that some of your expectations about other people could be overly pessimistic isn't going to be enough to put those insights into practice. Only experience calibrates your beliefs, showing where you might make *the choice* to connect with others differently and make connecting a habit that becomes part of your character rather than an opportunity you mistakenly avoid.

10

Being Wisely Social

> Men are not disturbed by things but the views which they take of them.
>
> —EPICTETUS

In a collection of posthumously published essays aptly titled *The Pessimist's Handbook,* the nineteenth-century philosopher Arthur Schopenhauer likened human social life to a group of porcupines huddling together in the winter.[1] Wanting to stay warm, they move close together, "but, as they began to prick one another with their quills, they were obliged to disperse." Getting cold again, they scuttle back together until their prickly quills force them apart again. After many rounds of "huddling and dispersing," they learn that they would be best off remaining a little distant from one another. Schopenhauer likens this to human society, where people want to be connected but are also "repelled by the many prickly and disagreeable qualities" that people possess, and therefore find it optimal to stay a moderate distance from each other. "By this arrangement," he concludes, "the mutual need of warmth is only very moderately satisfied; but then people do not get pricked."

This optimal distance analogy sounds compelling in theory but falls a bit flat in practice for both porcupines and people. In real life, porcupines take great care not to prick each other while huddling together very closely, both in dens and when mating. For people, the analogy implies that our social lives are precisely as good as they can be, with each of us finding our optimal balance of social connection through trial and error. But if that's true in practice, then why does reaching out and connecting with others, from strangers to acquaintances to friends and family, consistently leave us feeling better than we would have felt otherwise? Why does being asked to act more extroverted consistently leave people feeling more positive? Why do commuters enjoy their ride more when they talk to a stranger than they normally do? Why does expressing our gratitude, or performing a random act of kindness, or being open and honest leave people feeling good? There is indeed an optimal distance to keep between ourselves and others; it's likely to be closer than you might guess.

Porcupines may learn to manage their prickly parts more wisely because they live in a kind learning environment, wearing their quills on the outside and getting perfect feedback when they approach each other incorrectly. Finding our optimal distance from other people is distinctly more challenging because we live our social lives in a confusing learning environment with incomplete feedback. We don't wear our prickly parts on our skin and therefore have to guess how someone else might respond if we reach out to connect. If our guesses are overly pessimistic, then we avoid the very interactions we'd actually need to figure out what our optimal distance from others might be. Being overly optimistic gets corrected, but being overly pessimistic is self-fulfilling. Fearing the worst in others means never giving yourself the chance to learn what others are like at their best.

It's hard to overstate how empowering this insight can be. Connecting better can come from making *the choice* to be a little more social and thereby learning how to connect with others more wisely.

Testing Barriers

Avoiding interactions that might prick us is wise, but *mistakenly* avoiding interactions because we underestimate how much they would instead uplift and connect us is unwise. If we better understood how others would actually respond, then we could also choose to reach out more wisely.

Understanding exactly what you might do in your own life to be more wisely social, I'm afraid, isn't going to come from just reading the experiments I've covered in this book. I've now shared our research with countless people showing how our expectations about social interaction might be overly pessimistic. The most common reaction is resistance, and for good reason.

The fact is, "facts" derived from research are easy to question and sometimes difficult to apply to our own lives. We usually base conclusions from research on averages, but no single person is exactly average. It's hard to know where you might fall around the average. When I first spoke with Jessica Pan, the self-reportedly shy introvert from chapter 2 who spent a year making *the choice* to be more extroverted, she was very reluctant to try reaching out more often because she couldn't imagine it being anything other than a miserable experience. She thought she was the exception to the average rule. However, she was intrigued enough to test her beliefs. If you want to connect better, you'll also need to test the beliefs that might be keeping you from connecting positively with others a little more often.

Nobody understands this better than Stefan Hofmann, one of the world's experts at treating extreme cases of social anxiety using cognitive behavioral therapy. As Hofmann describes in his highly practical book, *CBT for Social Anxiety*, those who suffer from social anxiety disorder (SAD) have anxiety that is "excessive, persistent, and distressing or interferes with [their] life." Researchers have estimated that roughly 10 percent of Americans fit this criteria, with slightly higher rates among women than men.[2] Nobody's intense anxiety is alleviated by telling them that their fears are probably exaggerated, according to research. *Please*. The only thing that reliably alleviates debilitating social anxiety—Hofmann claims 70–75 percent success rates in reducing anxiety to manageable levels—is exposure therapy: repeatedly experiencing the very situation they're anxious about.

These "cost exposures," as psychologists describe them, get their power not from numbing people to the pain they experience but rather from allowing them to experience the gap between their pessimistic expectations and reality. "Only exposure to the situation will tell you whether the situation is indeed as bad as you expect it to be," Hofmann explains.[3] Those who avoid social interaction because of misplaced anxiety don't think their way into feeling better; they *feel their way to thinking better*.

Just as Jia Jiang learned when he went out and asked for purposefully outrageous favors, or Jessica Pan learned during her year of extroversion, or Claire Feuer learned from talking on the New York City subways, or Celine McGee learned when she went out love bombing strangers with compliments, experiencing the social interactions you might otherwise avoid allows you to feel what reality is like rather than what you imagine it to be. "This is exactly what drives treatment progress," Hofmann told me. "It's realizing that there's this discrepancy between how you expect other people will behave versus how other people actually behave."[4]

Research on social anxiety disorder makes it crystal clear that not all of our expectations about social interactions are misplaced. But when pessimistic expectations lead to avoidance and therefore the absence of experience to learn from, then you're back in the confusing learning environment where overly pessimistic beliefs can thrive. "Fear is like a parasite," Hofmann writes, "it can't live on its own; it can only survive if it is being fed and protected by avoidance."[5]

My goal in writing this book isn't to convince you that every research finding will apply perfectly to you. Instead, my goal is to invite you to consider what overly pessimistic beliefs might be keeping you from reaching out and connecting with people a little more often, and to gently start testing those barriers for yourself.

Testing Wisely

When I was a kid, my grandparents lived on a farm across the road from my great-aunt and great-uncle. Every now and then, Uncle Rufus's cows would break through their fence and end up on my grandparents' side of the road. The cows tested their barrier wisely. They didn't try to push over every fence post, because most of them were solid. Instead, they'd find the posts in the wet areas of the field that were likely to be wobbly and start leaning into them to test their strength. When they found a weak post, they'd lean in harder until it finally gave way. I don't think Rufus's cows understood the financial concept of return on investment, but they certainly acted like they did, testing the fence only where their effort would get the most in return.

If you're trying to be more wisely social, then I suggest following the cows' wisdom. Start by testing selectively, enriching your life by looking specifically for the opportunities that are likely to be *surprisingly* positive. Those are likely to be most rewarding because they're the opportunities you're currently missing. Your selective search can be helped by recognizing when you're making *the choice* to avoid reaching out and connecting in some way, picking easy opportunities to make *the choice* differently. This can identify places in your life where you might reach out more routinely in a way that turns connecting into a habit that then becomes part of your character. Reduced to its essence, my advice for living a more wisely social life is this: Recognize easy opportunities routinely.

Each of these four words describes a concept that is uniquely important. Understanding each could help you change the way you live your life in the way I've changed the way I live mine. Let me explain.

Recognize

Making *the choice* to approach or avoid other people is so quick and easy that you often miss that you're even making a decision. The first step to making *the choice* differently, then, is to recognize when you're actually making it.

Finding opportunities where you could choose to make your days a little more social isn't hard once you start looking. In one experiment, we asked a group of seventy-five people visiting our laboratory in downtown Chicago to think back on each hour of their previous day and indicate if they could have chosen to reach out to someone in a positive way but didn't.[6] On average, this group reported that they could have been more social in roughly half of the hours they were awake that day. The opportunities they spotted were mostly small things that would be easy and almost costless to do, like smiling at a stranger or chatting with someone at a bus stop, but some were more significant, such as "being more loving to my husband."

Recognizing every opportunity to connect doesn't mean that taking every opportunity would be a good idea, any more than recognizing times when you could physically exercise means you should be taking every available moment to do so. After all, you have other things to do! Indeed, when we asked the people in our study how they thought their day would have been if they had taken all of the opportunities to be more sociable, they thought they would be overdoing it, making their day worse overall. However, when we asked people to consider each opportunity in isolation, they estimated that each hour, on average, would have been more positive if they had chosen to reach out and connect instead. A good day comes not from taking every single social opportunity that exists but rather from choosing the best opportunities, being a little more social than you might have chosen otherwise.

Sometimes these opportunities will be little things. For instance, I recognized one day at work that I was walking about a hundred yards from the entrance to my office building, up the elevator, and past a dozen or so office doors without greeting anyone. Those were little moments of connection I was missing at the start of my day, so I started greeting people as I walked by (Hi, Jane; Hi, Erik; Good morning, Virginia!). I found it to be uplifting, and the friendliness I received in return suggests my colleagues did, too. I now get to my office feeling a little better than I would have otherwise, leaving a little friendliness in my wake that also left my coworkers feeling a little better, with barely an ounce of additional effort or a moment's delay.

At other times, recognizing *the choice* might prompt you to test a more substantial change. For instance, one of my former MBA students, Conor Sweeney, went through the gratitude letter exercise that I described in chapter 7 during my course. Inspired by this experience, Conor recognized that he often feels moved by books he reads or podcasts he listens to but wasn't doing anything about it. So, he decided to make that choice differently. Now when he feels moved by an author or speaker, he looks for their email ("usually it's pretty easy to track down," he tells me) and writes a letter expressing his appreciation. "The purpose isn't to get a reply," he tells me. This is a wise approach because prosociality feels more positive for both you and your recipient when it's done with a genuine interest in simply expressing your gratitude, without any sense of obligation or expectation of a response. Nevertheless, "they almost always write back," Conor tells me, a testament to the surprisingly positive impact that reaching out with appreciation can have. Conor feels great to have expressed his gratitude, and those he reaches out to feel better to have received it.

And sometimes, recognizing that you could be making *the choice* differently comes at the precise moment when you really need it. After hearing me speak about opportunities for deeper conversation as part of a podcast, for instance, one listener wrote to tell me that he had just been in the hospital during a very stressful experience and realized he was surrounded by people he could connect with if he tried. "I just started talking up anyone who was there. . . . Where are you from? How did you end up here?" He recognized that the conversations he typically had could be deeper if he made *the choice* to try. "We didn't talk about the weather, we talked about their lives, their hopes," he said. During one of the most difficult moments of his life, "these conversations were most uplifting."

Recognizing when you're making *the choice* is the first step to making it differently.

Easy

There's a mantra that every behavioral scientist can recite by heart: If you want people to do something, make it easy.[7] In so many different contexts, we're simply more likely to do easy things than hard things. The implication is that if you'd like to do something differently, make it easier to do. Want to eat better? Make sure you have veggies within easy reach when you open your fridge (and banish potato chips from your house altogether). Want to exercise more? Make it part of your daily routine, like biking to work rather than driving or taking the stairs up to your office instead of the elevator. Want to make it to meetings on time? Set a reminder on your calendar so you don't have to rely on your spotty memory.

Recognizing the importance of making things easy provides two important insights to help us be more wisely social. The first insight is to choose the easy opportunities you have to connect. Even small things like smiling and saying hello, passing along a compliment, or striking up a conversation are easy ways to brighten someone's day in a surprisingly powerful way. Although there's often a direct relationship between how much you put into something and how much you get out, reaching out to other people doesn't quite work that way. Even small acts of civility, kindness, and appreciation tend to leave people feeling nearly as positive as larger acts, meaning that the little things we do to connect tend to have the most surprisingly positive impact. The little note of appreciation you drop off in your colleague's mailbox that took you a minute to write might be something they keep in their office drawer for years. The small compliment you pass along might leave your recipient feeling better all day long. The bowl of soup you take to your sick friend might have required nothing more than taking the time to share dinner you were already making, but it's likely to feel much bigger to your friend. If you're trying to connect positively, then it's especially worth sweating the small social stuff that's easy to do.

You can also look for moments when it's easy to reach out. Life is a balancing act full of competing demands, so don't consider adding more to your plate by connecting in the busy times. Instead, look for the dead spaces in your life when you're choosing to do essentially nothing, but could easily be reaching out to someone to make that moment a little brighter. You might be waiting in line at the grocery store or sitting on a plane or commuting in the car. Those dead times are easy moments to make surprisingly better by being a little more social.

For instance, I don't drive a lot, but I've taken to using the times I do to call up my kids who are away at college, or my parents at home in Iowa, or friends far away whom I haven't spoken to in a while. I don't have to go out of my way to turn driving time into talking time, and my drives are better for it. Another example comes from Duncan Raban, a professional photographer in the U.K. known for taking candid photographs of celebrities including Mick Jagger, Elton John, and Grace Jones. He is becoming known these days for his "Just Say Hello" social media campaign in the U.K. The goal is simple: create moments of connection by encouraging Brits to just say hello more often to strangers as they pass throughout their day. "I'm passionately interested in people," Raban says. "People will say, 'Oh, I can't meet people,' but they're everywhere. You've just got to say hello with a compliment." Duncan isn't going out of his way or exerting any particular effort to greet people. Like me, Duncan also doesn't drive a lot, so he sprinkles hellos as he's walking around town to brighten moments that would otherwise be silent spaces. His walks, and those he walks by, are better for it.

Even one of my editors helping me with this book, Kassie Brabaw, has started spotting easy opportunities to connect that she might have overlooked before. "I think I told you when I first reached out," Kassie told me early in this book project, "that I used what I learned from covering your work to strike up a conversation at jury duty and that person became a friend! I also talk to more people than I ever would have when I take my dog to the park every morning." You might find there's lots of low-hanging happiness that could come from being a little more social once you start looking around for it.

The second insight from the "make it easy" mantra is to reduce any barriers that are keeping you from connecting with others. For instance, holding your cell phone in your hand or keeping it close in your pocket is likely to suck in your attention, the way black holes suck in stars. Removing that barrier makes it easier to notice people around you. So, consider carrying your phone in your backpack or purse, where it's likely to be less distracting. Many experiments confirm that your time in the presence of other people, from mealtimes to meetings to walking around town, will be better for it.[8] Or, you might want to express your gratitude when you feel it more often. I remove that barrier in my own life by keeping a stack of thank-you cards on top of the file cabinet next to my office chair so that I can easily express my appreciation when the mood strikes.

Or you might want to strike up a conversation with someone you've met in the neighborhood, but you can't remember their name. One way to reduce that barrier is by writing people's names down right after you meet them. The act of writing it down actually helps it to stick in your memory and also gives you a reminder you can return to later. I do this in the Notes app on my phone, where I keep separate lists of names of people I might see routinely ("On the Train," "At the Office," "Neighbors"). Along with their name, I jot down something to help me remember them after we talk: "Brenda: works in hospital, daughter on swim team"; "Vale: works for USPS"; "Laurie: volunteer at aquarium, evolutionary biologist." Once I've used their names a few times, they're no longer strangers and I don't need the note anymore. To help others in their conversations with me, I frequently start an interaction by reintroducing myself to help eliminate any potential awkwardness (a gift I sometimes appreciate when others do the same for me). A friend of mine, Todd Jones, has even taken this one step further by putting his name on his license plate: "IM TODD." "You'd be amazed," he told me, "how many people holler out to me, 'Hi, Todd!' when I'm out in the car, and how many fun little conversations that starts."

Although it might intuitively seem that the magnitude of the positive experiences you have will affect your happiness more ("We'll always have Paris," you might think), it's actually the frequency of positive experiences you have that better predicts your happiness.[9] Happiness is a mood, and moods fluctuate from one moment to the next. The wonderful feelings you have on a trip to the Caribbean aren't going to last very long when you're cleaning up the mess your kids left while you were away or are fighting traffic on your commute back to work.

Happiness isn't like height, which stays stable across time once you're fully grown. Happiness is instead like a leaky tire that you have to keep pumping up with frequent positive experiences. Easy things get done and hard things don't. If you want to live a consistently more connected life, take the easy opportunities you have to connect repeatedly.

Opportunities

Cars are for driving, lunch is for eating, and plane trips are for flying. Each context has its purpose. It's easy to think in singular terms about what opportunities a given context allows and therefore miss a key insight from psychology: that many contexts offer a wide range of different opportunities. For instance, a narrow focus that cars are for driving might keep you from thinking that a car trip can also allow you to call a friend. Lunch is for eating, but lunch is also an opportunity for connecting with others. This is why psychologists find that sharing a meal with someone makes it more likely that you'll cooperate with them in the future, and why dietary restrictions can be isolating and lonely.[10] And yes, plane trips are for flying, but they have also allowed me to have great conversations with people I never would have talked to otherwise.

On a recent trip to New York City, for instance, I walked onto a plane and a woman sitting in the aisle seat pointed to me and said, "You're Nick Epley, right?" It's very rare for me to be recognized like this, but she had been a student of mine years ago and recognized my curly hair. For the roughly ninety-minute flight, we talked about the trip she was making to see her socially conservative parents to talk about her daughter who had just come out as transgender. She was worried about how they might react, so we talked together about how she could approach a deep conversation to help it turn out better than she might have feared. It was not just a flight but a context that afforded a conversation I probably never would have had anywhere else, and a meaningful reconnection I never would have made otherwise. A week later I received an email thanking me for our conversation and encouragement. She told me, "[I had] more true conversations during my visit than I have had with [my parents] in as long as I can remember." Planes are for traveling, yes. They can be opportunities for deep conversations, too.

Taking an interest in connecting with other people can sometimes lead you to spot opportunities in contexts where you don't expect them, such as creating a compliment calendar for the holiday season instead of using chocolate. Taking an interest in connecting also led me to think very differently about a pear tree in our backyard one year. This is a tree I planted when it was tiny that is now so big that it overwhelms us with fruit every fall. The pears are terrific to eat, but they're also a terrific pain in the neck to pick. The tree is about twenty-five feet tall, requiring precariously balanced ladders and long fruit pickers to reach the top. We get about four wheelbarrows of fruit each year, roughly three more than even my hungry family of seven can possibly eat. One fall day while looking at the overloaded tree, I had an epiphany. We could make the pain of picking this tree a pleasure if we turned it into a party and got the whole neighborhood involved. From that insight was born our very first Pear Picking Party. It was terrific. I lifted kids (and a few adventurous adults) up into the tree in a tractor bucket. We raised ladders all around the tree so that the neighborhood kids could climb up into it. We got the wheelbarrow of pears we wanted, and everyone who visited walked away with their own bags of pears. Recognizing that this tree provided an opportunity for not only pear picking but also a party turned what was otherwise a burden into a social blast.

Rob Finlayson, who lives in Florida, wrote to tell me about a similarly unique social opportunity he spotted one day while walking along the beach. He realized that the small seashells along the beach could be made into lovely little gifts that might make someone smile, and possibly start a conversation. So, Rob started gluing small magnets to these beautiful little shells and now carries them everywhere. When he meets someone new, he pulls a handful from his pocket and allows the person to select one. "Many times during the week I am told by total strangers, 'you just made my day!'" Rob wrote to me. "Who gets that privilege?" he asked me. The answer is someone, like Rob, who understands that an object or activity can often be used for multiple purposes, including to create opportunities to connect that you might otherwise miss if you're not looking for them.

What are the seashells that could be turned into social connections in your own life? What is your Pear Picking Party? Almost every day I see people stuck in rather unpleasant situations that they could make better if they made *the choice* to be a little more social. Consider, for instance, the Department of Motor Vehicles (DMV). Everyone hates waiting there indefinitely. It's purgatory on earth. One day as I was writing this chapter, I had to visit the DMV to update my driver's license. I noticed that not a single person standing in the dreadfully long line had turned to their neighbor to simply say hello. Realizing that the person standing next to me was surely more interesting than doing nothing, I turned to him and used the most powerful line I have for starting a connection: "Hi, my name is Nick." With a smile and handshake, we started talking. Beyond commiserating about the DMV, we quickly found the things we had in common to talk about (farming and a love of the outdoors) because that's the way conversations tend to work (like trying to find a needle in a haystack *with a magnet,* you'll remember from chapter 3).

Our conversation was contagious. Once we started talking, others seemed to recognize that they could have a conversation, too, and pretty soon the whole line had come alive. We were still waiting in line at the DMV, but that dull experience was now better. The farmer I was talking to ended up getting done at the same time I did, and we raised our arms together in mock celebration to the line of people behind us, who then started cheering for us. By realizing that waiting in line could also be an opportunity to connect, I made a dull moment better.

If waiting in line at the DMV is a surprisingly positive opportunity to connect with someone, what other opportunities might emerge if you started looking out for them?

Routinely

It's often said that variety is the spice of life, but our regular routines are actually the most powerful ingredient for our happiness. As one pair of cognitive scientists summarized, "Most of the time we do what we do most of the time. Sometimes we do something new."[11]

Connecting with someone every now and then isn't going to meaningfully improve your life unless you make it a routine habit that you choose almost automatically. Because habits are typically regular routines, they are the most consistent source of our experience and, therefore, the most consistent source of our happiness and well-being. They also become the central feature of our character and personality. "We are what we repeatedly do," the philosopher Will Durant wrote as a summary statement of Aristotle's approach to ethics. "Excellence, then, is not an act but a habit."[12]

Although some people already think they're excellent in every way, the overwhelming majority of us, when asked, can find some aspect of our personality that we'd like to improve. Nathan Hudson, a personality psychologist at Southern Methodist University, reports that around 85–95 percent of the roughly seven thousand people he's surveyed would like to shift themselves in a more positive direction on at least one of the five traits measured by psychologists' most commonly used personality scale.[13] The two dimensions that people report wanting to change most often are also directly related to sociality: becoming a little more extroverted and a little less anxious and pessimistic (that is, a little less neurotic).[14] That is, becoming a little more social.

In works of fiction, character change comes through magic, such as in an overnight visit from three spirits for Ebenezer Scrooge or from the Fairy Godmother in Cinderella. In real life, change isn't magical; it comes from deliberately building a new habit. This requires picking some behavior that's consistently rewarding, and then doing it so frequently that you no longer have to think about trying to do it. A good way to get this going—which Charles Duhigg describes in much more detail as the "habit loop" in his book *The Power of Habit*—is by taking three steps.[15]

First, *identify your habit.* Start small and be precise. A habit isn't a vague character trait but rather a very specific action you do successfully and repeatedly until it becomes automatic. Don't commit yourself to a broad goal, like becoming more outgoing, but rather think about a very specific action that exemplifies the kind of person you want to become. Instead of "be more outgoing," perhaps try to create a habit out of having deeper conversations. Even that—"having deeper conversations"—is too broad because it doesn't specify exactly what to do. Instead, you might develop a habit of having deeper conversations by deciding to ask "why" in your conversations more often. Asking "why" connects more to deep and meaningful parts of people's lives, like their values, goals, and aspirations. Rather than talking about what someone does for a living, for instance, you'd ask why they do it. Rather than talking about what someone is feeling, you'd ask why they feel as they do. Rather than talking about what someone hopes to do in the future, you might ask why they hope to do it. Only with a specific action, such as "ask why," that you can perform repeatedly do you have an action that you can turn into a habit.

Second, *identify your cue.* A habit is triggered by a repeated association with the context you happen to be in. This, too, needs to be specific. If you're trying to have deeper conversations, be specific about which conversations you might do this in. Maybe it would be "when I'm meeting someone new." Or "when I'm on a plane" if you're a frequent flier. The context can also be a thought. Maybe you've decided that you'd like to express gratitude more often, in which case your cue would be "when I feel grateful" and your habit would be "then I'll write a thank-you note." The cue confines your habit to a specific moment in time that triggers you to think about the action you would like to follow.

Finally, *identify your reward.* The positive feeling you get from your habit is what encourages you to do it again. Sometimes the action that you're trying to turn into a habit isn't very fun to do (like exercising, eating healthy, and saving for the future), making it hard to get the repetitions you need to turn these actions into habits. Luckily, the social activities that connect us positively with others are usually surprisingly fun. You don't need to give yourself a chocolate bar after having a meaningful conversation with someone new or put off watching your favorite show until you've expressed your gratitude.

Most of the people I've covered in this book who have improved their lives by being a little more social have done so by recognizing an easy opportunity that they were missing, that was rewarding, and that they could do routinely. Jessica Pan pushed back on her avoidance fears by reaching out to almost everyone she encountered for a year and now does so every day without much thought. It's just part of her character now. Claire Feuer steps onto a train and automatically keeps an eye out for someone she could talk to without giving it any more thought than she dedicates to walking onto the train by putting one foot in front of the other. Dave Fleischer, the canvasser I described at the end of chapter 6 who seeks out deep conversations with people who disagree with him, can hardly help but go deep when he's having a conversation anymore. Jia Jiang asks for help when he needs it now without a moment's hesitation, and passing out thousands of compliments has given Celine McGee permanently rose-colored glasses to almost automatically see the best in others.

As just one example of how you might do this, I decided to develop a new habit myself about a year ago as I'm writing this, which I mentioned briefly in chapter 7. I realized that I often heard kind things being said about someone behind their backs, but rarely passed that appreciation along to the target of it directly. I therefore decided to create a habit of passing the compliments I overheard back to the person being complimented (anonymously, to protect privacy and because compliments feel even more positive when the source is anonymous). Building this habit of giving third-person compliments was especially easy because I got rewarded twice, once with the great feeling I had while writing my note and then again when the person I passed the compliment along to responded back to me. Nevertheless, to help cue the action as I was building the habit, I put a sticky note on my computer that said "pass it back." Eventually I stopped needing the sticky note.

Reaching out to connect when it's an easy opportunity that we'd otherwise overlook or avoid is a good way to have a good moment. Stringing those moments together is a good way to have a good day. Stringing those days together until they become a habit that becomes a part of your personality is a good way to have a good life.

Dolly Parton once said in an interview, "If you've got the money and you've got the heart and you're not too selfish, you can do a lot of good."[16]

Dolly is definitely right about that, but over the course of fifteen years, starting with a eureka moment on a train ride from the South Side of Chicago into work one morning and continuing through tens of thousands of data points in experiments, I've come to realize that you might not need as much as Dolly suggests in order to do a surprising amount of good for other people. It's not just a lack of money or heart or good intention that holds us back from being good to others. It's also the presence of overly pessimistic expectations about how others will respond that can keep us from reaching out and doing good for others, and in return, doing some good for ourselves, a little more often.

On that morning, during my normal commute, a delightful conversation with a woman in a memorable red hat led me to recognize that I had a surprisingly powerful ability to reach out and make someone's day brighter, and to create a moment of connection in return that made my day brighter as well. I also came to realize that I might not be using the power I have to connect as often as I could because I didn't think that reaching out would be as positive as it turned out to be. It wasn't a lack of money or heart or good intent that was keeping me from doing so; it was a mistaken barrier in my own mind that kept me from even trying to connect. I wasn't alone. Everyone else on the train that morning was doing the same thing. Were we all keeping ourselves isolated in a dull silent space because we failed to recognize how positive connecting with other people would feel if we reached out and tried?

That was just a big question to me then. In the fifteen years since, with the help of many collaborators, I've tested that question many times and in many ways. Across tens of thousands of people, I've seen a robust tendency over and over again for people to underestimate the good they can do by reaching out and being a little more social. I've seen grown men and women cry together after opening up to a stranger in a deep conversation. And I've heard countless stories from people who have cast aside their misplaced pessimism for a more realistic sense of optimism about other people. I often remember Jia Jiang's comment to me after trying to spend a hundred days in a row being rejected and learning that others are surprisingly helpful and surprisingly kind. "I feel I have this superpower, you know, I really do," he told me. "It's not like a Superman thing that I can do anything I want, because I still get a lot of rejections, but the superpower is a mindset I can fall back to."

The ability to do a surprising amount of good by reaching out and connecting with another person might be a superpower, but it is not a rare power that requires unusual resources. As Jia Jiang recognized, reaching out to connect a little more often is something you can do if you get over the misplaced barriers in your own mind that are holding you back. These barriers come in the form of doubt and pessimism about how others will respond if you make *the choice* to reach out and connect in some way. It can be a long list of doubts, coming in the form of question marks in your mind. Should I . . .

—Say hello? Talk to a stranger?

—Reach out and express support?

—Call up an old friend on the phone to reconnect?

—Have a deeper conversation?

—Reach out and express my gratitude?

—Pass along a compliment?

—Ask for help when I need it?

—Offer help when I can provide it?

—Perform a kind act when I'm able?

—Be open, authentic, and honest in conversation with someone?

In all of these cases, we've learned that the pessimism that can lead us to avoid reaching out to connect with others is somewhat misplaced. Testing your doubts by turning these question marks into periods is the first step to learning where misplaced pessimism might be keeping you from doing a little more good in your life by being a little more social.

Hello?

No. *Hello.*

Acknowledgments

It is a painful irony that writing a book about the importance of connecting would require me to spend so much time alone. Writing this book took several years longer than I had expected, interrupted in the beginning by the COVID-19 pandemic and then stuck for what seemed like ages by the difficulty of getting the nuances of our research right. What kept me going through seemingly infinite hours of isolation writing away on my computer were the many people I was connected to while going through this process.

First, I have had the unfair advantage of working with more wonderful collaborators than any researcher deserves. I am grateful to my literary agent, Max Brockman, who was able to sharpen random thoughts into a book proposal and then convince publishers that I had something worthwhile to say. When I describe research that "we" conducted in this book, I am expressing my gratitude to former PhD students and postdocs who did most of the truly hard work to get our research done, including Stav Atir, James Dungan, Margaret Echelbarger, Tal Eyal, Quinn Hirschi, Mike Kardas, Amit Kumar, David Munguia Gomez, Eliana Polimeni, Juliana Schroeder, Rui Sun, Kristina Wald, Adam Waytz, and Xuan Zhao. Over the course of fifteen years of research, I was also blessed to have three terrific lab managers overseeing the complicated work required to conduct scientific research, including Jasmine Kwong, Don Lyons, and Janice Im. I am also grateful for the nearly three decades of advice that Tom Gilovich and Dan Gilbert have given me about both work and life, to my many colleagues at the University of Chicago who make my daily life so much better because I'm connected to them, and to the Booth School of Business for funding my research for nearly twenty years.

Second, I had the great pleasure to meet many interesting and inspiring people over the course of writing this book whose stories I then got to describe. They include Claire Feuer, Dave Fleischer, Stefan Hofmann, Jia Jiang, Celine McGee, Jessica Pan, and Michael Slepian. I am also grateful to Charles Duhigg for encouragement, advice, and several sessions of deep conversation while I was writing. I began my conversations with every one of these people as strangers, and ended feeling like friends. I also had the opportunity to reconnect with some old friends and mentors who inspired me along the way, including one of the best teachers I've ever seen, Craig Aune, and my lifelong friend Todd Jones. Most workday mornings have been made better by talking about ideas with my friend and colleague Harold Pollack on my train ride to the office. I am also grateful to several people who reached out to me and provided their inspiring experiences of being a little more social, including Rob Finlayson, Duncan Raban, and Conor Sweeney. All of these interactions gave me energy and encouragement when I needed it.

Third, many people read worse versions of this book or provided ideas to help make your reading experience better. Stav Atir, Gus Cooney, Dave DeSteno, Tom Gilovich, Josh Jackson, Mike Kardas, Emma Levine, Todd Rogers, Juliana Schroeder, Michael Slepian, and Hal Weitzman all provided helpful comments on parts of the book. Amy Boonstra, Dan Gilbert, and Emmanuel Roman went above and beyond the call of both collegiality and friendship to provide helpful comments on an early draft of the entire book. Kassie Brabaw took a rambling first draft and helped me turn it into a more manageable second draft, providing inspiration that I was on the right track when I was less sure. Edward Kastenmeier, my editor at Knopf, expertly polished a later draft of this book, and patiently guided me across the finish line. Along the way, Lauren Carlson, Hadley Lange, Don Lyons, Janice Im, and Alex Schanne provided assistance of all kinds, from tracking down references to creating figures to giving me feedback on chapters or the entire book. I am grateful that

I have friends and colleagues who were so generous with their time, and who were both kind *and* honest in helping me to make this book better. I have valued their help more than they would guess. Any remaining mistakes are entirely my fault.

Fourth, my family provided a rock-solid base of support and encouragement from start to finish. Our "big kids"—Ben, Habtamu, Nathan, and Tsion—have contributed everything from eye rolls to interesting examples to thoughtful criticisms over years of dinner conversations and long car rides. Our "little one"—Lindsay—shows me the power of being a little more social every day. This book is being published in the same year that Jen and I are celebrating thirty years of marriage. Nobody has a more constant source of love, support, encouragement, and inspiration than I do. I'm excited for what our next thirty years together will bring. I love you all so very much.

Finally, I am grateful to have met one singularly inspiring person in the course of working on this book whose name I can no longer remember but whose image I can see clearly in my mind's eye: the woman in the lovely red hat who was surprisingly happy to talk to me one morning on the train and got me to start thinking, "Why?"

Notes

Preface: Social Enough Animals?

1. Marshall, A. (2017, Dec. 14). Elon Musk reveals his awkward dislike of mass transit. WIRED.com.
2. The full details of this experiment are described in the following paper: Epley, N., & Schroeder, J. (2014). Mistakenly seeking solitude. *Journal of Experimental Psychology: General, 143*(5), 1980–99.
3. To be more precise, the exact instructions we gave to people in the solitude condition were: "Please keep to yourself and enjoy your solitude on the train today. Take this time to sit alone with your thoughts. Your goal is to focus on yourself and the day ahead of you." The exact instructions in the control condition were: "Please do not make any changes to your normal commute. Your goal is to do as you would normally do." The exact instructions in the connection condition were: "Please have a conversation with a new person on the train today. Try to make a connection. Find out something interesting about him or her and tell them something about you. The longer the conversation, the better. Your goal is to try to get to know your community neighbor this morning."
4. To give you a little more detail about this experiment, after you agreed to participate and we explained what we wanted you to do on the commute that day, we'd hand you an envelope containing your gift card and a survey to complete at the end of your commute and return in the mail to us, and send you on your way to do whatever we asked you to try. We were most interested in the first four questions on the survey.

   Three of these questions asked you to report how positive your experience was. Specifically, how pleasant your commute was compared with normal, how happy you felt after your commute, and how sad you felt after your commute. We combined these three measures into a single overall measure of positivity (reverse scoring the sadness item because it's negative). The three bars on the left side of the figure below show you how people, on average, thought they would feel if they were in each of our conditions. People reported having the most positive experience in the connection condition and the least positive in the solitude condition. The three bars on the right, in contrast, show how a separate group of people recruited from the same train station *actually* felt in each of those conditions. Although our commuters thought they would have the most positive commute in the solitude condition and the least positive commute in the connection condition, commuters' actual experiences showed exactly the opposite pattern, having the most positive commute in the connection condition and the least positive commute in the solitude condition.

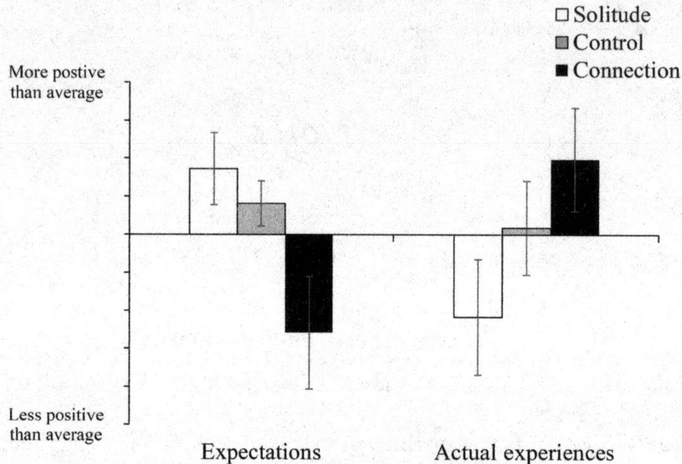

The fourth question asked about what might be seen as a potential cost of talking to someone while commuting: being unproductive. Specifically, this question asked people to rate how productive they found their commute to be compared with normal. As you can see in the three bars on the left in the figure below, people *thought* they would have the least positive commute in the connection condition. However, we found no meaningful differences in how productive people actually found their commute to be in each of these experimental conditions. This doesn't mean, of course, that talking to someone doesn't take time away from doing other things. It obviously does. It just means that talking to someone wasn't seen as a less productive use of one's time than whatever people were doing in the solitude or control conditions that day.

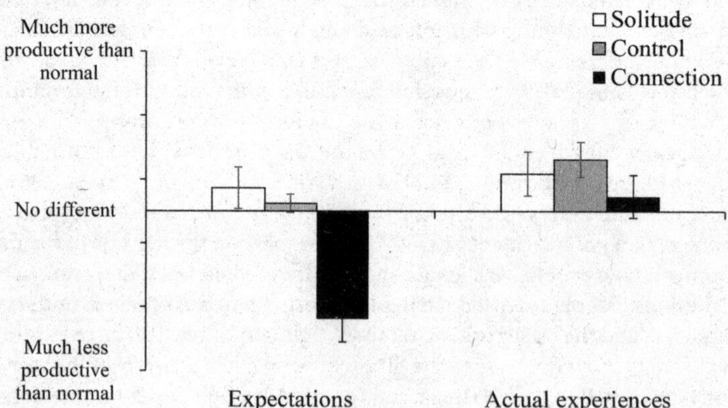

1. *Homo Socialis*

1. Ventura, M. (2022, Feb. 8). "Marinella Beretta e la sua storia storia: Morta invisibile da 3 anni, scoperta solo grazie al vento" [Marinella Beretta and her story: Dead, unseen for three years, discovered only by the wind]. *Il messaggero* (www .ilmessaggero.it).
2. Anderson, L., Washington, C., Kreider, R. M., & Gryn, T. (2023, June 8). "Share of one-person households more than tripled from 1940 to 2020." Census.gov.
3. Alberti, F. B. (2018). This "modern epidemic": Loneliness as an emotion cluster and a neglected subject in the history of emotions. *Emotion Review, 10*(3), 242–54.

   This article is expanded on in her book: Alberti, F. B. (2019). *A biography of loneliness: The history of an emotion*. Oxford: Oxford University Press.
4. As Alberti documents, how often the term "loneliness" appears in books over time has dramatically increased since the 1800s, as you can see in the figure below. (Courtesy of www.books.google.com/ngrams.)

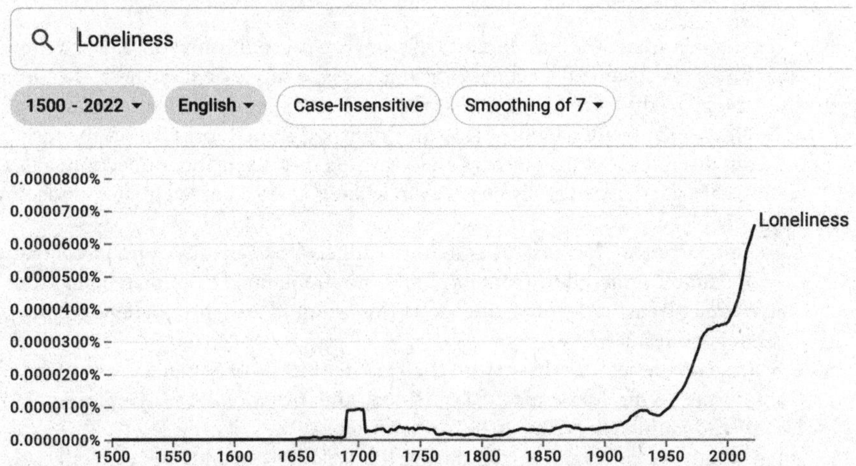

The change in meaning associated with loneliness is also reflected in the frequency of other related words used over time. Alberti notes, for instance, that the term "solitude" follows a very different historical trajectory than "loneliness," peaking in the 1700s and declining recently. She attributes this pattern at least partly to the shift in the meaning of "loneliness" to refer to both the physical state of being alone and the psychological state of feeling alone. Note that the term "alone" in published writing also follows a very different historical path than "loneliness," although experiencing a bit of an uptick in popularity starting around 1975.

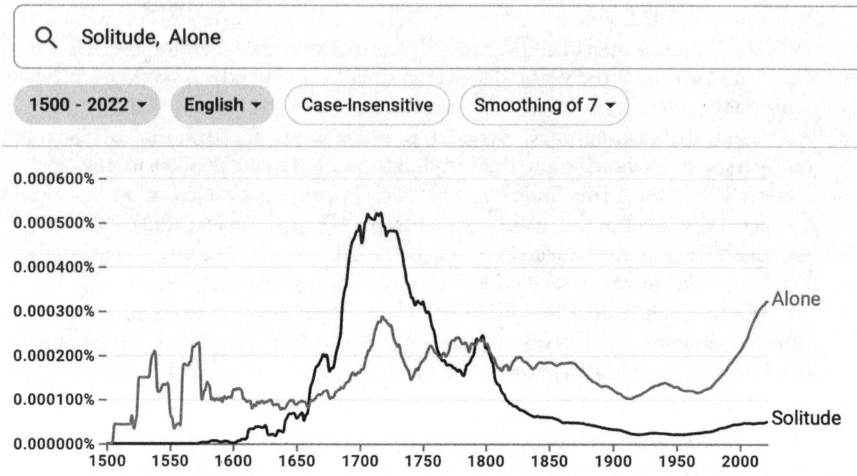

5. Alberti notes that Thomas Blount's *Glossographia*, published in 1656, defined "loneliness" as a state of "oneliness, or loneliness, a single or singleness." Not long after, the 1676 edition of Elisha Coles's *English Dictionary* defined loneliness simply as "solitude." Only after 1800, at least in English, did the term take on the feeling of being disconnected from others and yearning or hunger for connection, a psychological state that can easily be felt even when you are completely surrounded by other people.
6. *Merriam-Webster's*, for instance, defines "lonely" as "being without company (lone)," "cut off from others (solitary)," and "not frequented by human beings (desolate)," but also as "sad from being alone (lonesome)," and "producing a feeling of bleakness or desolation."
7. U.S. Surgeon General's Advisory on the Healing Effects of Social Connection and Community. "Our Epidemic of Loneliness and Isolation." U.S. Department of Health and Human Services, 2023 (www.hhs.gov).
8. Interestingly, research conducted during the COVID-19 pandemic generally documented large increases in loneliness at the first three months of the lockdown phase of the pandemic, at least in the United States and western Europe, where the measures were collected, followed by a return to pre-pandemic levels for many as people adjusted to their new circumstances and figured out other ways to stay connected to each other even when required to stay physically distanced. Aknin, L. B., et al. (2022). Mental health during the first year of the COVID-19 pandemic: A review and recommendations moving forward. *Perspectives on Psychological Science, 17*(4), 915–36.
9. The UCLA Loneliness Scale measures how often you experience particular feelings of social isolation versus connection (never, rarely, sometimes, or always). Sample items include "How often do you feel that you are 'in tune' with the people around you?," "How often do you feel that you are no longer close to anyone?," "How often do you feel that people are around you but not with you?," and "How often do you feel that there are people you can talk to?" Analyzing responses to

this scale from 124,855 young adults aged eighteen to twenty-nine between 1976 and 2019 found an increase in reported loneliness of 0.56 standard deviations. To put this increase in perspective, the Centers for Disease Control estimates that the average woman in the United States is 63.5 inches tall with a standard deviation of 5.2 inches (meaning that the average person deviates from that average height by 5.2 inches). The average man is 69 inches tall with a standard deviation of 5 inches. If height in the United States had changed as much as loneliness between 1974 and 2019, women would have grown 2.9 inches taller and men would have grown 2.8 inches taller.

Psychologists, like everyone else, have become more interested in understanding loneliness relatively recently, meaning that most of the loneliness surveys included in this analysis were conducted after the year 2000 (a total of 365 surveys, compared with 81 before 2000). We therefore have more confidence in the more recent estimates of loneliness, but there is no statistical difference in the rate that loneliness has increased before versus after 2000. Buecker, S., Mund, M., Chwastek, S., Sostmann, M., & Luhmann, M. (2021). Is loneliness in emerging adults increasing over time? A preregistered cross-temporal meta-analysis and systematic review. *Psychological Bulletin, 147*(8), 787–805.

The height estimates are based on data from "Anthropometric Reference Data for Children and Adults: United States, 2015–2018." Centers for Disease Control, Jan. 2021 (www.cdc.gov).

10. Baumeister, R., & Leary, M. (1995). The need to belong: Desire for interpersonal attachments as a fundamental human need. *Psychological Bulletin, 117*(3), 497–529.
11. Darwin, C. (1871). *The descent of man, and selection in relation to sex* (Vol. 1, p. 156). New York: D. Appleton.
12. Eriksson, K., Vartanova, I., Strimling, P., & Simpson, B. (2020). Generosity pays: Selfish people have fewer children and earn less money. *Journal of Personality and Social Psychology, 118*(3), 532–44.
13. As one of the world's leading experts on loneliness, John Cacioppo, once put it, "Physical pain protects the individual from physical dangers. Social pain, also known as loneliness, evolved for a similar reason: because it protected the individual from the danger of remaining isolated." From Cacioppo, J. T., & Patrick, W. (2008, p. 7). *Loneliness: Human nature and the need for social connection.* New York: W. W. Norton.
14. Wahba, M. A., & Bridwell, L. G. (1976, p. 212). Maslow reconsidered: A review of research on the need hierarchy theory. *Organizational Behavior and Human Performance, 15*(2), 212–40.

Maslow himself even seemed aware that his theorizing lacked empirical support. In 1954, he presented some ideas on self-actualization "with due apologies to those who insist on conventional reliability, validity, sampling, etc." Maslow, A. M. (1954). *Motivation and personality.* New York: Harper & Row. That's a little like your doctor giving you advice "with due apologies to the truth."

Just a moment's reflection makes Maslow's predictions of a hierarchy seem implausible, at best. Someone without a home can still surely care about being loved and respected by others just as much as someone safely housed in the suburbs. A hungry person can still be deeply hurt by a broken marriage, or deeply desire to have stronger relationships with those they should love. Survey results confirm this intuition: The importance that people place on needs at different levels tends to be positively related to each other, or not correlated with each other at all, rather than being negatively correlated as a hierarchy would predict. The more accurate description is that we have a collection of basic needs that we try to keep satisfied all at once. When you're hungry, you look for food. When you're lonely, you look for kind and accepting people. If you're hungry and lonely, you look for someone to have lunch with. The need for positive social connection is not a luxury that we only care about once other basics are met, but is rather one of several needs that we care about and monitor continuously.

A moment's reflection also makes it clear that Maslow's hierarchy is somewhat dehumanizing, because it suggests that those who don't have the basic needs of food, shelter, and security met—namely, those who are of lower socioeconomic status—do not care about the higher-level needs of love, esteem, and autonomy. Having a sense of meaning, autonomy, and purpose in life, based on Maslow's theory of a hierarchy of needs, is only a concern for the C-suite crowd.

In a study that Juliana Schroeder and I conducted, we found that people's beliefs about others' needs are consistent with Maslow's beliefs about a hierarchy of needs, at least for other people if not for themselves. In particular, we found that people tend to say that they care more about high-level needs like autonomy and purpose (the pinnacle of Maslow's self-actualization needs) than other people do, and that those who are very low in socioeconomic status (like homeless people or drug addicts) are perceived to be motivated primarily by satisfying only their most basic physical needs at a level that they report is similar to nonhuman animals (like chimpanzees).

For instance, in one experiment at a crisis-management center in Chicago, we found that charity donors to a holiday gift drive (and hence of higher socioeconomic status) believed that the charity recipients cared more about satisfying their physical needs of hunger and housing than they cared about being loved or having a sense of meaning in life, whereas the actual charity recipients reported caring about these needs equally (in the same way that charity donors reported about themselves). When asked to rank the three needs (food, love, meaning) in their order of importance, the charity donors thought the recipients would rank food as the most important need by far, with love coming next and meaning a close third. The actual charity recipients, in contrast, ranked the need for meaning and purpose in their lives as the most important, with love and food tied, on average, in second place, which is the same order of rankings that the charity donors reported for themselves.

In another experiment, we found that University of California, Berkeley, students (a higher socioeconomic group) believed that homeless people would prefer a program that met their physical needs by providing food over a wellness program that satisfied their psychological need for self-esteem and meaning, whereas actual homeless people reported a similar level of interest in both programs. Psychological needs like love and meaning are internal states and experiences that can be hard to observe in others, but that doesn't mean that others don't feel them just as you do. Failing to recognize the importance of these psychological needs in others inaccurately diminishes their importance, a process that demeans others' needs because it fails to recognize the importance of high-level psychological needs like meaning and love.

Although it might seem that a person who is hungry cares only about eating, or that a criminal won't be that upset by the pain of solitary confinement and hence can be treated like a nonhuman animal, the hungry and incarcerated still have a human mind that tends to care about the same basic needs that you do. Studs Terkel, the great chronicler of the ordinary worker and author of the classic book *Working*, realized this only after interviewing hundreds of people about their jobs and their needs. "I was constantly astonished," Terkel wrote, "by the extraordinary dreams of ordinary people. No matter how bewildering the times, no matter how dissembling the official language, those we call ordinary are aware of a sense of personal worth—or more often a lack of it—in the work they do." Schroeder, J., & Epley, N. (2020). Demeaning: Dehumanizing others by minimizing the importance of their psychological needs. *Journal of Personality and Social Psychology, 119*, 765–91; Terkel, S. (Ed.). (1974). *Working: People talk about what they do all day and how they feel about what they do*. New York: Pantheon Books.

15. Harlow's experiments with baby monkeys were momentous. He separated infant macaques from their mothers in a laboratory he ran in Madison, Wisconsin, and then raised them with two surrogate mothers instead. One was a "wire mother," made of steel mesh with a wooden head and a "unibreast" sticking out of its "chest" that provided all of the calories the baby monkey needed to survive. The other was a "cloth mother," in the same shape but made of a wooden block covered with sponge rubber, upholstered in terry cloth, and warmed by a small lightbulb behind its monkey-mannequin head. A slightly warm upholstered block may not seem very loving and cuddly, but it was definitely better than the alternative. If the only reason that an infant cuddled their mother was that she provided food, then the baby monkeys would be spending all their time on the wire mother, who provided milk, and completely ignoring the cloth mother, who only provided cuddly warmth.

    What actually happened was precisely the opposite: The infants spent only about 30 minutes a day on the wire mother and spent roughly 960 minutes a day cuddling up to the cloth mother. When put side by side, the infants would cling to the cloth mother while moving just enough to feed from the wire mother, and then quickly return to cuddling the cloth mother once they were full. The babies would have presumably spent even less time on the wire mother if they could have eaten faster. Even Harlow himself seemed to underestimate the power of social connection. "We were not surprised to discover that contact comfort was an important basic affectional or love variable," he later said in his presidential address to the American Psychological Association, "but we did not expect it to overshadow so completely the variable of nursing."

    Harlow learned in other experiments that the infants would almost universally flee to the cloth mother when startled or scared, and avoid the wire mother almost completely. When the monkeys were raised only in a wire cage that provided every calorie the infant could ever need, Harlow learned that his baby monkeys survived with "difficulty, if at all, during the first days of life." The infant monkeys that did survive those conditions grew into maladjusted adults who rocked in the corners of their cages, struggled to socialize or connect with other monkeys, and usually died young.

16. John Bowlby's observations of the long-lasting damage of isolation in infancy and young childhood led him to formulate attachment theory, a set of now well-supported principles describing how different types of attachments in young

childhood can establish norms and habits that linger well into adulthood. Most damaging is being deprived of social connection early in life.

In a famous report written for the WHO in 1951, Bowlby noted that the numerous studies involving direct observation of children deprived of parental care in institutional settings "make it plain that, when deprived of maternal care, the child's development is almost always [seriously impaired]—physically, intellectually, and socially—and that symptoms of physical and mental illness may appear." Bowlby's report, *Maternal Care and Mental Health,* noted a consistent pattern to the symptoms shown by children separated from their parents. First was the distress known by every parent who leaves their child with a babysitter for the first time to go out for a date. Prolonged separation is followed by a kind of despair and helplessness, leading children to withdraw from social interaction and become emotionally deadened. Over time, as children adjusted to their separation, they would return to their daily activities but would remain withdrawn, in a state that Bowlby referred to as detachment. Bowlby, J. (1951). Maternal care and mental health. *Bulletin of the World Health Organization, 3,* 355–533; Harlow, H. F. (1958). The nature of love. *American Psychologist, 13*(12), 673–85; Zayas, V., & Sakman, E. (2020). Human attachment and affiliation. In *Oxford research encyclopedia of psychology.*

17. Burden, B. (2023, June 30). Was I married to a stranger? *New York Times.*
18. One experiment, in fact, found that being isolated and alone for eight hours led people to feel just as tired and fatigued as being deprived of food for eight hours, again highlighting similarities in the biological response to being deprived of these two basic needs. Another experiment conducted during two different lockdown phases of the COVID-19 pandemic in 2020 found that people reported feeling more tired and fatigued on the days when they had no contact with other people. This is why "languishing"—the psychological opposite of flourishing—became such a popular word in 2020. Being starved for social contact produces a similar fatigued response as being starved for food. Stijovic, A., Forbes, P. A., Tomova, L., Skoluda, N., Feneberg, A. C., Piperno, G., Pronizius, E., Nater, U. M., Lamm, C., & Silani, G. (2023). Homeostatic regulation of energetic arousal during acute social isolation: Evidence from the lab and the field. *Psychological Science, 34*(5), 537–51; Keyes, C. L. (2002). The mental health continuum: From languishing to flourishing in life. *Journal of Health and Social Behavior, 43*(2), 207–22; Grant, A. (2021, April 27). Those blah feelings have a common name. *New York Times,* sec. D, p. 6.
19. To see this similarity in brain regions underlying basic needs more directly, consider an experiment that I think you'll be happy you didn't sign up for. In this experiment, people were randomly assigned over the course of several days to fast for ten hours on one day (from 9:00 a.m. to 7:00 p.m.) and to sit alone in a psychology lab's equivalent of solitary confinement for ten hours on another day (again, from 9:00 a.m. to 7:00 p.m.). On the solitary day, people arrived at the laboratory by 8:30 a.m. and handed over every bit of technology they had on them. They then walked into a room that contained an all-you-can-eat buffet of snacks and drinks, some toys and games, a few text articles if they had sent the researchers anything they wanted to read beforehand, and a laptop that could only be used to ask the researchers to refill the buffet. Like Harlow's baby monkeys with a wire mother, they had everything they needed to survive physically for the next ten hours, but

had no social contact whatsoever. On the fasting day, these people were simply asked to fast from 9:00 a.m. until 7:00 p.m., when they came to the psychology lab, but were given no restrictions on what they could do otherwise (aside from exercising, which they were asked to avoid for health reasons).

After ten hours of fasting or isolating, it's not hard to imagine that hungry people craved food and isolated people craved other people. Harder to imagine is exactly what's going on inside people's brains. Is "starving for food" the same kind of craving as "starving for human contact," or are these just the same ways of talking about very different things? To find out, each person was slid headfirst into an fMRI scanner at the end of their ten hours of fasting or isolating and shown pictures of food (pizza, pasta, cake, chocolate), friendly people (talking, laughing, smiling, greeting), and pretty flowers (as a control condition). After each set of pictures, each person was asked how much they wanted whatever was shown in the pictures (that is, wanted to eat, wanted social contact, and wanted flowers).

Not surprisingly, people indicated that they wanted more of whatever they had just been deprived of (with no differences in how much each group wanted flowers). More surprising, perhaps, is that the neural regions of the dopaminergic system, essentially right in the very center of your brain, responded to social craving and food craving in highly similar ways, even though other regions of the brain that had nothing to do with craving easily distinguished between the details of thinking about other people versus thinking about food. As the authors put it, "A common signal at the core of the 'craving circuit' in the [dopaminergic system] responds selectively to motivationally salient deprived cues, independent of their specific content. By contrast, food and social craving led to dissociable responses almost everywhere else in the brain." Non-neuroscience translation: Craving food looks the same in your brain as craving people, even though your brain is fully capable of recognizing that food and people are not the same things. Tomova, L., Wang, K. L., Thompson, T., Matthews, G. A., Takahashi, A., Tye, K. M., & Saxe, R. (2020). Acute social isolation evokes midbrain craving responses similar to hunger. *Nature Neuroscience, 23,* 1597–605.

20. Vaillant, G. (2009, July 16). Yes, I stand by my words, "happiness equals love—full stop." *Positive Psychology News.*

    You can read more comprehensive reports of this study, sometimes also called the Grant Study (named after its original funder, William T. Grant), in George Vaillant's book (2012), *Triumphs of Experience: The Men of the Harvard Grant Study.* You can also read another report of the results including an additional ten years of study from the current director of this study, Robert Waldinger, in his book with Marc Schulz (2023), *The Good Life: Lessons from the World's Longest Scientific Study of Happiness.*
21. Gaffigan, J. (2013, p. 165). *Dad is fat.* New York: Crown Archetype.
22. Herrmann, E., Call, J., Hernandez-Lloreda, M. V., Hare, B., & Tomasello, M. (2007). Humans have evolved specialized skills of social cognition: The cultural intelligence hypothesis. *Science, 317,* 1360–66.
23. Leary, M. R., Tambor, E. S., Terdal, S. K., & Downs, D. L. (1995). Self-esteem as an interpersonal monitor: The sociometer hypothesis. *Journal of Personality and Social Psychology, 68,* 518–30.
24. Nearly three decades of research now provide solid evidence that self-esteem is

indeed a sociometer. Perhaps the clearest evidence is the very tight relationships between our own self-esteem and how socially desirable we think we are: how likable, competent, attractive, and moral we think others see us. For instance, in one particularly intensive study of 229 Chicagoans surveyed for at least five years, the correlation between people's reported loneliness and their self-esteem was very large (a correlation of -0.57, meaning more loneliness was associated with lower self-esteem), and loneliness and self-esteem emerged as the strongest predictors of happiness (-0.43 for loneliness and 0.48 for self-esteem, with more loneliness being associated with less happiness and more self-esteem being associated with more happiness). Cacioppo, J. T., Hawkley, L. C., Kalil, A., Hughes, M. E., Waite, L., & Thisted, R. A. (2008). Happiness and the invisible threads of social connection: The Chicago Health, Aging, and Social Relations Study. In M. Eid & R. J. Larsen (Eds.), *The science of subjective well-being,* pp. 195–219. New York: Guilford Press.

Extensive reviews of the research documenting how self-esteem operates like a sociometer can be found in the following articles: Leary, M. R. (2012). Sociometer theory. In L. Van Lange, A. W. Kruglanski, & E. T. Higgins (Eds.), *Handbook of theories of social psychology* (Vol. 2, pp. 141–59). Los Angeles: Sage; Leary, M. R., & Guadagno, J. (2011). The sociometer, self-esteem, and the regulation of interpersonal behavior. In R. F. Baumeister & K. Vohs (Eds.), *Handbook of self-regulation* (2nd ed.). New York: Guilford; Leary, M. R. (2006). Sociometer theory and the pursuit of relational value: Getting to the root of self-esteem. *European Review of Social Psychology, 16,* 75–111.

25. Cooley anticipated objections from the more independent-minded among us, who might not think that others' impressions matter much. "Possibly some will think that I exaggerate the importance of social self-feeling by taking persons and periods of life that are abnormally sensitive. . . . Many people of balanced mind and congenial activity scarcely know that they care what others think of them, and will deny, perhaps with indignation, that such care is an important factor in what they are and do. But this is an illusion." Cooley turned to novels of the day to support his theory, but stronger evidence comes from experiments conducted nearly a century later indicating that our beliefs about how much they are impacted by others' evaluations is not meaningfully correlated with how much they are actually impacted by them. These quotations from Cooley are on page 208 of the revised edition of his 1902 book, *Human Nature and the Social Order,* published in 1922. The absence of correlations between how much you might think you're affected by others' evaluations and your actual sensitivity is reported in Leary et al. (1995). Self-esteem as an interpersonal monitor.
26. Rosenberg, M. (1986). Self-concept from middle childhood through adolescence. In J. Suls & A. G. Greenwald (Eds.), *Psychological perspectives on the self* (Vol. 3, p. 126). Hillsdale, N.J.: Lawrence Erlbaum.
27. Although monitors do their work at all times, they also tend to respond asymmetrically, reacting more to negative signals than positive ones (such as how the fuel gauge alarm in your car only goes off when you're close to being empty). If you've ever posted something on social media and anxiously monitored the likes, or written anything online and made the mistake of reading the comments section, then you know that our sociometer is more sensitive to negative evaluations than it is to positive ones. I experience this every time I read through my teaching evaluations,

where the barbed comments stand out and sting much more than the kind words feel good, making me feel bad overall even if the harsh words are much less common than the kind words. Even negative signals from people who shouldn't matter to us—strangers we'll never see again, for instance—affect us because they could be giving us useful information about our value in relationships that do matter. If my students don't like me, then maybe my friends and family don't think I'm all that great, either? Being ostracized by others in experiments, even something as trivial as not being looked at on the street or not having a digital ball thrown to you in an online game of catch, not only hurts in the moment (firing the same neural regions that signal physical pain) but also produces a cascade of negative thoughts about yourself that can linger for a long time. Williams, K. (2002). *Ostracism: The power of silence.* New York: Guilford Press.

28. Kahneman, D., & Deaton, A. (2010). High income improves evaluation of life but not emotional well-being. *Proceedings of the National Academy of Sciences, 107*(38), 16489–93.
29. Every study I've ever seen shows diminishing returns of increasing income on well-being. Even an experiment in which two wealthy people donated $10,000 to two hundred randomly selected people around the world showed diminishing returns of income on happiness. In this rather amazing experiment conducted in 2021, in coordination with the TED organization (made famous for its TED Talks), those with the smallest income experienced the biggest boost to their well-being, an effect that lasted for at least six months after receiving the cash (long after it was spent by many, and as long as the researchers tracked well-being). The impact of a $10,000 windfall on people's well-being, however, steadily declined as a person's annual income increased. Beyond an annual salary of $123,000, there was no statistically significant impact of receiving the windfall compared with a control condition that did not receive any money.

    However, whether well-being continues to rise indefinitely as you make more and more money, even if the changes are very small, is currently a matter of scientific debate. In the analysis by Kahneman and Deaton, no discernible increases in experienced well-being could be found beyond the income category that ranged from $60,000 to $90,000, which led many media outlets at the time to report that happiness doesn't increase once you make $75,000 per year (the midpoint of this income range). It even led one financial services company—Gravity Payments—to increase all of their employee's salaries to a minimum of $70,000 (after the CEO, Dan Price, misread the widely reported figure that would have cost the company a little more for each employee).

    Additional analyses conducted on the Gallup World Poll, a survey of a little more than 1.7 million people from 164 countries around the world, found that the point at which income fails to increase experienced well-being—what is sometimes referred to as the "income satiation point"—depends a bit on where in the world you are measuring it, with wealthier countries showing higher satiation points. All regions of the world, though, showed some satiation point, with some parts of the world (such as Latin America and East Asia) showing an actual decline in experienced well-being at the highest income levels beyond the satiation point. However, these Gallup surveys measure happiness in a rather coarse way, simply asking if you felt a particular emotion, like happiness, the prior day or not. These surveys cannot differentiate, then, between feeling somewhat happy and feeling deliriously happy. Studies that ask people about their well-being using more sensitive measures that can differentiate between different levels of positive emotions, such as asking how you feel on a scale ranging from "very bad" to "very good," do not find a point at which well-being stops increasing as income increases. Those increases tend to be small, but they are increases nonetheless.

The take-home message from all of this research is that money does indeed bring some happiness, mostly by diminishing some of the miseries that come from lacking money, but once you're out of poverty, there are definitely better ways of increasing your happiness than pursuing more money for its own sake. Dwyer, R. J., & Dunn, E. W. (2022). Wealth distribution promotes happiness. *Proceedings of the National Academy of Sciences, 119*(46), e2211123119; Jebb, A., Tay, L., Diener, E., & Oishi, S. (2018). Happiness, income satiation, and the turning points around the world. *Nature Human Behaviour, 2,* 33–38; Killingsworth, M. A. (2021). Experienced well-being rises with income, even above $75,000 per year. *Proceedings of the National Academy of Sciences, 118*(4), e2016976118.

30. The longer story is in the table below. Please let your eyes wander over it somewhat quickly so that I can then walk you through the whole thing in the paragraphs below it.

		Positive Mood	Not Negative	Stress Free	Life Eval.	Avg. Ratio
More positive →	**Regression coefficient** High income ($4k+ per month vs. lower)	0.03	-0.06	-0.03	0.64	
	Ratio vs. high income					
	Old (60+ vs. younger)	0.79	0.93	6.28	0.50	2.13
	Weekend (Saturday/Sunday vs. weekday)	1.13	0.72	4.83	0.01	1.67
	Insured (Have health insurance vs. not)	0.40	0.92	1.19	0.59	0.78
	Religious (Religion Important vs. not)	1.16	-0.02	1.21	0.35	0.68
	Obese (BMI 30 or larger vs. lower)	-0.38	-0.14	-0.42	-0.31	-0.31

← **More negative**	Graduate (College degree vs. not)	0.03	0.01	-1.93	0.48	-0.35
	Divorced (Yes vs. no)	-0.38	-0.27	-0.88	-0.32	-0.46
	Female (vs. male)	0.16	-0.60	-1.89	0.29	-0.51
	Children at home (Yes vs. no)	0.08	-0.37	-2.47	-0.11	-0.72
	Caregiver (Yes vs. no)	-0.49	-1.02	-2.99	-0.25	-1.19
	Smoker (Yes vs. no)	-1.01	-0.84	-2.85	-0.70	-1.35
	Health condition (Bad diagnosis vs. not)	-1.36	-1.22	-3.15	-0.48	-1.55
	Alone (No social contact vs. any)	-7.13	-2.10	-3.73	-0.75	-3.43
	Headache (Yes vs. no)	-4.45	-3.41	-9.82	-0.78	-4.62

Don't worry. It's not as complicated as it initially looks. The first row in the table shows the effect of being in roughly the upper half of income in their sample (making $4,000 per month or more, equivalent to $48,000 per year or more) versus being in the bottom half (making less than $4,000 per month, or less than $48,000 per year) on the three measures of happiness "in your life" (positive mood, negative mood, and stress) and the one measure of happiness "with your life" (ladder).

Those in the high-income group are making, on average, roughly four times more in annual salary than those in the low-income group (I estimate roughly $27,000 a year versus $100,000 a year). If you're the kind of person who really cares about the statistics, then the numbers in the first row are regression coefficients. If you're not a stats person, then the numbers in the first row simply show that higher income leads to more positive well-being (more positive mood, less negative mood, less stress, and better life satisfaction), but that the effects of money on happiness in your life are fairly small (except for the effect of money on happiness "with your life"—life evaluation—which is quite large).

Now to the more interesting part. What you can now do is take that difference in the effect of being relatively high versus low in income and compare it with the effect of being relatively high or low on any of the other variables. You can then calculate a ratio of how important those other variables are compared with a fourfold increase in your annual salary (between an average of roughly $27,000 and $100,000). Look at the next row in the table labeled "Old," which will give you some good news if you're planning to grow older: Your best days may be ahead of you. This row shows reported well-being of those aged sixty or older compared with those under sixty, indicating that those sixty and over experience more positive mood than those under sixty, and that the effect is 79 percent the size of being high versus low in income. The next row—weekend—compares reported well-being when it's measured on a weekend versus a weekday, showing that people are in a more positive mood on the weekend than on a weekday, an effect that is actually a bit larger than a fourfold difference in your salary. The ratios in this table are positive numbers if the effect on the reference group described in each row (older people, on the weekend, those with health insurance, and so on) is a positive outcome (more positive mood, less negative mood, less stress, and more positive life evaluation), and are negative numbers if the effect on the reference group is negative. I've ordered the table from the variables that produce the most consistently positive effects on well-being at the top to those having the most consistently negative effects at the bottom.

Continue looking down that first column and you'll note the *really* big effect on people's positive mood: "Alone." This question asked people to indicate how many hours they spent in social contact the day before, with the table above comparing the 5 percent of this sample who had no social contact with the rest who spent an hour or more with others. The difference between those who spent the day alone versus with other people for any amount of time is more than seven times bigger on your reported happiness, enjoyment, and smiling than a fourfold increase in your salary. Across all of the well-being measures, on average, the only thing a bit worse than spending a day alone is spending a day with a headache. Ouch.

31. Research from this same Gallup poll has been published in "Happiness Is Love—and $75,000" by Jennifer Robinson on Gallup.com on November 17, 2011. These findings consistently suggest we become more energized and excited when we're in the presence of other people, but are more tired and fatigued as we spend more time alone or isolated. This helps to explain why researchers consistently find that fun activities are more fun when you're with others than when you're alone. Researchers have documented this effect in a few different ways. One simple way is to text people over the course of the day, ask them if they're having fun or not, and ask if they are alone or with others (among other things, usually). In two studies that did this, people reported being with another person 80 percent of the time they were having fun in one study and 61 percent of the time in another.

The problem with this kind of study, however, is that people might be doing very different things with others than they're doing alone. The best way to test how the presence of other people affects positive experience, then, is to ask people to do the same fun activity by themselves or with another person. People in one experiment were asked to play Jenga—a game that involves removing wooden blocks from a tower until it falls—alone or with either a friend or a stranger. If you've ever played this game, you know it's both fun and exciting as you remove blocks to watch the tower teeter. Although people playing alone reported having quite a lot of fun, it was more fun when played with a stranger, and even more fun when played with a friend. Being in the presence of close others not only seems to make the activities you do together more positive and fun; it even seems to make the world itself look a little more positive. In one experiment, people looked at a series of moderately positive pictures either alone, with a stranger, or with a friend and indicated how much they liked each of the pictures. Results showed that people liked the pictures more when they rated them in the presence of a friend than in the presence of a stranger or alone. Being with friends not only makes the things we do feel a little more positive but also seems to make the world look a little more positive. Reis, H. T., O'Keefe, S. D., & Lane, R. D. (2017). Fun is more fun when others are involved. *Journal of Positive Psychology, 12*(6), 547–57.

32. The results from the Gallup Wellbeing Survey might inflate the importance of social connection for our well-being compared with income because spending a day without any social contact is quite rare, but they're not alone in suggesting that social connection may be the most critical variable for our happiness and well-being. Another large-scale study using what might be a better approach to measuring well-being surveyed 33,391 people multiple times throughout the day using an app that asked people to report what they were doing and how they were feeling at the moment on a linear scale across a number of different measures. Across a total of more than 1.7 million reports, how lonely people reported feeling at any given moment was much more strongly related to how happy they were feeling (a correlation of -0.49) than to how much money people reported making (a correlation of 0.09 with the log of their reported income). This analysis puts the relationship between loneliness and happiness at roughly five times larger than between income and happiness.

    The author of this research, Matt Killingsworth, also told me in an email exchange that how often people reported interacting with other people in any given moment is also more strongly correlated with how happy they report feeling (a correlation of 0.2) than with (the log of) how much money people report making. As in the Kahneman and Deaton analysis, Killingsworth also found that social variables were more strongly correlated with how happy people reported feeling in their lives than they were with broader evaluations of how happy people were with their lives (such as a measure of how satisfied people were with their lives). In this case, interaction frequency was correlated with life satisfaction to about the same extent as income was (correlations of 0.19 and 0.17, respectively).

    Killingsworth noted that you might expect two measures of a person's feelings (happiness and loneliness) to be more strongly correlated with each other than one measure of some objective state and a person's feelings (like income and happiness), which means that the interaction frequency may be a somewhat more objective measure of the value of social contact for well-being compared with income. However, loneliness is more than just how often you are around other people; it's about how connected you are feeling to others. There is no way of measuring loneliness without asking people how they are feeling in the moment. Killingsworth (2020). Experienced well-being rises with income, even above $75,000 per year.

33. Diener, E., & Seligman, M. E. P. (2002). Very happy people. *Psychological Science, 13*(1), 81–84.

34. A follow-up analysis of nearly 1.5 million people from 166 nations representing more than 98 percent of the world's population found highly similar results. In this analysis, 94 percent of the happiest people around the world reported having someone they could rely on to help when in trouble compared with only 43 percent of the least happy people, and 98 percent of the happiest people reported being treated with respect the previous day compared with only 52 percent of the least happy people. Diener, E., Seligman, M. E. P., Choi, H., & Oishi, S. (2018). Happiest people revisited. *Perspectives on Psychological Science, 13*(2), 176–84.

35. If you're curious, here's the full table of results, showing how positive and negative each category of activities made people feel. The researchers also asked people

who they were with when doing each activity. Those results are in the second table below. People generally felt more positive when they were with others than when they were alone, except when spending time with their boss. Bosses, take note:

Activities	Positive	Negative	Balance	Ratio
Intimate relations	5.1	0.36	4.74	100%
Socializing	4.59	0.57	4.02	85%
Relaxing	4.42	0.51	3.91	82%
Pray/worship/meditate	4.35	0.59	3.76	79%
Eating	4.34	0.59	3.75	79%
Exercising	4.31	0.5	3.81	80%
Watching TV	4.19	0.58	3.61	76%
Shopping	3.95	0.74	3.21	68%
Preparing food	3.93	0.69	3.24	68%
On the phone	3.92	0.85	3.07	65%
Napping	3.87	0.6	3.27	69%
Computer/email/ internet	3.81	0.8	3.01	64%
Caring for children	3.86	0.91	2.95	62%
Housework	3.73	0.77	2.96	62%
Working	3.62	0.97	2.65	56%
Commuting	3.45	0.89	2.56	54%

Interaction Partners	Positive	Negative	Balance	Ratio
Friends	4.36	0.67	3.69	100%
Relatives	4.17	0.8	3.37	91%
Spouse/SO	4.11	0.79	3.32	90%
Children	4.04	0.75	3.29	89%
Clients/customers	3.79	0.95	2.84	77%
Co-workers	3.76	0.92	2.84	77%
Alone	3.41	0.69	2.72	74%
Boss	3.52	1.09	2.43	66%

Kahneman, D., Krueger, A. B., Schkade, D., Schwarz, N., & Stone, A. A. (2004). A survey method for characterizing daily life experience: The Day Reconstruction Method (DRM). *Science, 306*, 1776–80.

36. This study, conducted with just over four hundred adults in Michigan, replicated this pattern of enjoying time with friends slightly more than romantic partners and children, but also found that these differences could be entirely explained by the different kinds of activities we do with our friends versus family members. Socializing, for instance, was the activity people tended to rate as the most consistently positive, and people reported socializing 65 percent of the time when they were with their friends, but only 28 percent of the time with their romantic partners and 27 percent of the time with their kids. In contrast, housework was among the least positive things people reported doing, and they reported doing this only 5 percent of the time with their friends—still a surprisingly high figure to me—but spent 11 percent of their time with their romantic partners doing housework.

    Anyone who wants to keep friends knows that you don't invite the gal pals or your buddies over for a fun night of vacuuming. When the researcher equated for these activities statistically, a very different pattern of how positive our experiences are with other people emerged. As the authors write, "When isolating the effects of the people who are present (by statistically controlling for the activities being performed), individuals do not appear to respond more favorably to the mere presence per se of their friends, rather than that of their partners or children. To the contrary—it appears that, when activities are statistically controlled, the presence of children predicts the largest differences in momentary positive emotions." It's not whom we're with that seems to matter for our happiness, but rather what we're doing with those we're with. This also helps to explain why being alone is so consistently less positive than being with others: Most of us don't seem to do that much when we're all alone. Hudson, N. W., Lucas, R. E., & Donnellan, M. B. (2020). Are we happier with others? An investigation of the links between spending time with others and subjective wellbeing. *Journal of Personality and Social Psychology, 119*(3), 672–94.
37. Curry, O. S., Rowland, L. A., Van Lissa, C. J., Zlotowitz, S., McAlaney, J., & Whitehouse, H. (2018). Happy to help? A systematic review and meta-analysis of the effects of performing acts of kindness on the well-being of the actor. *Journal of Experimental Social Psychology, 76,* 320–29.
38. Dunn, E. W., Aknin, L. B., & Norton, M. I. (2014). Prosocial spending and happiness: Using money to benefit others pays off. *Current Directions in Psychological Science, 23*(1), 41–47.
39. Scale these positive social actions up to the level of a country, and happy people become members of a happy country. In 2019, the World Happiness Report concluded that the happiest countries on the planet—places like Finland and Denmark—are those where people's sense of social support, connection to others, and trust in their government and fellow citizens is high. Places where the social fabric is torn apart by conflict as extreme as civil war, like Yemen and Syria, are the most unhappy places in the world.

    Helliwell, J., Layard, R., & Sachs, J. (2019). *World happiness report 2019.* New York: Sustainable Development Solutions Network. (Also available at www.worldhappiness.report.)

    Lok, I., & Dunn, E. W. (2020). Under what conditions does prosocial spending promote happiness? *Collabra: Psychology, 6*(1), 5; Aknin, L. B., Dunn, E. W., & Whillans, A. V. (2022). The emotional rewards of prosocial spending are robust and replicable in large samples. *Current Directions in Psychological Science, 31*(6),

536–45; Aknin, L. B., Dunn, E. W., Proulx, J., Lok, I., & Norton, M. I. (2020). Does spending money on others promote happiness? A registered replication report. *Journal of Personality and Social Psychology, 119*(2), e15–e26.

40. Dunn, E. W., Gilbert, D. T., & Wilson, T. D. (2011). If money doesn't make you happy, then you probably aren't spending it right. *Journal of Consumer Psychology, 21*(2), 115–25.
41. House, J. S., Landis, K., & Umberson, D. (1988). Social relationships and health. *Science, 241*(4865), 540–45.
42. The figure below, taken from a meta-analysis of 148 studies, shows the estimates of the increased odds of survival (versus death) associated with various risk factors. Being relatively well connected to others versus poorly connected is on par with the effect of smoking fewer than fifteen cigarettes a day versus more than fifteen. It is also notably bigger than whether you're classified as lean versus obese on the BMI, or live in an area with relatively low versus high air pollution.

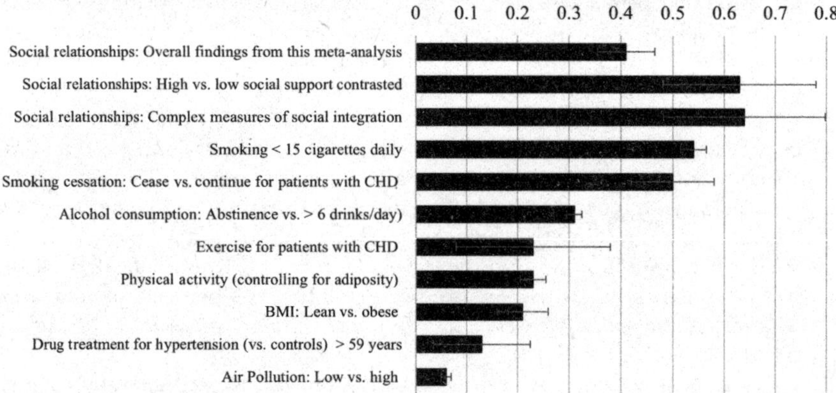

Holt-Lunstad, J., Smith, T. B., & Layton, J. B. (2010). Social relationships and mortality risk: A meta-analytic review. *PLOS Medicine, 7*(7), e1000316.

43. Research comparing the mortality risks from being alone versus feeling alone, sometimes referred to as received support versus perceived support or objective isolation versus subjective isolation, has found similar odds ratios for death associated with each type of isolation, working through distinct mechanisms. Uchino, B. (2009). Understanding the links between social support and physical health: A life-span perspective with emphasis on the separability of perceived and received support. *Perspectives on Psychological Science, 4*(3), 236–55; Holt-Lunstad, J., Smith, T. B., Baker, M., Harris, T., & Stephenson, D. (2015). Loneliness and social isolation as risk factors for mortality: A meta-analytic review. *Perspectives on Psychological Science, 10*(2), 227–37.
44. Research indicates that it's even better for your health, and your happiness, if the person you're around is also positive, happy, and satisfied with their life. Chopik, W., & O'Brien, E. (2017). Happy you, healthy me? Having a happy partner is independently associated with better health in oneself. *Health Psychology, 36*(1), 21–30.
45. Klinenberg, E. (2015). *Heat wave: A social autopsy of disaster in Chicago*. University of Chicago Press.

46. This warning sounds much funnier when you hear Laurie read it at hyperspeed on her podcast, *The Happiness Lab,* in the episode titled "Mistakenly Seeking Solitude" (2019, Season 1, Episode 4).
47. Cohen, S., Janicki-Deverts, D., Turner, R. B., & Doyle, W. J. (2015). Does hugging provide stress-buffering social support? A study of susceptibility to upper respiratory infection and illness. *Psychological Science, 26*(2), 135–47.
48. Cacioppo & Patrick (2008). *Loneliness.*
49. Whillans, A. V., Dunn, E. W., Sandstrom, G. M., Dickerson, S. S., & Madden K. M. (2016). Is spending money on others good for your heart? *Health Psychology, 35,* 574–83.

    Charles Darwin even shared a story consistent with this result, noting that his father—Robert, a medical doctor—once told him of an observant patient "who certainly had heart-disease and died from it," but who also seemed disappointed that his heart never acted irregularly when Darwin's father was around to check on it. Just like a car that starts working perfectly as soon as you take it to the shop, this patient, Darwin wrote, "positively stated that his pulse was irregular to an extreme degree yet to his great disappointment it invariably became regular as soon as my father entered the room."
50. Aristotle. (2014, p. 141). *Nicomachean ethics* (R. Crisp, Trans. & Ed.). New York: Cambridge University Press.
51. Daniel Gilbert quoted in "What Technology Can't Change About Happiness" by Adam Piore, published on September 10, 2015, on Nautilus (www.nautil.us).
52. Robinson, J. (2011, Nov. 17). "Happiness is love—and $75,000." Gallup.com.

2. The Choice

1. Pan, J. (2019). *Sorry I'm late, I didn't want to come: One introvert's year of saying yes.* Kansas City, Mo.: Andrews McMeel Publishing.
2. "Darwin on Marriage." Darwin Correspondence Project. University of Cambridge. (www.darwinproject.ac.uk).
3. Darwin, E. (1882). Reminiscences of Charles Darwin's last years. Darwin Online. Interestingly, Darwin's surprisingly peaceful experience at the end of life does not seem to be especially unusual. Although approaching death seems like it would be a terrifying and unpleasant experience for many people, those who are actually knowingly preparing for death tend to feel more positive than you might imagine. In one very clever experiment, researchers asked a group of healthy people to imagine that they were terminally ill with cancer, and had them create a blog post to describe their experience. These healthy participants were instructed, "Write a post for your blog, keeping in mind that you only have a few months left to live." Researchers then collected actual blog posts from people who were truly in the last few months of their lives with cancer (or with amyotrophic lateral sclerosis—ALS), and compared these actual blog posts with the imagined blog posts.

    Results indicated that the imagined blog posts used more negative words than the actual blog posts, and a separate group of people who read these posts indicated that the actual posts contained more positive emotions and less negative emotions than the imagined posts. In fact, the actual blog posts got even more positive and less negative as the patient's actual time until death got shorter. Getting even a bit more morbid, the researchers found similar results when they asked people to write what they thought would be their last words on death row if they were about to be executed "in a few days" for committing a capital offense. These imagined last words contained less positive emotion and more negative emotion than the actual last words, on average, of 396 inmates who were actually executed in Texas between 1982 and 2013. As the authors conclude, "Our results suggest that death is more positive than people expect: Meeting the grim reaper may not be as grim as it seems." Goranson, A., Ritter, R. S., Waytz, A., Norton, M. I., & Gray, K. (2017). Dying is unexpectedly positive. *Psychological Science, 28*(7), 988–99.

4. Bentham not only thought his theory described what people actually do—their actual choices and behavior—but also thought these two masters could be used to identify what people *should* do in any given situation. That is, he saw these two forces as the essence of morality. Figuring out the right thing to do in any situation was therefore reduced to a deceptively simple math problem: Add up the total amount of pleasure or positive outcomes from a decision across all people along with the total amount of pain or negative outcomes and then subtract, choosing whatever brings the most good for the most people. This is the foundational principle of utilitarianism. Bentham, J. (1780/2012, p. 1). *An introduction to the principles of morals and legislation.* Mineola, N.Y.: Dover Publications.
5. Gable, S. L., & Berkman, E. T. (2013). Making connections and avoiding loneliness: Approach and avoidance social motives and goals. In A. J. Elliot (Ed.), *Handbook of approach and avoidance motivation,* pp. 203–16. New York: Taylor & Francis.
6. Carver, C. S., Suton, S. K., & Scheier, M. F. (2000). Action, emotion, and personality: Emerging conceptual integration. *Personality and Social Psychology Bulletin, 26*(6), 741–51.
7. Gorman, A. (2022, Jan. 20). Why I almost didn't read my poem at the inauguration. *New York Times.*
8. This "first step" metaphor can even be quite literally true. Studies of marathon runners find that more people finish just ahead of round-numbered times (such as three hours) than just after those times, because those round-number times serve as a goal that runners speed up to achieve right at the end of the race. Allen, E., Dechow, P., Pope, D., & Wu, G. (2016). Reference-dependent preferences: Evidence from marathon runners. *Management Science, 63*(6), 1657–72.
9. Gilovich, T., Kerr, M., & Medvec, V. H. (1993). Effect of temporal perspective on subjective confidence. *Journal of Personality and Social Psychology, 64*(4), 552–60.
10. Pan, interview by author, March 23, 2022.
11. Carver, C. S., & White, T. L. (1994). Behavioral inhibition, behavioral activation, and affective responses to impending reward and punishment: The BIS/BAS Scales. *Journal of Personality and Social Psychology, 67*(2), 319–33.
12. These relationships between extroversion and approach, and neuroticism and avoidance, are typically very strong, in the ballpark of the relationship between height and weight in men. To see this, first note that the simplest way such relationships are measured statistically is through a correlation coefficient, which simply indexes the degree of relationship between two variables. A correlation coefficient can range anywhere from 1 (indicating a perfect positive relationship between two variables) to 0 (indicating no relationship at all between two variables) to -1 (indi-

cating a perfect negative relationship between two variables, such that high scores on one variable perfectly correspond to low numbers on another variable).

The typical correlation coefficient between height and weight in men is around 0.5. In one thorough survey of 329 college students, for instance, the observed correlation between scores on extroversion and approach orientation was 0.45, and the correlation between extroversion and avoidance orientation was only -0.13. In contrast, the observed correlation between scores on neuroticism and avoidance orientation was 0.59, and the correlation between neuroticism and approach orientation was only 0.13. Extroverts tend to be more approach oriented, just as taller men also tend to be heavier, while those who are more anxious (or neurotic) tend to be more avoidance oriented.

13. This quotation is the opening line of a paper reporting the results of five studies documenting that people tend to feel more positive when they are acting extroverted compared with when they are acting introverted. Wilt, J., Noftle, E. E., Fleeson, W., & Spain, J. S. (2012). The dynamic role of personality states in mediating the relationship between extraversion and positive affect. *Journal of Personality, 80*(5), 1205–36.

    This is a familiar refrain. Another group of researchers opens a paper by noting "there is a sizable research base documenting that more extraverted individuals experience greater positive affect" before citing thirty-two separate papers documenting this result. McNiel, J. M., Lowman, J. C., & Fleeson, W. (2010). The effect of state extraversion on four types of affect. *European Journal of Personality, 24*(1), 18–35.
14. Steel, P., Schmidt, J., & Shultz, J. (2008). Refining the relationship between personality and subjective wellbeing. *Psychological Bulletin, 134*(1), 138–61.
15. Lucas, R. E., Diener, E., Grob, A., Suh, E. M., & Shao, L. (2000). Cross-cultural evidence for the fundamental features of extraversion. *Journal of Personality and Social Psychology, 79*(3), 452–68.
16. Here's the way Will Fleeson, a psychologist at Wake Forest University and one of the world's experts on how personality affects well-being, put it in an email when I asked him if the impact of extroversion on well-being varied by culture: "I do believe that the relationship between extraversion and positive affect does vary across cultures, but I do not believe that the relationship varies substantially across cultures. There may be exceptions, of course, and there will always be some variation across cultures, sometimes even meaningful variation. In every country it has been investigated in which I am aware, a positive relationship has been found." Personal communication, Jan. 10, 2023.
17. Naidu, E. S., Paravati, E., & Gabriel, S. (2022). Staying happy even when staying 6 ft apart: The relationship between extroversion and social adaptability. *Personality and Individual Differences, 190,* 111549; Götz, F. M., Gvirtz, A., Galinsky, A., & Jachimowicz, J. M. (2021). How personality and policy predict pandemic behavior: Understanding sheltering-in-place in 54 countries at the onset of COVID-19. *American Psychologist, 76*(1), 39–49.

    Interestingly, the relationship between extroversion and COVID-19 infections in one large-scale analysis of people in the United States and Germany was small and inconsistent, suggesting that extroverts might have moved around more during the COVID-19 pandemic, especially as it became more prolonged, but did so in a way that did not spread the disease as much as one might have expected.

Neuroticism, however, did serve as a protective factor against COVID-19 spread, suggesting that the happiest and healthiest people during the pandemic were the small number of people who score highly both on extroversion and on neuroticism. Peters, H., Götz, F. M., Ebert, T., Müller, S. R., Rentfrow, P. J., Gosling, S. D., Obschonka, M., Ames, D., Potter, J., & Matz, S. C. (2023). Regional personality differences predict variation in early COVID-19 infections and mobility patterns indicative of social distancing. *Journal of Personality and Social Psychology, 124*(4), 848–72.

18. Fleeson, W., & Gallagher, P. (2009). The implications of Big Five standing for the distribution of trait manifestation in behavior: Fifteen experience-sampling studies and a meta-analysis. *Journal of Personality and Social Psychology, 97*(6), 1097–114.
19. Wilt et al. (2012). Dynamic role of personality states in mediating the relationship between extraversion and positive affect.
20. Fleeson, W., Malanos, A. B., & Achille, N. M. (2002). An intraindividual process approach to the relationship between extraversion and positive affect: Is acting extraverted as "good" as being extraverted? *Journal of Personality and Social Psychology, 83,* 1409–22.
21. Meuller, S., Ram, N., Conroy, D. E., Pincus, A. L., Gerstorf, D., & Wagner, J. (2019). Happy like a fish in water? The role of personality-situation fit for momentary happiness in social interactions across the adult lifespan. *European Journal of Personality, 33,* 298–316.
22. Kuijpers, E., Pickett, J., Wille, B., & Hofmans, J. (2022). Do you feel better when you behave more extraverted than you are? The relationship between cumulative counterdispositional extraversion and positive feelings. *Personality & Social Psychology Bulletin, 48*(4), 606–23.
23. Margolis, S., & Lyubomirsky, S. (2020). Experimental manipulation of extraverted and introverted behavior and its effects on well-being. *Journal of Experimental Psychology: General, 149*(4), 719–31.
24. From Sonja Lyubomirsky, speaking on Sanjay Gupta's podcast, *Chasing Life* (Episode 450, "The Habits of Happy People").
25. Even the researchers themselves were surprised at this result. "Overall, and in contrast to what could have been expected," they concluded, "our results did not suggest that counter-trait behavior would be particularly depleting. Although this contradicts the common view that sociability is especially depleting for introverts, it is in line with previous research." Leikas, S. L., & Ilmarinen, V. J. (2017). Happy now, tired later? Extraverted and conscientious behavior are related to immediate mood gains, but later fatigue. *Journal of Personality, 85*(5), 603–15.
26. To provide a little more detail, these researchers did find some evidence that acting out of character was cognitively taxing, but it didn't come from acting introverted rather than from acting extroverted. Specifically, extroverts who were told to act introverted in a small group conversation performed a little worse after the conversation on a test of cognitive functioning (namely, they had more difficulty inhibiting intrusive thoughts on a Stroop task). Apparently, being more outgoing in a conversation was not more mentally taxing for introverts, but being quiet in a small group conversation took some mental effort for extroverts. Zelenski, J. M., Santoro, M. S., & Whelan, D. C. (2012). Would introverts be better off if they acted more like extraverts? Exploring emotional and cognitive consequences of counterdispositional behavior. *Emotion, 12*(2), 290–303.

27. Fleeson, W., & Wilt, J. (2010). The relevance of Big Five trait content in behavior to subjective authenticity: Do high levels of within-person behavioral variability undermine or enable authenticity achievement? *Journal of Personality, 78*(4), 1353–82; Ching, C. M., Church, A. T., Katigbak, M. S., Reyes, J. A. S., Tanaka-Matsumi, J., Takaoka, S., Zhang, H., Shen, J., Arias, R. M., Rincon, B. C., & Ortiz, F. A. (2014). The manifestation of traits in everyday behavior and affect: A five-culture study. *Journal of Research in Personality, 48,* 1–16; Sherman, R. A., Nave, C. S., & Funder, D. C. (2012). Properties of persons and situations related to overall and distinctive personality-behavior congruence. *Journal of Research in Personality, 46*(1), 87–101.
28. Cooper, A. B., Sherman, R. A., Rauthmann, J. F., Serfass, D. G., & Brown, N. A. (2018). Feeling good and authentic: Experienced authenticity in daily life is predicted by positive feelings and situation characteristics, not trait-state consistency. *Journal of Research in Personality, 77,* 57–69; Wilt, J., Sun, J., Jacques-Hamilton, R., & Smillie, L. D. (2023). Why is authenticity associated with being and acting extraverted? Exploring the mediating role of positive affect. *Self and Identity, 22,* 896–931.
29. Kuijpers et al. (2022). Do you feel better when you behave more extraverted than you are?
30. Jacques-Hamilton, R., Sun, J., & Smillie, L. D. (2019). Costs and benefits of acting extraverted: A randomized controlled trial. *Journal of Experimental Psychology: General, 148*(9), 1538–56.
31. In fact, if you consistently change how you make *the choice,* then you are likely to change your personality as well. In the experiment I described earlier in this chapter, where 131 people were asked to act extroverted one week and introverted another week, these participants also scored higher in trait extroversion (as measured by two different personality tests) after their extroverted week and scored lower on trait extroversion after the introverted week. Changing the choices people made over the course of a week also changed the type of person they reported being.

    The professional golfer Greg Norman tells an interesting story about changing himself from being more avoidant to more approach oriented, in a single moment, early in his career. In an interview with the economist Steve Levitt on his podcast, *People I (Mostly) Admire,* Norman recalls his early days playing professional golf. Norman recalled that some people at the top of their game really seemed to be open and welcoming of the social attention that came from being a top player, whereas some seemed to withdraw and hold back from it in a way that made the attention more difficult and unpleasant to manage.

    Norman noted that when he won his first professional tournament in 1976 (his fifth PGA tournament), "I was an introvert and I couldn't get up in front of the microphone and speak. When I went into the clubhouse to be with the members of the golf club at the end for presentation, I was a shy kid standing in the corner. And I, actually, said to myself, 'If I want to be a great golfer, I have to change the way I feel right now.' It was a snap decision I made because I had to get up right there in front of [a lot of] people inside the clubhouse, all celebrating. And right there and then, I pulled myself out from being an introvert into being a public figure." Although Norman might be unique in changing his personality habits in a single moment, research definitely indicates that becoming consistently more approach oriented and sociable is possible. Margolis & Lyubomirsky (2020). Experimental manipulation of extraverted and introverted behavior and its effects on well-being.

3. Unexpected Values

1. Einstein, A. (1936). Physics and reality. *Journal of the Franklin Institute, 221*(3), 349–82.
2. In fact, researchers find that a person's face can convey as wide a range of first impressions, depending on the expression they make, as the range of first impressions made across different people showing the same facial expression. In other words, your own face can vary so much from one expression to another that you can go from looking completely friendly and trustworthy in one moment to completely unfriendly and untrustworthy in another moment. This means that you should be careful about drawing any kind of inference about what someone is generally like from their facial expression or appearance. Todorov, A., & Porter, J. (2014). Misleading first impressions: Different for different images of the same person. *Psychological Science, 25*, 1404–17.
3. In the actual experiment, the scenario people considered was slightly different. They were simply told about the $50 gift card (to a Barnes & Noble bookstore) with the two-week use restriction and asked how much they would be willing to pay for it, or were told about a 50 percent chance of getting either a $50 or a $100 gift card with a two-week restriction and asked how much they would be willing to pay for it. In another experiment conducted with University of Chicago undergraduates, using real gift certificates to a bookstore and real money rather than a hypothetical scenario, these students said they would be willing to pay, on average, $66.15 for a $100 gift certificate, $38 for a $50 certificate, but only $28 for a fifty-fifty chance to win either a $100 gift card or a $50 gift card. The uncertainty of the coin flip made the chance to win more money *less* attractive rather than more attractive. Gneezy, U., List, J. A., & Wu, G. (2006). The uncertainty effect: When a risky prospect is valued less than its worst possible outcome. *Quarterly Journal of Economics, 121*(4), 1283–309.
4. Not realizing that the $100 lottery is available, or misunderstanding the odds of a coin flip, does not seem to explain the uncertainty effect because making sure everyone is aware of the better option, and removing anyone who misunderstands the odds, still yields the effect.

   Nor does it seem to be that people are trying to avoid feeling disappointed by not winning the substantially better option, or even any aversion to playing a "lottery," because the uncertainty effect still emerges even when the two options are quite similar (for example, a fifty-fifty chance of winning a $50 versus a $55 gift certificate) and when there is no mention of gambling or a "lottery." Simonsohn, U. (2009). Direct risk aversion: Evidence from risky prospects valued below their worst outcome. *Psychological Science, 20*(6), 686–92; Newman, G., & Mochon, D. (2012). Why are lotteries valued less? Multiple tests of a direct risk-aversion mechanism. *Judgment and Decision Making, 7*(1), 19–24.
5. The less you know about other people, the bigger your uncertainty, and the more your expectations warp toward pessimism and avoidance. As we get to know people over repeated positive experiences, that uncertainty diminishes, and our reluctance to reach out fades. This is surely a large part of why we'd be reluctant to talk with a stranger but will happily reach out and connect to our friends. In one online survey of Americans that quantifies this rather obvious point, 93 percent of respondents said they would talk to a friend seated next to them in a waiting

room but only 3 percent said they'd talk to a stranger. Every single person in this survey said they would talk to a friend sitting next to them on a train, on a plane, or in a cab, but only 24 percent, 32 percent, and 49 percent, respectively, said they would talk to a stranger in each of these locations. Are these strangers likely to be ax murders, kidnappers, or overly judgmental jerks who should be avoided? No. But even if you knew *exactly* the odds of experiencing positive or negative outcomes in a social interaction, the nonzero chance that they *might* be will nudge you toward keeping your distance. Epley & Schroeder (2014). Mistakenly seeking solitude.

6. Gouldner, A. W. (1960). The norm of reciprocity: A preliminary statement. *American Sociological Review, 25,* 161–78; Fehr, E., Fischbacher, U., & Gächter, S. (2002). Strong reciprocity, human cooperation, and the enforcement of social norms. *Human Nature, 13*(1), 1–25; Fehr, E. & Fischbacher, U. (2003). The nature of human altruism. *Nature, 425,* 785–91.
7. Jamil Zaki quoted in "Our Fear of Rejection Is Like Our Fear of Sharks . . . Totally Out of Proportion to the Real Risks" on Laurie Santos's blog (www.drlauriesantos.com), Aug. 1, 2024.
8. Fiske, S. T., Cuddy, A. J., & Glick, P. (2007). Universal dimensions of social cognition: Warmth and competence. *Trends in Cognitive Sciences, 11*(2), 77–83.
9. Wojciszke, B., Bazinska, R., & Jaworski, M. (1998). On the dominance of moral categories in impression formation. *Personality and Social Psychology Bulletin, 24*(12), 1251–63.
10. For instance, in one experiment, volunteers viewed pictures of human faces either for a hundred milliseconds or for as long as they wanted and then evaluated how trustworthy the person seemed (a measure of their warmth), or how competent the person seemed. Judgments made without any time limits give a good sense of what you might consider a fully formed impression of the person, allowing researchers to measure how closely your judgments based on just a brief hundred-millisecond snapshot of someone approximate what you'd think of them if you had as much time as you wanted. These researchers found that judgments of trustworthiness after just a hundred-millisecond snapshot were considerably more consistent with the judgment you would make with as much time as you wanted than were judgments of someone's competence. Willis, J., & Todorov, A. (2006). First impressions: Making up your mind after a 100-ms exposure to a face. *Psychological Science, 17*(7), 592–98.
11. Willis & Todorov (2006). First impressions.
12. Cogsdill, E. J., Todorov, A. T., Spelke, E. S., & Banaji, M. R. (2014). Inferring character from faces: A developmental study. *Psychological Science, 25*(5), 1132–39.
13. William James's actual assertion was, "My thinking is first and last and always for the sake of my doing, and I can only do one thing at a time." James, W. (1950). *The principles of psychology* (Vol. 2, p. 333). New York: Dover Publications.
14. Hur, J., Ruttan, R., & Shea, C. T. (2020). The unexpected power of positivity: Predictions versus decisions about advisor selection. *Journal of Experimental Psychology: General, 149*(10), 1969–86.
15. Gretzky, W. (2012). *Gretzky: An autobiography*. (With R. Reilly). Toronto: HarperCollins Publishers.
16. Feiler, D., Tong, J., & Larrick, R. (2013). Biased judgment in censored environments. *Management Science, 59*(3), 573–91.

17. Gary Becker's Nobel Memorial Prize in Economics address (delivered Dec. 9, 1992) can be found online at the Nobel Prize website (www.nobelprize.org).

4. Hello, Stranger

1. The quotations from Claire in this chapter come from a conversation we had on September 16, 2022, and several follow-up emails afterward. I confirmed Claire's memory by talking with her dad, Loren, on September 26, 2022. You can read more about Claire's experience talking to people on the trains in an interview by Sirena He: "Kindness of Strangers on the Train," published on June 26, 2022, on the online platform Medium (www.medium.com).
2. Just in case you spot one on the New York City subway one day, here's an honorary badge that Claire sent to me:

3. In an even more extreme example, in the midst of a larger unfolding terrorist attack, Rachel Edri returned to her home in Ofakim, Israel, on October 7, 2023, after air raid sirens had sent her to a bomb shelter, and found a group of Hamas militants waiting. Unknown to Rachel, these militants were part of a wave of horror spreading from Gaza into Israel, killing Israeli citizens—men, women, children, and babies—almost indiscriminately. She said, "One of the terrorists said to me: 'you remind me of my mother.' I told him, 'I am really like your mother. I will help you; I will take care of you. What do you need?' "

   Unaware of the horrors happening outside her home, she did her best to treat the men as kindly as she could, even trying to calm one after he struck her across the face with the butt of his rifle. She fed them and gave them Coke Zero to drink, which they said they liked more than regular Coke. "After they drank and ate, they became much calmer," she said. "I started having conversations, and at one point I even forgot for a moment that they were terrorists." After seventeen hours, Rachel's son, Eviatar, was able to give a local rescue team information about the house that allowed them to rescue both her and her husband unharmed. Alone in the house, the militants were eventually shot and killed by the rescue team.

   After the attack, Rachel was celebrated around the world as a shining example of the legendary Jewish mother who wraps up family, friends, and strangers alike in warmth while overfeeding every one of them. Edri's brother was not at all surprised by his sister's actions; she was known for her generosity while serving meals to soldiers at a nearby military base. Speaking of their upbringing in a working-class family with twelve children, her brother said, "We learned to survive and acquired the wisdom of life like street cats. You can see that in how [Rachel] acted." If you'd like to read more about Edri, Julia Frankel wrote a piece on her, "Woman Becomes Israeli Folk Hero for Plying Hamas Militants with Snacks Until Rescue Mission Arrives," *AP News*, Oct. 18, 2023.

4. To be a little more specific, the people in this experiment were romantic couples who participated in each session with another couple. These people were paired up to have a conversation either with their own partner or with the opposite-sex person from the other couple, to keep the gender pairings the same. The people in this experiment thought they'd have a more positive experience with their own partner, but they actually enjoyed the conversations equally regardless of whom they were talking with. Dunn, E. W., Biesanz, J. C., Human, L. J., & Finn, S. (2007). Misunderstanding the affective consequences of everyday social interactions: The hidden benefits of putting one's best face forward. *Journal of Personality and Social Psychology, 92*(6), 990–1005.
5. Mallett, R. K., Wilson, T. D., & Gilbert, D. T. (2008). Expect the unexpected: Failure to anticipate similarities leads to an intergroup forecasting error. *Journal of Personality and Social Psychology, 94*(2), 265–77.
6. Sandstrom, G. M., & Boothby, E. J. (2020). Why do people avoid talking to strangers? A mini meta-analysis of predicted fears and actual experiences talking to a stranger. *Self and Identity, 20*(1), 47–71.
7. The authors of this research also noted that the increase in positive mood before versus after the conversation occurred for people across the lifespan, from age twenty to seventy, contradicting anyone who thinks (sometimes, like me) that kids these days don't know how to talk to each other. The graph below shows that the mismatch between expectations and experiences is fairly consistent across age groups. The bigger problem may be that we're not trying to talk to each other as much as would be optimal for our own well-being.

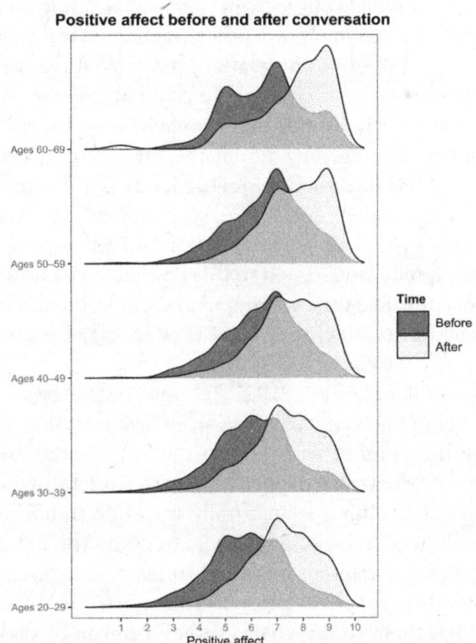

This figure is reprinted from Reece, A., Cooney, G., Bull, P., Chung, C., Dawson, B., Fitzpatrick, C., et al. (2023). The CANDOR corpus: Insights from a large multimodal dataset of naturalistic conversation. *Science Advances* 9(13), eadf3197.

8. Sandstrom, G. M., & Dunn, E. W. (2014). Is efficiency overrated? Minimal social interactions lead to belonging and positive affect. *Social Psychological & Personality Science, 5*(4), 437–42.
9. Gunaydin, G., Oztekin, H., Karabulut, D. H., & Salman-Engin, S. (2021). Minimal social interactions with strangers predict greater subjective well-being. *Journal of Happiness Studies, 22*(4), 1839–53.
10. Ascigil, E., Gunaydin, G., Selcuk, E., Sandstrom, G. M., & Aydin, E. (2023). Minimal social interactions and life satisfaction: The role of greeting, thanking, and conversing. *Social Psychological and Personality Science, 16*(2), 202–13.
11. Epley & Schroeder (2014). Mistakenly seeking solitude.
12. Epley & Schroeder (2014). Mistakenly seeking solitude.
13. The belief that another person's mind directly matches their action is so routine that psychologists have a name for it: the correspondence bias. However, the link between what's on our minds and how we act is far more complicated than our snap judgments might presume. In fact, this bias is mistaken so often that psychologists have a second name for it: the fundamental attribution error. You can learn the precise details of this two-named bias here: Gilbert, D. T., & Malone, P. S. (1995). The correspondence bias. *Psychological Bulletin, 117*(1), 21–38.
14. Bill Nye captures this philosophy in Lesson 6 of his Science and Problem-Solving Master Class (www.masterclass.com): "Everyone You'll Ever Meet Knows Something You Don't." He also passed this wisdom along in a commencement address he gave at Goucher College on May 24, 2019 (transcript available at www.goucher.edu).
15. I talked with this wonderful couple from the moment they sat down next to me (I was in the window seat) to the moment we walked off the plane on our two-hour flight. Right at the end of our conversation, they asked me if I had a place to stay in Washington, D.C., and if I might be interested in staying with them while I was visiting. That gesture surely sounds odd or maybe even inappropriate just hearing about it through my writing now, but at the time, after a nearly two-hour deep conversation, we all felt like good enough friends that heading to their place for dinner and unpacking in their guest room seemed perfectly reasonable. I, however, was going downtown to speak at a conference and felt unable to take them up on their kind offer. I regret that decision to this day because I now know I would have had a much more enjoyable time visiting with them in their home than I did sitting alone that evening in my hotel room. If I ever have the great fortune of meeting them again, I'll make *the choice* differently.
16. Atir, S., Wald, K. A., & Epley, N. (2022). Talking to strangers is surprisingly informative. *Proceedings of the National Academy of Sciences, 110*(34), e2206992119.
17. Underestimating the amount we'll learn in a conversation also doesn't seem to depend on whether we're trying explicitly to learn something or not, I think mostly because learning is something we naturally try to do in almost any conversation and therefore don't need to be explicitly told to do it. The figure below shows how much people in one experiment expected to learn and how much they actually learned when we asked people to do their best to learn in the conversation (learning goal) or just left them to do whatever they'd normally do in the conversation (control goal). The figure below also shows that people, as we find time and time again, expected to find the conversations to be less interesting and enjoyable than

they actually did, expected to like their partner less than they actually did, and also expected to feel less lucky to have been paired up with their conversation partner than they actually did. These results also did not depend on whether people were trying to learn something in their conversation or not. Atir, Wald, & Epley (2022). Talking to strangers is surprisingly informative.

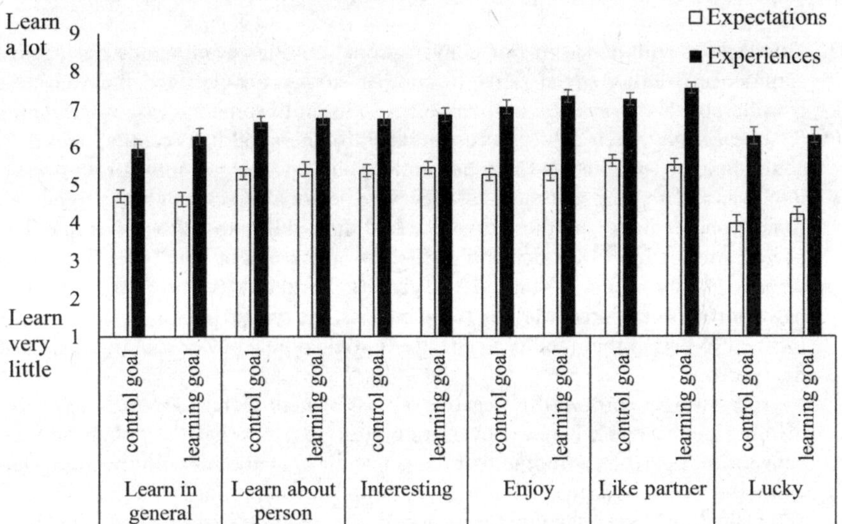

18. We found a similar result in another experiment where we asked people to either spend ten minutes talking with another person in the experiment or spend ten minutes surfing the internet. A conversation can wander back and forth to some shared interest with another person that you might never have anticipated, whereas surfing the internet is largely under your own control and hence is a little easier to guess where it might go. We found that people reported learning more in their ten-minute conversation than they did in their ten-minute web surf, but they did not anticipate this outcome beforehand. These participants actually expected to learn the same amount, on average, in their conversation as they did surfing the web, again meaning that they underestimated how much they would learn in conversation more than they underestimated how much they would learn surfing the web. Atir, Wald, & Epley (2022). Talking with strangers is surprisingly informative.
19. The only time we've ever found that people didn't underestimate how much they would learn in an open-ended conversation with a stranger was when their conversation was too short to learn something, because learning something requires time. In one experiment we conducted with passengers in ride-sharing vehicles (using Uber or Lyft) leaving Midway Airport, those who were able to have a more than ten-minute conversation with their driver tended to learn more than they expected while those who had too short of a ride did not. As far as we can tell, the only consistent way to learn very little from talking with a stranger is to not have much of a conversation at all. Atir, S., Wald, K. A., & Epley, N. (2022). Unpublished data, University of Chicago.

20. Hume, D. (1751/1777). *An enquiry concerning the principles of morals.* In L. A. Selby-Bigge (Ed.), *Enquiries concerning human understanding and concerning the principles of morals,* pp. 268–69. Oxford: Clarendon Press.
21. The author, Hugo Reid, wrote this book under the pen name Roger Boswell. Boswell, R. (1867). *The art of conversation, giving hints, suggestions, and rules for cultivating and promoting pleasant social intercourse.* London: Cassell, Petter, & Galpin.
22. This lack of confidence in our conversational abilities even stands out against confidence in other social skills. In another survey, people rated themselves as considerably above average in their ability to listen to someone who is struggling (71st percentile), their ability to cooperate with others (69th percentile), and their ability to express gratitude (67th percentile), but "engaging in informal conversation" was still a virtue that most felt they were personally lacking (45th percentile). In fact, people in yet another survey ranked their ability to talk with people they haven't met before (48th percentile) slightly below "doing new types of manual labor (e.g., "shoveling, sawing"; 54th percentile) and only slightly above "playing new sports" (40th percentile). By these metrics, the typical person would be more inclined to bet on their ability to effectively wield a new power tool than talk to a new person.

    Interestingly, some of this negative self-assessment seems to stem from people blaming themselves when a conversation goes poorly rather than blaming their conversation partner, a finding that is again somewhat at odds with the more general self-serving pattern of accepting responsibility when things go well in our lives and deflecting blame when things go poorly. In one study, people who looked back on a past conversation that went well reported being just as responsible for the good outcome as their partner, but when they recalled a conversation that went poorly, people said they were more responsible for the bad outcome than their partner was. After having an actual conversation with a new person in a laboratory setting, people blamed themselves for the low points in the conversation while claiming their partner was largely responsible for the high points.

    "Together," the authors summarize (p. 565), "these studies indicate that people approach the common activity of engaging in informal conversation with an unusual level of self-doubt." Welker, C., Walker, J., Boothby, E., & Gilovich, T. (2023). Pessimistic assessments of ability in informal conversation. *Journal of Applied Social Psychology, 53*(7), 555–69.
23. Another group of researchers found a similar result in cross-generational conversations. This experiment, led by Gillian Sandstrom in coordination with the U.K.'s Economic and Social Research Council, recruited a little over two hundred people from the United States and the U.K. who were either twenty-five to thirty years old or sixty-five to seventy years old and asked them to have a conversation with either someone of the same generation or someone of a different generation. As researchers observe over and over again, people's expectations before their conversation were more pessimistic than their actual experiences warranted. In particular, people underestimated how much they would enjoy their conversation, like their partner, and have in common with their partner (especially when talking with someone of a different generation).

    As we found in our experiments, people also reported learning more from their partner than they thought their partner had learned from them. Although people reported learning more when having a conversation with someone of a different generation, the gap between how much people reported learning and how much they thought their partner learned was a similar size regardless of whom people were having a conversation with. Sandstrom, G. M., Moreton, J., Ebert, J., Boothby, E., & Cooney, G. (2023). Cross-generational conversations: Expectations and experiences. Unpublished Manuscript, University of Essex. Available for download at www.gilliansandstrom.com.

24. Boothby, E. J., Cooney, G., Sandstrom, G. M., & Clark, M. S. (2018). The liking gap in conversations: Do people like us more than we think? *Psychological Science, 29*(11), 1742–56; Mastroianni, A., Cooney, G., Boothby, E. J., & Reece, A. G. (2021). The liking gap in groups and teams. *Organizational Behavior and Human Decision Processes, 162,* 109–22; Wolf, W., Nafe, A., & Tomasello, M. (2021). The development of the liking gap: Children older than 5 years think that partners evaluate them less positively than they evaluate their partners. *Psychological Science, 32*(5), 789–98.
25. *Independent,* Dec. 17, 2015 (www.independent.co.uk/us).
26. Schroeder, J., Lyons, D., & Epley, N. (2022). Hello, stranger? Pleasant conversations are preceded by concerns about starting one. *Journal of Experimental Psychology: General, 151*(5), 1141–53.
27. One interesting and unexpected finding in our London experiment was that these commuters actually *did* expect that they would enjoy their commute more if they talked to a stranger. Although they still underestimated how much they would enjoy connecting with a stranger, they didn't expect to enjoy their experience less than keeping to themselves or doing whatever they normally do. I think this difference stemmed from an important change we made to the experiment itself. In contrast to what we did in Chicago, where a separate group of people merely imagined how they would feel if they tried to have a conversation with a stranger, the same group of people in London predicted how they would feel if they were able to follow the instructions and then reported how they actually felt after having a conversation.

    Whereas those in Chicago were imagining trying to start a conversation and possibly not finding someone who wanted to talk, those in London imagined a conversation they were actually going to have. Again, the barrier to having a conversation wasn't in thinking that talking would necessarily be unpleasant, but rather thinking that almost nobody else on the train would be willing to talk if you tried. Indeed, our London commuters in an additional experiment were even more pessimistic than our Chicago commuters, estimating that only 25.4 percent of their fellow riders would be willing to talk (compared with 46.4 percent in our Chicago experiment). It's hard to know whether this pessimism about starting a conversation stemmed from being in a different location, or in a different time—roughly nine years later, when earbuds seem to have become surgically implanted in almost everyone's ears. Schroeder, Lyons, & Epley (2022). Hello, stranger?
28. In one series of experiments, for instance, those who were more introverted expected that they would feel less positive if they were asked to act extroverted in a laboratory task (such as participating in an interview, or working in a group), but they felt more positive than those instructed to act more introverted, meaning

that introverts underestimated how positive they would feel acting extroverted. Zelenski, J. M., Whelan, D. C., Nealis, L. J., Besner, C. M., Santoro, M. S., & Wynn, J. E. (2013). Personality and affective forecasting: Trait introverts underpredict the hedonic benefits of acting extraverted. *Journal of Personality and Social Psychology, 104,* 1092–108.

We observed a similar result on the trains in Chicago, where those who were more extroverted thought they'd feel more positive in the connection condition than those who were more introverted, but extroversion wasn't meaningfully related to how people actually felt after talking with a stranger. We did not, however, observe this result on buses in Chicago or on the trains in London. Epley & Schroeder (2014). Mistakenly seeking solitude; Schroeder, Lyons, & Epley (2022). Hello, stranger?

29. Specifically, people in this experiment were asked to have a roughly fifteen-minute conversation with a stranger. After three minutes of talking, the people in the experiment indicated on a survey how much they were enjoying the conversation. Roughly half of these people were then asked to imagine that they continued having their conversation for another twelve minutes, and predicted how they thought they would feel after each three-minute session in the conversation. The other half instead continued having their conversation, and indicated how much they were enjoying it in three-minute intervals.

Those who merely imagined having their conversation expected that they would enjoy it a little less with each passing three-minute period, whereas those who actually had their conversation reported no decrease in their enjoyment as the conversation went on. The researchers observed this result both in open conversations when people could talk about whatever they wanted and when people were given short icebreaker questions to discuss. Kardas, M., Schroeder, J., & O'Brien, E. (2022). Keep talking: (Mis)understanding the hedonic trajectory of conversation. *Journal of Personality and Social Psychology, 123*(4), 717–40.

30. For instance, in a group of multiple apartment buildings where each building had only eight units, four on the first floor and four on the second floor, 44 percent of residents named their next-door neighbor as their closest friend. Just another twenty-two feet to the next neighbor's door cut the friend rate in half, to only 22.5 percent, and moving three doors away cut it in half again, to 10 percent. Buildings within each community were only forty-five feet apart, but most people (≈65 percent) indicated that their closest friend lived in the same building, even though there were very few people in each building compared with the entire graduate housing community.

To put it another way, the odds in this study of being friends with someone in a unit within your own building were 20 percent, or one in five, whereas the odds of being friends with someone in any given unit outside their own building were only 0.003 percent, or three in a thousand. It's no surprise to me why my own family is much better friends with our next-door neighbors than we are with the families who live across the street, or around the block from us, or on the other side of town. Most people are likable, meaning that the people you tend to like are also those you come in contact with the most. Festinger, L., Schacter, S., & Back, K. (1950). *Social pressures in informal groups: A study of human factors in housing.* Stanford, Calif.: Stanford University Press.

31. Segal, M. W. (1974). Alphabet and attraction: An unobtrusive measure of the effect of propinquity in a field setting. *Journal of Personality and Social Psychology, 30*(5), 654–57.
32. Reis, H. T., Maniaci, M. R., Caprariello, P. A., Eastwick, P. W., & Finkel, E. J. (2011). Familiarity does indeed promote attraction in live interaction. *Journal of Personality and Social Psychology, 101*(3), 557–70.
33. The most reliable limits we've found so far on the positive consequences of sociality after looking carefully with our microscopes are overly negative expectations in our own minds. Being somewhat pessimistic about how positively others are likely to respond when we reach out to them can keep us from reaching out to people we'd otherwise enjoy and learn from, needlessly narrowing our social circles by as much as 50 percent, according to one experiment we conducted online.

    In this experiment, we asked people in groups of five to first introduce themselves to each other and then report how much they thought they would enjoy talking to each of the other four people in their group for twenty minutes, and to also report how much they thought they would enjoy just taking a break and doing whatever they wanted for the next twenty minutes (which meant not talking to any of the other people in the group). We also asked them to rank order what they wanted to do for the next twenty minutes, including talking to each of the other four people and also not talking to anyone by taking a break.

    We found that people ranked taking a break, on average, right in the middle, meaning that they thought two people in the group were worth talking to but the other two would be less preferable than taking a break and not talking at all. However, when we actually randomly assigned people to do one of the five options, these same people found talking to any person in the group—even the person they least wanted to talk to—more enjoyable than taking a break alone for twenty minutes. If given the opportunity, these people would have avoided half of the conversations they had, and would have ended up being less happy for choosing to avoid these conversations. Hirschi, Q., & Epley, N. (2023). Overly pessimistic expectations narrow social networks. Unpublished data, University of Chicago.
34. Here are the actual results from this cab experiment, with the talkers' and loners' expectations on the left and their experiences on the right. These results are described in experiment 3 of Epley & Schroeder (2014). Mistakenly seeking solitude.

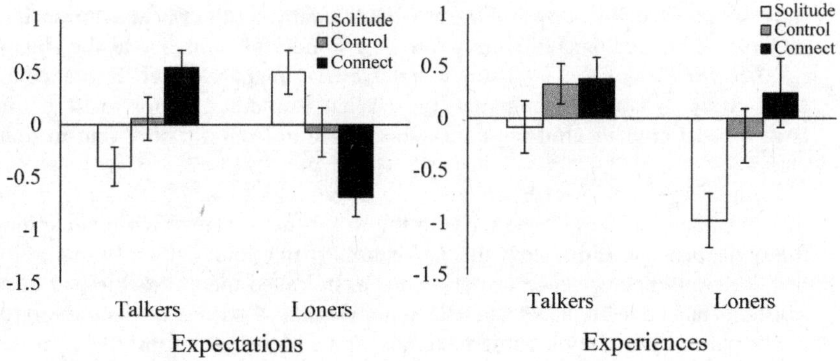

35. Sandstrom, G. M., Boothby, E. J., & Cooney, G. (2022). Talking to strangers: A week-long intervention reduces psychological barriers to social connection. *Journal of Experimental Social Psychology, 102,* 104356.
36. More completely, Milgram wrote, "The requirements of appropriate social behavior on the subway are, on the face of it, simple. One rule of subway behavior is that seats are filled on a first-come, first-served basis. Another implicit rule is one that discourages passengers from talking to one another. Even though riders are often squeezed into very close proximity, they are rarely observed to converse." Milgram, S., & Sabini, J. (1978). On maintaining social norms: A field experiment in the subway. In A. Baum, J. E. Singer, & S. Valins (Eds.), *Advances in environmental psychology: Vol. 1. The urban environment,* pp. 33–34. Hillsdale, N.J.: Erlbaum.

5. The How of Connection

1. Smith, A. (1759/1982). *The theory of moral sentiments.* D. D. Raphael & A. L. Macfie (Eds.). Liberty Fund.
2. Leonard C. Bruno's "Mr. Watson, Come Here" documents Bell's notebooks and personal correspondence and can be found through the Library of Congress (www.loc.gov).
3. Tomlinson is quoted as saying that the first email test messages were "completely forgettable" in his *New York Times* obituary, "Ray Tomlinson, Who Put the @ Sign in Email, Is Dead at 74," March 7, 2016.
4. Malinowski, B. (1923, p. 310). The problem of meaning in primitive languages. In C. K. Ogden & I. A. Richards (Eds.), *The meaning of meaning,* pp. 296–336. London: K. Paul, Trend, Trubner.
5. Cooney, G., & Reece, A. (2024). NaturalTurn: A method to segment transcripts into naturalistic conversational turns. Unpublished manuscript, University of Pennsylvania. arxiv.org/abs/2403.15615.
6. Reece et al. (2023). CANDOR corpus.
7. One of the most eye-opening research presentations I have ever seen was Provine presenting his research on laughter in the Psychology Department at Cornell University when I was a young PhD student. I remember it like a lightning bolt of energy to my sometimes sputtering mind. Provine, as many scientists do, started by trying to jettison any preconceived notions he had about laughter in order to study why we laugh just by looking at what the data had to say. "My approach to understanding laughter," Provine wrote in a wonderful summary in the *American Scientist,* "is one that a visiting extraterrestrial might take were it to encounter a group of laughing human beings. What would the visitor make of the large bipedal animals emitting paroxysms of sound from a toothy vent in their faces?"

   One of Provine's most basic questions as an alien to laughter was, when do people laugh? It makes all the sense in the world that we laugh when something funny happens around us, but this isn't what Provine found at all. In one of his first "sidewalk neuroscience" experiments, as he called them, Provine had three assistants hang out "in places where laughter was likely," such as student unions or public places where people gathered to talk, and told them to record the comment that immediately preceded the laughter. Documenting twelve hundred instances of laughing, Provine observed that speakers laughed 46 percent more often than listeners did, indicating that laughter was not most often a response to something funny, and that only 10–15 percent of the comments that preceded laughter were actually seen as being even remotely funny when the researchers carefully evaluated them. "Banal comments like 'where have you been' or 'it was nice meeting you, too' were the typical fare," Provine noted. "Most prelaugh dialogue is like that of an interminable television situation comedy scripted by an extremely ungifted writer."

In another study, Provine asked university students to document every time they laughed as best they could over the course of the week in a diary. Each day, students had about a 1 percent chance of laughing when they were alone, but a nearly 40 percent chance of laughing when they were with someone else. This ratio, if anything, was actually larger than the difference between smiling when alone versus with someone else (7.4 percent versus 47.3 percent) or talking when alone versus with someone else (16.8 percent versus 72.1 percent). This result was a revelation to me and an example of what psychological research can do at its best: to reveal the ways in which our understanding of each other might be misleading and shine a light directly on the truth. Provine, R. R. (1993). Laughter punctuates speech: Linguistic, social, and gender contexts of laughter. *Ethology, 95*, 291–98; Provine, R. R. (1996). Laughter. *American Scientist, 84*, 38–45; Provine, R. R., & Fischer, K. R. (1989). Laughing, smiling, and talking: Relation to sleeping and social context in humans. *Ethology, 83*, 295–305.

For more on Provine's research, I encourage you to read his book, *Laughter: A Scientific Investigation* (2001). If you'd like to laugh along while reading it, then I suggest reading it out loud with a friend.

8. Reece et al. (2023). CANDOR corpus.
9. This typical speed of turn taking seems to be fairly universal. In one interesting study that analyzed turn-taking speed in natural conversations across ten different cultures from all around the world, the researchers found a very similar pattern across cultures, with an average around 200 milliseconds that includes both some overlaps and gaps in conversation that are roughly similar. You can see this high level of universality in the figure below, which shows the distribution of turn-taking speeds in milliseconds. Negative numbers indicate overlaps, when one person was speaking before another person stopped speaking. Positive numbers indicate gaps, when one person speaks after the other person stops responding. Japanese speakers had the quickest average turn time at a lightning-speed average of 7 milliseconds, whereas Danish speakers had the slowest at roughly 470 milliseconds, but even these most extreme differences deviate by only a quarter second from the overall average across all cultures. As the authors summarize, "The findings suggest a strong universal basis for turn-taking behavior, in that all languages show a similar distribution of response offsets." Although some languages move back and forth a little more quickly than others, the authors note that the difference they find "is not of the kind that would imply fundamentally different types of turn-taking systems in the different languages, as the cultural variability hypothesis would suggest." The main result across all cultures was that conversations move back and forth really fast.

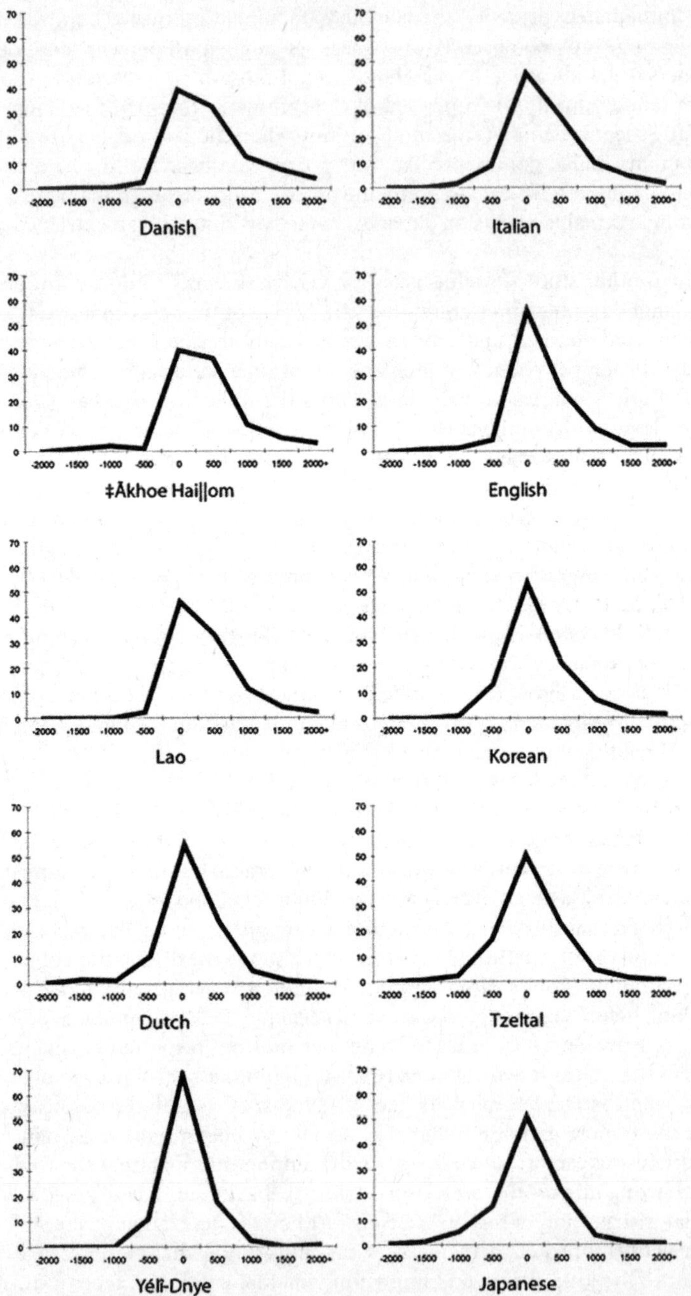

This figure is reprinted from Stivers, T., Enfield, N. J., Brown, P., Englert, C., Hayashi, M., Heinemann, T., Hoymann, G., Rossano, F., De Ruiter, J. P., Yoon, K. E., & Levinson, S. C. (2009). Universals and cultural variation in turn-taking in conversation. *Proceedings of the National Academy of Arts and Sciences, 106*(26), 10587–92.

10. As you might imagine, researchers find that the speed of turn taking isn't taken as a sign of a conversation partner's interest when we're speaking with friends, because we already know that our friends are interested in talking with us and therefore aren't looking for moment-to-moment signals for it. Templeton, E. M., & Wheatley, T. (2023). Listening fast and slow. *Current Opinion in Psychology,* 101658; Templeton, E. M., Chang, L. J., Reynolds, E., Cone LeBeaumont, M., & Wheatley, T. (2023). Long gaps between turns are awkward for strangers but not for friends. *Philosophical Transactions of the Royal Society B, 378*(1875), 20210471; Templeton, E. M., Chang, L. J., Reynolds, E., Cone LeBeaumont, M., & Wheatley, T. (2022). Fast response times signal social connection in conversation. *Proceedings of the National Academy of Sciences, 119,* e2116915119.
11. There is, of course, some question about cause versus effect in these response times. Are we feeling more positive and connected in an interaction because we're responding faster, or are we responding faster because we're feeling more positive and connected? In real conversations, you can't run the experiment in which you assign some people to respond quickly and others to respond slower, as if we had a dial on the back of our heads that could speed us up or slow us down. However, thanks to technology you can easily take audio clips from a conversation and edit them so that responses come at whatever speed you'd like them to, from blisteringly fast to painfully slow, and then have a separate group of people listen to the audio clip and guess how connected and enjoyable the original conversation partners seemed to be. In one experiment that did this, researchers took audio clips from real conversations and created one version where the response delay was blisteringly fast (one-fifth of the original length) and another where it was painfully slow (double the original length). Compared with the unaltered audio, cutting the response time by one-fifth made it seem as if the conversation were more enjoyable, whereas doubling the delay made it seem less enjoyable. Templeton et al. (2022). Fast response times signal social connection in conversation.
12. Interestingly, there's a little more nuance to how the speed of responses affects our sense of enjoyment and connection in conversation. It's not that faster is always better, but rather that longer gaps or silences seem to be worse. Having an average response time of two hundred milliseconds in a typical conversation means that some actual response times are much slower than two hundred milliseconds—there's a gap between when one person stops and the other person starts—whereas others are much faster. Some response times are so fast that they start before another person stops talking. It's as if they've read your mind and already know how you're going to finish your sentence before you actually finish it. In the study involving more than three thousand conversations, the degree of overlap in response times was not related to how enjoyable the conversation seemed, but degree of delay was. The bigger the gaps, the less enjoyable the conversation left people feeling. Reece et al. (2023). CANDOR corpus.
13. Kardas, M., & Epley, N. (2024). Surprisingly in sync: Overlooking responsiveness in conversation as a source of social connection. Unpublished manuscript, University of Chicago.
14. Kardas & Epley (2024). Surprisingly in sync.
15. Yudelson, L. (2020, Dec. 22). The Yiddish word of 2020. *Jewish Standard.*
16. That said, transmission delays are surely not the only thing that can lead to Zoom fatigue and might not even be the biggest thing. Constant eye contact, being able

to see yourself (if you have this option enabled), being trapped at your computer, having to exaggerate your expressions to communicate clearly, having to manage distractions—like your kid wandering into the midst of a meeting—all take their toll. Imperfect synchrony is just one of the challenges. Other experiments examining the impact of adding delays to response times over the telephone and in video interactions in the laboratory also confirm that these delays, even if as slow as a hundred milliseconds, can disrupt the synchrony of conversation, increasing the amount of time people spend talking over each other and increasing the amount of silence as people try to figure out when it's their turn to talk. If you've ever tried to have a cell phone conversation with a bad connection, constantly trying to figure out when to speak and when to be quiet, then you know how frustrating even split-second delays can be. Boland, J. E., Fonseca, P., Mermelstein, I., & Williamson, M. (2022). Zoom disrupts the rhythm of conversation. *Journal of Experimental Psychology: General, 151*(6), 1272–82; Templeton et al. (2022). Fast response times signal social connection in conversation.

17. Keller, H. (1933, pp. 68–69). *Helen Keller in Scotland: A personal record written by herself.* London: Methuen.
18. Zaki, J., Bolger, N., & Ochsner, K. (2009). Unpacking the informational bases of empathic accuracy. *Emotion* 9(4), 478–87.
19. In fact, even visual cues can sometimes be misleading. In another experiment, people were slightly more accurate in understanding their partner's thoughts and feelings in a conversation when they talked in a pitch-dark room compared with when they talked with the lights on. Some research even suggests we're better able to detect lies when we're only hearing what someone has to say because the body language we see can mask cues to dishonesty that are present in someone's voice. Although I'd be reluctant to advise CIA agents to conduct their interrogations with the lights off or over the telephone because these experimental effects are fairly small, and plenty of other bad things can happen when it's dark, scientific research makes it clear that the visual cues we get through body language and facial cues reveal surprisingly little beyond what's contained in our voice. Kraus, M. W. (2017). Voice-only communication enhances empathic accuracy. *American Psychologist, 72*(7), 644–54.
20. Indeed, sign language includes the very same kinds of paralinguistic cues that exist in our voices but instead replicates them in the way signers communicate. Just like the voice, sign language can reflect your conscious experience as you're having the experience, with changes in tone and pacing and volume reflected in the way gestures are signed. Everything I say in this section about the power of voice is likely true for the power of signing, too, although there is unfortunately less of the research I describe in this section comparing sign language with text alone. For more about how human gestures replicate our voices and are used in amazing ways for communication, see Susan Goldin-Meadow's book *Thinking with Your Hands* (2023).
21. Waytz, A., Schroeder, J., & Epley, N. (2013). The lesser minds problem. In P. Bain, J. Vaes, & J. P. Leyens (Eds.), *Are we all human? Advances in understanding humanness and dehumanization*, pp. 49–67. New York: Psychology Press.
22. More specifically, we asked five Clinton and five Trump voters to explain whom they'd be voting for roughly a week before the election, and to explain why they were voting for their chosen candidate. These voters provided their explanation both in a written statement and in a videotaped statement. This allowed us to

obtain four different media versions from each person, two that included a person's voice (video or audio only) and two that included only text (the transcript of the video recording or their written statement). We then presented each of the resulting versions to roughly twenty volunteers (eight hundred in total to evaluate all forty explanations), who then reported how mindful they found the voter to be. Finally, we asked them to report their impression of the voters' capacity to think (such as how sophisticated and rational the voter is) and the voter's capacity to feel (such as how emotional, warm, and responsive the voter is).

Interestingly, whether volunteers heard a voter's voice including video or without it didn't matter for how mindful the voter seemed. Again, you can't see someone else's mind, but you can hear it. Whether volunteers read a voter's written statement or read the transcript of the videotaped statement also didn't matter for how mindful the voter seemed. What mattered for how rational, thoughtful, and caring someone seemed was whether you heard what the voter had to say or only read it. Schroeder, J., Kardas, M., & Epley, N. (2017). The humanizing voice: Speech reveals, and text conceals, a more thoughtful mind in the midst of disagreement. *Psychological Science, 28,* 1745–62.

23. Ronson, J. (2015). *So you've been publicly shamed.* London: Picador.
24. Kruger, J., Epley, N., Parker, J., & Ng, Z. (2005). Egocentrism over email: Can we communicate as well as we think? *Journal of Personality and Social Psychology, 89,* 925–36.
25. Schroeder, Kardas, & Epley (2017). The humanizing voice.
26. Kumar, A., & Epley, N. (2021). It's surprisingly nice to hear you: Misunderstanding the impact of communication media can lead to suboptimal choices of how to connect with others. *Journal of Experimental Psychology: General, 150*(3), 595.
27. Bevis, B., Schroeder, J., & Yeomans, M. (2025). Spoken conversation facilitates constructive disagreement. Unpublished manuscript, University of California, Berkeley.
28. Smith (1759/1982). *Theory of moral sentiments.*

6. Going Deeper

1. R.E.M. (1988). Pop song 89. On *Green.* Warner Bros. Records.
2. The pleasure of sharing information doesn't stop at information about yourself. In one experiment, people were given the chance to reveal the answer to a difficult math problem to another person. Not only did people's brains show the neural signature of reward when they had a chance to pass along the right answer to another person, but their wallets also showed the reward because they were willing to forgo making some money themselves in order to reveal the right answer to another person. Teaching other people things is a rewarding experience, as almost any teacher will tell you. Tamir, D. I., & Mitchell, J. P. (2012). Disclosing information about the self is intrinsically rewarding. *Proceedings of the National Academy of Sciences, 109*(21), 8038–43; Tamir, D. I., Zaki, J., & Mitchell, J. P. (2015). Informing others is associated with behavioral and neural signatures of value. *Journal of Experimental Psychology: General, 144*(6), 1114–23.
3. Kardas, M., Kumar, A., & Epley, N. (2022). Overly shallow? Miscalibrated expectations create a barrier to deeper conversation. *Journal of Personality and Social Psychology, 122*(3), 367–98.

4. Aron, A., Melinat, E., Aron, E. N., Vallone, R. D., & Bator, R. J. (1997). The experimental generation of interpersonal closeness: A procedure and some preliminary findings. *Personality and Social Psychology Bulletin, 23*(4), 363–77.
5. Another way to compare expectations about deep conversations with actual experience is to calculate the percentage of people who underestimate how much they'll enjoy the conversation, overestimate it, or estimate it exactly right based on their expectations going into the conversation. Below is the percentage who do each based on how much they expected they would enjoy the conversation on a scale ranging from 0 (not at all) to 10 (extremely). The more pessimistic people's expectations, the more they tend to underestimate how positively they'll feel. The highest percentage of people who predict their experiences exactly right are those who are the most optimistic about their conversation to begin with. Overall, 78 percent of people underestimated how much they would enjoy their deep conversation.

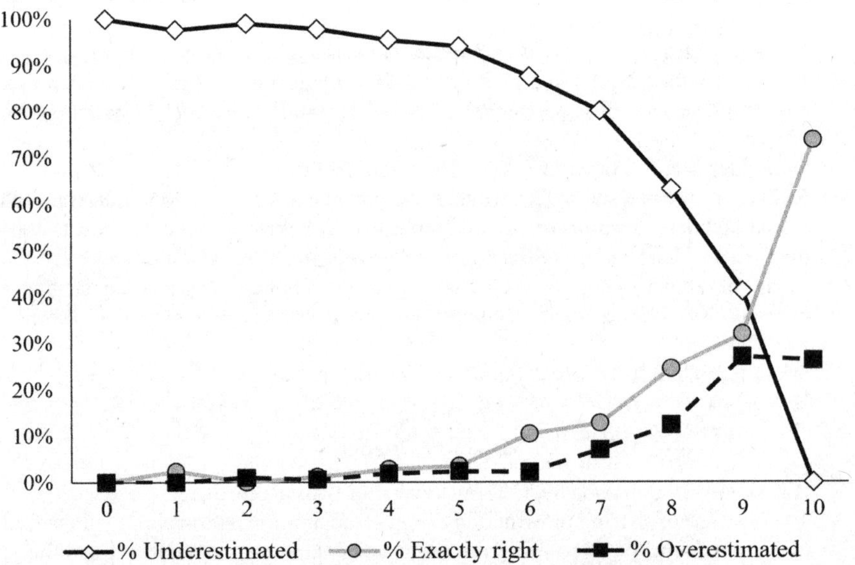

6. We've also asked some of these deep talkers (3,146 of them) to tell us the extent to which their conversation went better or worse than they expected, on a scale ranging from -5 (much worse than they expected) to 5 (much better than they expected). What they tell us mirrors the ratings I described earlier that we obtained from everyone before and after their conversation. A full 83 percent say it went better than expected to some extent, with 22 percent giving the highest rating. Only 2 percent say it went worse than they expected. Not everyone is surprised to have the best conversation they've ever had. However, the range is almost entirely on the better-than-expected side of the spectrum. That imbalance shows that deep conversations weren't just good; they were *surprisingly* good.

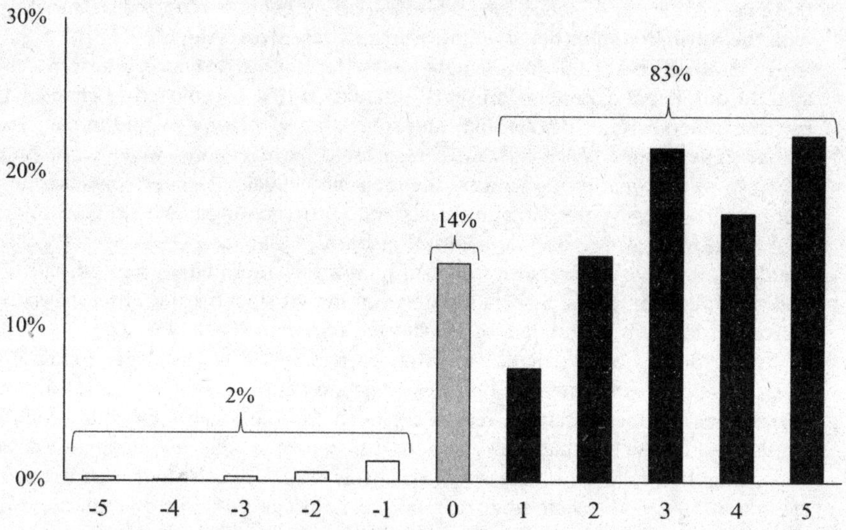

7. This desire for having deeper conversations seems wise. When we ask people in experiments to discuss shallower topics—less intimate but still novel questions like "Do you like to get up early or stay up late—why?" or "What is the best TV show you've seen in the last month?" or "How often do you come here?"—the conversations are still quite positive, and even more positive than people expect, but generally not quite as surprisingly positive as the deeper conversations. And when we ask people in an experiment to have both a shallow *and* a deep conversation, they tend to think they'll enjoy the deep conversation less beforehand but actually end up afterward saying they enjoyed it more.

When other researchers track the conversations people have over the course of their day, the days with more deep conversations tend to be more positive than those with fewer deep conversations (regardless, by the way, of how introverted people report being). The days with more small talk, in contrast, aren't consistently better than days with less small talk. In this study, the researchers analyzed the experiences of five separate groups of people (486 people in total)—university students, breast cancer patients and their spouses, adults from Atlanta participating in an unrelated experiment, and recent divorcées—who walked around for a series of days or weeks wearing a device that unobtrusively recorded bits of their conversations over the course of their day from the time they woke up to the time they went to bed. The device enabled researchers to measure both the number of conversations each person had on any given day and whether the conversations were deep and substantial or shallow and inconsequential (by listening in and rating each conversation). The researchers found that people reported feeling happier on days when they had more conversations, felt happier on days when they had more deep conversations, and felt considerably less happy when they spent more time alone.

People did not feel meaningfully more or less positive depending on the number of shallow conversations they had. The researchers also measured whether any of these consequences of social interaction varied by people's reported personality, with their primary focus being on introversion and extroversion.

In another nod to the surprisingly weak effects of extroversion and introversion on our actual experience in social interaction that we covered in chapter 2, the researchers wrote, "Interestingly and somewhat surprisingly—and in contrast to our expectations specifically with regards to extraversion—we did not find evidence of personality moderating the identified effects." Deeper conversations were positive experiences for introverts and extroverts alike. Milek, A., Butler, E. A., Tackman, A. M., Kaplan, D. M., Raison, C. L., Sbarra, D. A., Vazire, S., & Mehl, M. R. (2018). "Eavesdropping on happiness" revisited: A pooled, multisample replication of the association between life satisfaction and observed daily conversation quantity and quality. *Psychological Science, 29*(9), 1451–62.

Interestingly, this particular research project was a much larger follow-up to a small-scale experiment of only seventy-nine people that this same group of researchers conducted several years earlier. This initial small-scale study found similar results, except that they also found that people were less happy on days when they had relatively more small talk. This result is consistent with people's claim that they tend to hate small talk, but the failure of this effect to replicate in a much larger sample means that it's not likely to be a very reliable result. The strongest conclusion that this entire body of research can offer at this point is that deep talk is typically more positive than small talk, but small talk is still better for your happiness than no talk at all. The original small-scale study is reported here: Mehl, M. R., Vazire, S., Holleran, S. E., & Clark, C. S. (2010). Eavesdropping on happiness: Well-being is related to having less small talk and more substantive conversations. *Psychological Science, 21,* 539–41.

8. Deeper conversations often involve discussing the very kinds of personally meaningful topics we'd want to talk about with others because they're genuinely more interesting, but they're also the topics that we fear that others don't want to talk about with us. Researchers find that these fears are also likely to be exaggerated. In a series of experiments, people who were *asking* questions of another person thought that sensitive questions—"Have you ever cheated on a partner?" or "What are your views on abortion?" or "Have you ever had financial problems?"—would generally produce a worse experience than asking more mundane questions: "Are you a morning person?" or "How did you get your current job?" or "What season do you like best?" However, the people who were being asked these questions actually preferred the sensitive questions over the mundane ones. Although it's pretty clear when reading those questions that the more sensitive ones would be more interesting to talk about than the mundane ones, uncertainty about how another person might respond can lead you to fear that others might think differently. Hart, E., VanEpps, E., & Schweitzer, M. E. (2021). The (better than expected) consequences of asking sensitive questions. *Organizational Behavior and Human Decision Processes, 162*(1), 136–54.
9. Bruk, A., Scholl, S. G., & Bless, H. (2018). Beautiful mess effect: Self–other differences in evaluation of showing vulnerability. *Journal of Personality and Social Psychology, 115*(2), 192–205.
10. This quotation comes from an interview Brooks did with the Commonwealth Club

on November 16, 2023, talking about his book *How to Know a Person: The Art of Seeing Others Deeply and Being Deeply Seen* (2023).

11. Brophy, I. N. (1945). The luxury of anti-Negro prejudice. *Public Opinion Quarterly, 9*, 456–66.
12. Wilner, D. M., Walkley, R. P., & Cook, S. W. (1955). *Human relations in interracial housing: A study of the contact hypothesis.* Minneapolis: University of Minnesota Press.
13. Wald, K., Kardas, M., & Epley, N. (2024). Misplaced divides? Discussing political disagreement with strangers can be unexpectedly positive. *Psychological Science, 35*(5), 471–88.
14. Specifically, when we asked nearly five hundred people to imagine they were about to have a conversation with a stranger who agreed or disagreed with them on one of these topics, people thought that talking to someone they agreed with would be a much more positive experience (for example, they'd enjoy discussing the topic more, think they'd learn more, like their partner more, feel more connected to their partner, find it to be less awkward, think their partner would be less hostile) than talking with someone they disagreed with. The gap in people's expectations was massive: People expected that talking with someone they agreed with would be pretty good compared with talking with someone they disagreed with. You can see those gaps below, as well as the size of those gaps reported as an effect size statistic (a Cohen's *d*). To put those effect sizes in perspective, an effect size (*d*) of 1.0 is typically considered in the behavioral sciences in the "large" category. The effect sizes in expectations of someone you agreed versus disagreed with varied from what would typically be considered "large" to nearly three times that size. It's then not surprising that when we asked people how interested they would be in having this conversation versus trying to avoid it, people overwhelmingly said they'd try hard to avoid the conversation with someone they disagreed with. Consistent with all of the advice you've ever heard, most people know that they don't want to talk about politics or religion with a stranger.

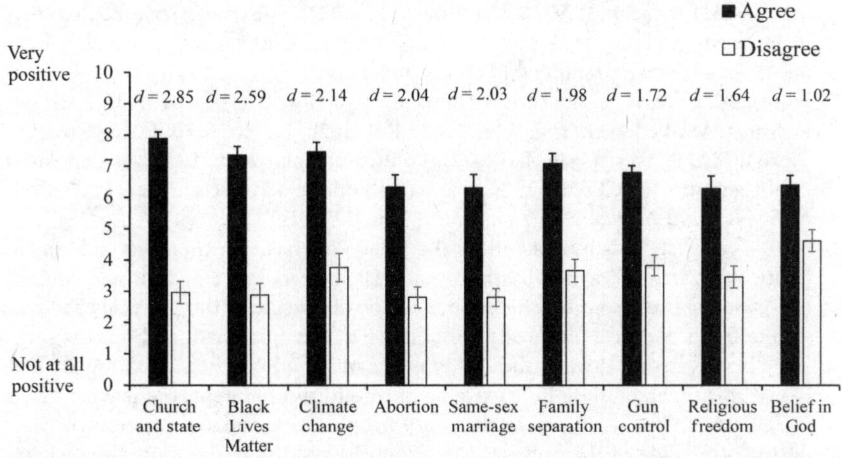

15. Specifically, we assigned people in this experiment to one of three conditions: that they were about to have a conversation with someone they disagreed with or some-

one they agreed with, or we did not tell them about their partner's views. The black bars in the figure below show that people expected to have a more positive conversation experience when they agreed with their partner than when they disagreed, with expectations in the uncertain condition falling in the middle. The white bars, however, show that how positive these conversations actually felt was similar, regardless of whether the conversation partners agreed or disagreed with each other. This meant that talking with someone they disagreed with was surprisingly pleasant.

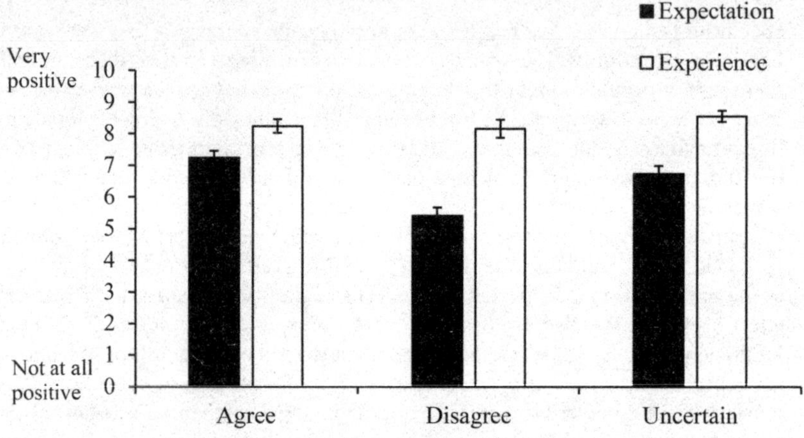

16. Westfall, J., Van Boven, L., Chambers, J., & Judd, C. M. (2015). Perceiving political polarization in the United States: Party identity strength and attitude extremity exacerbate the perceived partisan divide. *Perspectives on Psychological Science, 10,* 145–58; Fernbach, P. M., & Van Boven, L. (2022). False polarization: Cognitive mechanisms and potential solutions. *Current Opinion in Psychology: People Watching: Interpersonal Perception and Prediction, 43,* 1–6.
17. Flores, A., Cole, J. C., Dickert, S., Eom, K., Jiga-Boy, G. M., Kogut, T., Loria, R., Mayorga, M., Pedersen, E. J., Pereira, B., Rubaltelli, E., Sherman, D. K., Slovic, P., Västfjäll, D., & Van Boven, L. (2022). Politicians polarize and experts depolarize public support for COVID-19 management policies across countries. *Proceedings of the National Academy of Sciences, 119*(3), e2117543119.
18. In this research, misunderstanding the minds of those on the other side of the political spectrum was a bipartisan issue: Democrats and Republicans similarly overestimate the extent to which those on the other side of the political spectrum dislike them. Political animosity exists more in our imagination about the other side's beliefs than it does in the reality of the other side's beliefs. The tragedy here is that misunderstanding how extreme our political opponents are is what drives people apart. In this research, the more people overestimated how much those on the other side of the political spectrum disliked them, the more they wanted to avoid interacting with those on the other side. Unfortunately, believing that someone hates you and therefore avoiding them also keeps you from ever learning that your beliefs might be mistaken. Moore-Berg, S. L., Ankori-Karlinsky, L.,

Hameiri, B., & Bruneau, E. G. (2020). Exaggerated meta-perceptions predict intergroup hostility between American political partisans. *Proceedings of the National Academy of Sciences, 117*(26), 14864–72.

19. Specifically, people in this experiment who were interacting with someone they disagreed with expected their conversation partner to have more extreme views before their conversation than they believed they actually had after their conversation. We did not see this same effect when people were interacting with someone they agreed with.

20. One obvious concern with both of the experiments I've described in this section is that they were taking place in a laboratory setting, with people who knew they were in an experiment and being studied, and hence might be on their best behavior. I'm afraid you can't ethically conduct an experiment like the ones I've described without people giving their informed consent to be studied, so this constraint is somewhat inescapable. However, this feature of our experiments is also obvious to the people who are participating in them, so if being in an experiment is altering how they're actually talking with one another, then they don't seem to be anticipating it beforehand. Most of the time we don't record the conversations, because we want to make sure that the people in our experiments are free to have whatever conversation they would normally have. It's also not practical to record many of them because these conversations happen in city parks, large classrooms, private lab rooms, or in private breakout rooms online.

    Our results are consistent across these contexts. It doesn't seem to matter. In almost all cases, the people in these experiments are anonymous to us because they never report their names in our survey, and they know the survey is anonymous, in order to make it easy for people to respond honestly as we explicitly ask them to.

21. These quotations from and about Daryl Davis come from an article written by Nicholas Kristof in *The New York Times* titled "How Can You Hate Me When You Don't Even Know Me?" (June 6, 2021), and from episode 1419 of *The Joe Rogan Experience* (titled "Daryl Davis," Jan. 30, 2020). I first learned of Daryl's experiences from the PBS documentary featuring him titled *Accidental Courtesy* (Feb. 13, 2017).

22. Dungan, J., & Epley, N. (2024). Surprisingly good talk: Misunderstanding others creates a barrier to constructive confrontation. *Journal of Experimental Psychology: General, 153*(3), 779–97.

23. More specifically, we asked 160 people in this experiment to recall a time when someone confronted them about some issue in their lives, to indicate who confronted them, and to indicate how they felt when they were confronted (such as how angry, how hostile, how guilty, and how ashamed). The issues people remembered being confronted about ranged from very serious (cheating on their partner, drug use, lying) to more minor (cutting in line at a concert, refilling a fountain drink without paying for it, stealing a pen from the office). We then described each recalled issue to one person from a new group of people. We asked this new group to imagine having this issue in the same kind of relationship that the original "confronted" participant described and to predict how the person would respond if they actually confronted that person in real life. Those who imagined confronting someone in the future expected more anger and less guilt than those who were actually confronted in these events reported experiencing. This is described as experiment 1 in Dungan & Epley (2024). Surprisingly good talk.

24. Just to make sure that our pairs ended our experiment on a high note, we also asked the roommates to think about something they liked about the other person and the romantic couples to think about something they felt grateful to their partner about. They shared these positive things in a conversation at the end of the experiment.
25. Fleischer describes his method of deep canvassing, and the effect if can have on prejudice, in his TEDx talk titled "How to Fight Prejudice Through Policy Conversations" (Oct. 31, 2018).
26. Not only did these deep conversations tend to turn out surprisingly positively, but researchers who studied the long-term consequences of having a deep conversation with a transgendered person found that these conversations also dramatically reduced prejudice against them. The average decrease in prejudice was about as large after a ten-minute conversation as the average decline in prejudice against transgendered people that occurred over a period of increasing acceptance of the LGBTQ+ community between 1998 and 2012. This decrease in prejudice was also more durable than any other intervention researchers have found to date for decreasing prejudice, lasting for at least three months after the conversation (which is the last point at which attitudes were measured in the experiment). In fact, the one bad conversation that David Fleischer could recall when I asked him about it came while he was conducting one of the control condition conversations of this experiment in which he was talking to people about paying for plastic bags at stores. Broockman, D., & Kalla, J. (2016). Durably reducing transphobia: A field experiment on door-to-door canvassing. *Science, 352*, 220–24.
27. You can find the exchange between Fleischer and Newsome in the article titled "What Helps Us Connect with People Who Are Different from Us" at davefleischer .substack.com.

7. Choosing Thankfulness

1. James was surely being a little overly dramatic in his show of affection for his students' appreciation, but he also told his students not to "take all this too jocosely" (meaning too wittily, humorously, or facetiously). James was sincerely moved. He ends the letter warmly: "Believe in the extreme pleasure you have caused me, and in the affectionate feelings with which I am and shall always be faithfully your friend." James, W. (1896/1920). *The letters of William James.* H. James (Ed.). London: Longmans, Green.
2. While we're on the topic of appreciation, I became aware of Celine thanks to Alfred Lubrano, a reporter for *The Philadelphia Inquirer* who wrote a nice story about Celine's "compliment hobby." Lubrano's article was published on the *Philadelphia Inquirer* website on November 12, 2023, under the title "This Woman Roams the City, Handing Out Compliments to Strangers." The quotations from Celine all come from a conversation we had on December 18, 2023.
3. Brooks, D. (2023). *How to know a person: The art of seeing others deeply and being deeply seen.* New York: Random House.
4. I don't have Celine's original compliment cards, but she did send me images of her more recent cards. Count yourself lucky if you get one while in Philadelphia and do your best to pass it on.

5. Emmons, R. A. (2007). *Thanks! How the new science of gratitude can make you happier.* New York: Houghton Mifflin.
6. Cousin, L., Redwine, L., Bricker, C., Kip, K., & Buck, H. (2021). Effect of gratitude on cardiovascular health outcomes: A state-of-the-science review. *Journal of Positive Psychology, 16*(3), 348–55; Gu, Y., Ocampo, J. M., Algoe, S. B., & Oveis, C. (2022). Gratitude expressions improve teammates' cardiovascular stress responses. *Journal of Experimental Psychology: General, 151*(12), 3281–91.
7. In fact, behavioral scientists think the primary function of appreciation is relational, motivating us to form new relationships or deepen existing relationships through both direct and indirect reciprocity. Sara Algoe, one of the world's experts on the feeling of gratitude and appreciation, finds in her research that gratitude is primarily a social experience that is triggered most commonly by noticing someone else being responsive to our needs. This might be a teacher who reached out to help at just the right moment, a friend who believed in you when others didn't, or a spouse or parent who loves us despite our shortcomings. As Algoe notes, "From within a sea of social contacts, a responsive gesture stands out from the rest: it signals that the person understands, approves, or cares about the self." By making us feel good and motivating us to be good to other people, Algoe argues, "the emotion of gratitude appears to have evolved as a mechanism to fuel upward spirals of mutually-responsive behavior between individuals, thereby placing everyday gratitude right at the heart of the most important relationships of our daily lives." Algoe, S. B. (2012). Find, remind, and bind: The functions of gratitude in everyday relationships. *Social and Personality Psychology Compass, 6*(6), 455–69.
8. Simmel, G. (1950). *The sociology of Georg Simmel.* Glencoe, Ill.: Free Press.
9. Bartlett, M. Y., & DeSteno, D. (2006). Gratitude and prosocial behavior: Helping when it costs you. *Psychological Science, 17*(4), 319–25.
10. DeSteno, D., Duong, F., Lim, D., & Kates, S. (2019). The grateful don't cheat: Gratitude as a fount of virtue. *Psychological Science, 30*(7), 979–88; Kates, S., & DeSteno, D. (2021). Gratitude reduces consumption of depleting resources. *Emotion, 21*(5),

1119–23; Vayness, J., Duong, F., & DeSteno, D. (2020). Gratitude increases third-party punishment. *Cognition and Emotion, 34,* 1020–27.

11. DeSteno, D., Condon, P., & Dickens, L. (2016). Gratitude and compassion. *Handbook of Emotions, 4,* 835–46; Ma, L., Tunney, R. J., & Ferguson, E. (2017). Does gratitude enhance prosociality? A meta-analytic review. *Psychological Bulletin, 143*(6), 601–35.
12. Emmons, R. A. (2008, p. 480). Gratitude, subjective well-being, and the brain. In Eid & Larsen, *Science of subjective well-being,* pp. 469–89.
13. Layous, K., Sweeny, K., Armenta, C., Na, S., Choi, I., & Lyubomirsky, S. (2017). The proximal experience of gratitude. *PLOS ONE, 12*(7), e0179123.
14. Zhao, X., & Epley, N. (2021). Insufficiently complimentary? Underestimating the positive impact of compliments creates a barrier to expressing them. *Journal of Personality and Social Psychology, 121,* 239–56.
15. In this survey, we asked a group of Americans recruited online to take what you might call a Goldilocks Test of their social habits, considering how often they, and others, perform a series of social behaviors compared with how much they "should" perform them. They answered on a scale ranging from -3 (much less often than I should) to 3 (much more often than I should), with 0 being exactly as often as I should. As you can see in the figure below, people indicated that they gave compliments and expressed gratitude, on average, a little less often than they should but were closer to being just about exactly right for the other social behaviors. Interestingly, our survey respondents felt uniquely deficient in their compliment giving and gratitude expressing compared with others, whom they felt were closer to doing these activities exactly as often as they should. We find the same results when we ask how often people "would like" to perform these activities.

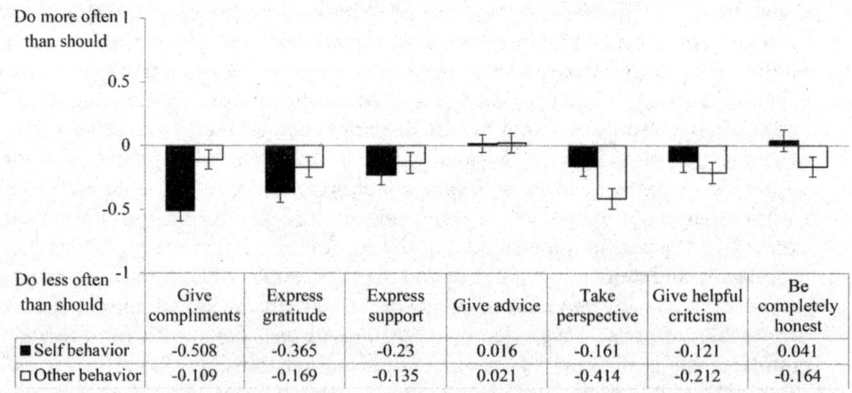

	Give compliments	Express gratitude	Express support	Give advice	Take perspective	Give helpful criticsm	Be completely honest
■ Self behavior	-0.508	-0.365	-0.23	0.016	-0.161	-0.121	0.041
□ Other behavior	-0.109	-0.169	-0.135	0.021	-0.414	-0.212	-0.164

Zhao, X., & Epley, N. (2021). Insufficiently complimentary? Underestimating the positive impact of compliments creates a barrier to expressing them. *Journal of Personality and Social Psychology, 121,* 239–56.

16. Although I'm a Regina Spektor fan, I'm grateful to Shai Davidai and Tom Gilovich for opening a paper with this terrific lyric to remind me of it. Davidai, S., & Gilovich, T. (2016). The headwinds/tailwinds asymmetry: An availability bias in assess-

ments of barriers and blessings. *Journal of Personality and Social Psychology, 111*(6), 835–51.

17. Dickens wrote this encouragement to stave off the doom and gloom that he saw polluting people's enjoyment of the Christmas holiday, which foreshadowed the headwinds/tailwinds distinction that I'll be talking about later in this section. "There are people who will tell you that Christmas is not to them what it used to be; that each succeeding Christmas has found some cherished hope, or happy prospect, of the year before, dimmed or passed away; that the present only serves to remind them of reduced circumstances and straitened incomes—of the feasts they once bestowed on hollow friends, and of the cold looks that meet them now, in adversity and misfortune. Never heed such dismal reminiscences." He did not, though, think that this gloom-inducing nostalgia was restricted to holidays: "There are few men who have lived long enough in the world, who cannot call up such thoughts any day in the year." From Dickens's book *Sketches by Boz: Illustrative of Every-Day Life and Every-Day People*, published in 1903 and available on the Project Gutenberg website (www.gutenberg.org).
18. Hume, D. (1739). *A treatise of human nature*. London: printed for John Noon. This quotation is in book 3, part 1, section 1.
19. You can find a video of Tom describing his "enemies of gratitude" on Cornell University's website (www.cornell.edu). Or, you can listen to him talk about them with Shankar Vendatem on the *Hidden Brain* podcast (www.hiddenbrain.org).
20. Wilson, T. D., Wheatley, T. P., Meyers, J. M., Gilbert, D. T., & Axsom, D. (2000). Focalism: A source of durability bias in affective forecasting. *Journal of Personality and Social Psychology, 78*, 821–36.
21. Study 2 from Gilbert, D. T., Pinel, E. C., Wilson, T. D., Blumberg, S. J., & Wheatley, T. (1998). Immune neglect: A source of durability bias in affective forecasting. *Journal of Personality and Social Psychology, 75*, 617–38.
22. Converse, B. A., & Fishbach, A. (2012). Instrumentality boosts appreciation: Helpers are more appreciated while they are useful. *Psychological Science, 23*, 560–66.
23. Commenting on the 2024 Summer Olympics in Paris, the *New York Times* journalist Juliet Macur suggested another good-bet hypothesis about the importance of comparisons that researchers have not yet tested (as far as I know): "Fourth place is always a hard pill to swallow." Medvec, V. H., Madey, S., & Gilovich, T. (1995). When less is more: Counterfactual thinking and satisfaction among Olympic medal winners. *Journal of Personality and Social Psychology, 69*, 603–10.
24. Lyubomirsky, S., & Ross, L. (1997). Hedonic consequences of social comparison: A contrast of happy and unhappy people. *Journal of Personality and Social Psychology, 73*, 1141–57.
25. Davidai & Gilovich (2016). Headwinds/tailwinds asymmetry.
26. Amit and I described our first experiments involving gratitude in this paper: Kumar, A., & Epley, N. (2018). Undervaluing gratitude: Expressers misunderstand the consequences of showing appreciation. *Psychological Science, 29*, 1423–35.
27. This is what an experience that feels really good looks like in a figure. After sending or receiving their letter, the letter writers and their recipients were asked to indicate how positive or negative they felt compared with normal on a scale that ranged from -5 (much more negative than normal) to 5 (much more positive than normal), with 0 indicating no more positive or negative than normal. The percentage

of gratitude expressers and their recipients giving each response is shown below. Expressing appreciation led letter writers to feel considerably more positive than they normally feel, but it led recipients to feel dramatically more positive than they normally feel.

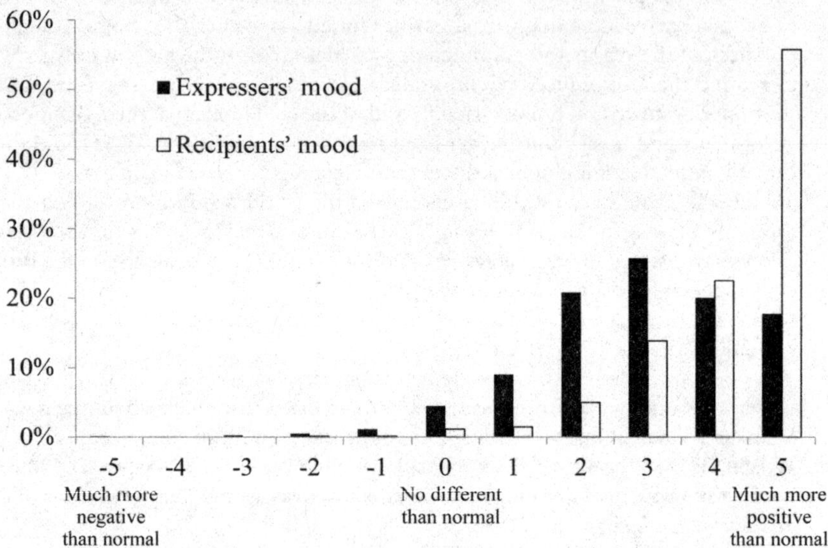

28. One issue in this experiment is that not everyone who expresses their gratitude is willing to let me reach out to their recipient to find out how the letter made them feel, and not all recipients respond when I reach out to them. This could create a problem for interpreting our results if the recipients who don't respond feel differently than those who do, such as if they felt more negative about the experience than the recipients who did respond. Unfortunately, there is no way of knowing how the recipients who don't respond feel. However, there are two reasons to think that they may not feel differently, on average, than those who respond do. First, gratitude expressers who have a recipient who responded ("paired") do not have different expectations from those whose recipient did not respond ("unpaired"). At the very least, this suggests that the gratitude expressers aren't anticipating more negative responses from recipients whom they would prefer we not contact, or who do not respond. Second, and perhaps more persuasively, if the people who don't respond have more negative evaluations than those who do, then the gap between letter writers' expectations and the recipients' experiences should be even larger when fewer people respond in a given experiment (because more of the negative responses are missing and only the more positive ones remain). Across nineteen iterations of this experiment, with varying response rates, we did not find this to be true.

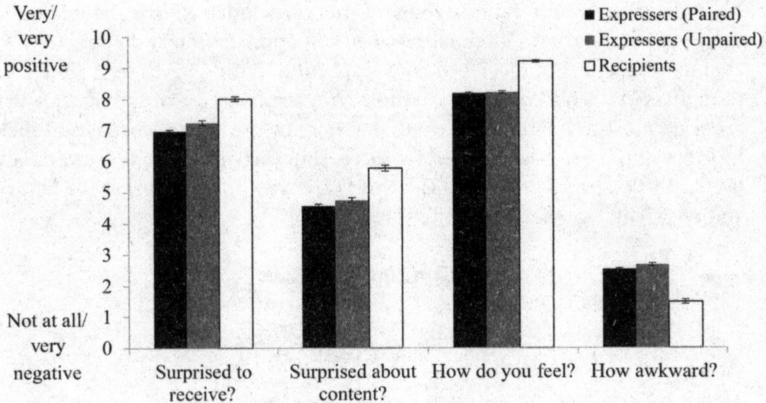

Epley, N., Kumar, A., Dungan, J., & Echelbarger, M. (2023). A prosociality paradox: How miscalibrated social cognition creates a misplaced barrier to prosocial action. *Current Directions in Psychological Science, 32*, 33–41.

29. We can get a little better picture of this gap between letter writers' expectations and their recipients' experiences if we look more closely at the entire range of their emotional responses. Letter writers' expectations were so positive, an average of 3.19 on the -5 to 5 scale, that it almost seems like what researchers would consider a "ceiling effect," a situation in which people report the highest score on a given measure. But it's not letter writers who are showing the ceiling effect; it's the recipients. If you look at the graph below, what you see is the range of letter writers' expectations compared with the range of the letter recipients' actual evaluations. Nineteen percent of letter writers expected their recipients would report the most positive mood possible on this scale (a 5), but 55 percent of the letter recipients actually did so. If anything, we're underestimating just how positive the recipients likely feel because our scale doesn't go all the way to 11 (I've been so deliriously happy that I've been wetting my pants for the past week).

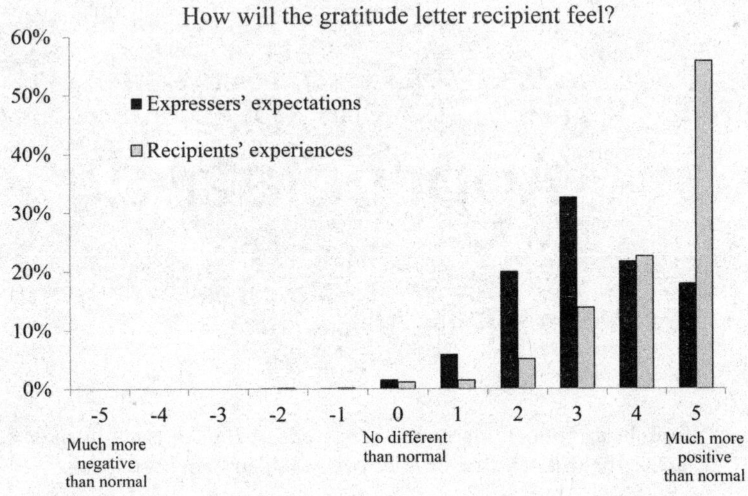

30. It's impossible to fully capture the sentiments included in what people write about their experiences, both after expressing their appreciation and after being appreciated by someone. For me, it's the most uplifting writing I ever read. One way to try, though, is to simply count up the most commonly used words and see which ones are used most frequently. I've done that here by creating a word cloud that shows how commonly words are used by increasing their font size (excluding all words used only two times or fewer). The words are very positive, just as the letter writers and recipients say they are in the surveys.

How Gratitude Expressers Feel

How Gratitude Recipients Feel

31. You can hear more of this story on the podcast *Hidden Brain* in an episode titled "You 2.0: The Gift of Other People" (www.hiddenbrain.org).

32. Boothby, E. J., & Bohns, V. K. (2021). Why a simple act of kindness is not as simple as it seems: Underestimating the positive impact our compliments have on others. *Personality and Social Psychology Bulletin, 47*(5), 826–40.
33. Zhao, X., & Epley, N. (2021). Kind words do not become tired words: Undervaluing the positive impact of frequent compliments. *Self and Identity, 20,* 25–46.

8. Choosing Kindness

1. You can find Jia's book, and even links to all of the videos of his rejection attempts online, at www.rejectiontherapy.com. I highly recommend watching some of the videos, particularly Jia's experience just moments before each request and often his surprise, at least in his early videos, after his request. You can also learn more by watching Jia's TEDx talk titled "What I Learned from 100 Days of Rejection" (uploaded May 2015 on www.ted.com).
2. Jia told me that this experience on day 3 is what really changed his mind about human nature. He realized that if someone is willing to do this when he asks, then what else would be possible if he wasn't holding himself back from asking? This video went viral on Jia's blog, with countless calls being placed the next day to the store. Jackie Braun, the Krispy Kreme employee who made Jia's rings, was home the day after but quickly learned of the stir she had caused online. Jia went back to Jackie on day 12 to ask her to talk about her experience in front of the "millions" who were following Jia's blog by then (of course, she accepted that request). Jia and Jackie went on television and radio programs together, Jackie was praised by Krispy Kreme on social media and received a call from the CEO, and Jia started a Facebook campaign to get Jackie a raise (which she likely got given the call from the CEO). Jia even heard that his video had become part of employee training at Krispy Kreme. None of this would have happened if Jia had not overcome his fear of reaching out to ask another person for help.
3. One of my favorite examples of one of these "mixed" reactions is when Jia took a request from a fan of his blog to challenge a random person to a staring contest. Jia upped the ante a bit and decided instead to walk into a random local business in Boston, where he happened to be visiting at the time, and challenge the CEO of that business to a staring contest. Yes, a staring contest. At the welcome desk, the CEO's assistant laughs at the request but does indeed take it to the CEO. A few minutes later, the VP of marketing at the company—Heidi—walks out to apologize that the CEO is unable to do this now. Eventually Jia asks if she would be willing to have a staring contest with him instead. Moments later, after going to get another employee to serve as an unbiased judge, they're locked in a death stare until Jia gives a half blink and the contest is called in Heidi's favor. What strikes you when watching Jia's experiences is both how often people are willing to do something you wouldn't imagine either with him or for him and how much fun they have while doing it.
4. To be more precise, my collaborator, Don Lyons, watched all of Jia's videos and scored the overall tone of the interaction as very negative, negative, neutral, positive, or very positive. Although the tone of the fifty-one acceptances was clearly more positive than the tone of the forty-eight rejections, even being rejected wasn't very negative. Mostly people turned Jia down nicely, with people trying their best to accept or even doing something else for Jia (like the Costco manager who

wouldn't allow him to talk on the store intercom to say how much he loved Costco, but who did pay for his lunch and sit with him for a nice conversation), or neutral, with people simply saying they couldn't do whatever Jia was asking of them.

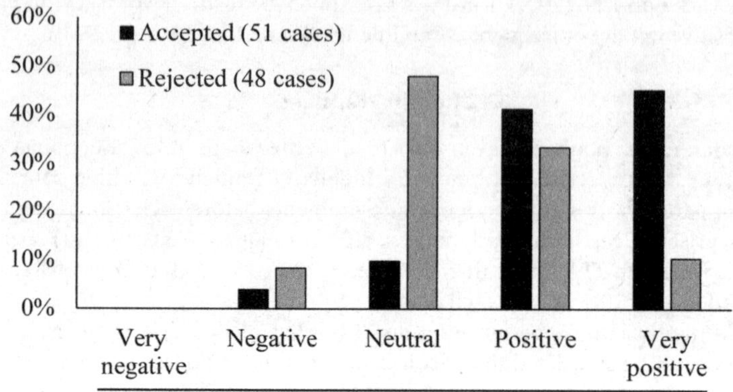

5. Flynn, F. J., & Lake (Bohns), V. K. (2008). If you need help, just ask: Underestimating compliance with direct requests for help. *Journal of Personality and Social Psychology, 95*(1), 128–43.
6. Andreoni, J. (1990). Impure altruism and donations to public goods: A theory of warm-glow giving. *Economic Journal, 100,* 464–77.
7. Roghanizad, M. M., & Bohns, V. K. (2022). Should I ask over Zoom, phone, email, or in-person? Communication channel and predicted versus actual compliance. *Social Psychological and Personality Science, 13*(7), 1163–72.
8. DellaVigna, S., List, J. A., & Malmendier, U. (2012). Testing for altruism and social pressure in charitable giving. *Quarterly Journal of Economics, 127*(1), 1–56.
9. These quotations come from an interview the Santa Clara Valley Historical Association conducted with Jobs in 1994. The interviewer's prompt was, "Correct me if I'm wrong. When you were starting Apple, or maybe beforehand, the rumor that I heard was that you went to talk to like Gordon Moore and Bob Noyce, and at Xerox PARC. And actually, these doors were open to you, which is unusual. I believe it's unusual compared to other places in the world where you can call the CEO of a company and say . . . ," and Jobs jumped right in.

   His full response is worth reading: "I've actually always found something to be very true, which is most people don't get those experiences because they never ask. I've never found anybody that didn't want to help me if I asked them for help. I always call them up. I called up, this will date me, but I called up Bill Hewlett when I was 12 years old, and he lived in Palo Alto. His number was in the phone book. And he answered the phone himself and said, 'Yes?' And I said, 'Hi, I'm Steve Jobs. I'm 12 years old. I'm a student in high school, and I want to build a frequency counter. And I was wondering if you had any spare parts I could have.' And he laughed and he gave me the spare parts to build this frequency counter, and he gave me a job that summer in Hewlett-Packard working on the assembly line putting nuts and bolts together on frequency counters. He got me a job in the place that built them. And I was in heaven. And I've never found anyone who said no or hung up the phone when I called. I just asked. And when people ask me, I try to be as responsive. You know, to pay that debt of gratitude back. Most people never pick up the phone and call. Most people never ask. And that's what separates sometimes people who do things from people who just dream about them. You've got to act, and you've got to be willing to fail. You've got to be willing to crash and burn, you know, with people on the phone, with starting a company, with whatever. If you're afraid of failing, you won't get very far."

10. The Sandberg quotations in this section come from an interview she did with the National Public Radio program (www.npr.org) *All Things Considered* on April 25, 2017: "'Just Show Up': Sheryl Sandberg on How to Help Someone Who's Grieving." She also describes her experience of grieving, and what she learned about expressing support, in her book (co-authored with Adam Grant), *Option B: Facing Adversity, Building Resilience, and Finding Joy* (2017).
11. To be precise, the correlation between these three psychological barriers and how likely they thought they were to express support was more than double the size of the correlation between the recipient's perceived need and their likelihood of expressing support (-0.54, 0.49, and 0.48 for awkwardness, mood, and support, versus only 0.21 for perceived need). Dungan, J. A., Munguia Gomez, D. M., & Epley, N. (2022). Too reluctant to reach out: Receiving social support is more positive than expressers expect. *Psychological Science, 33*(8), 1300–312.
12. As you might imagine, it's a little unusual to receive a letter of support out of the blue followed up by a request from me to complete a confidential survey asking how the letter made you feel. These recipients didn't sign up to be in the experiment in the first place, and so it's also not surprising that not all of them responded to our request to tell us how they felt. Out of the 120 people who sent their recipients a letter of support, we heard back from 50, giving us a 42 percent response rate. It could be that people who respond to the survey are different from the people who don't, and it would be especially concerning if the people who responded felt more positive than the people who didn't.

    There are two ways we can address this. First, the ratings of expressers whose recipients responded do not look meaningfully different in any way from the ratings of expressers whose recipients did not respond. That is, the expressers whose recipients did not respond did not expect a less positive response, or indicate that the recipient they were reaching out to was any more negative or positive than the expressers whose recipients did respond to us. The second, and more compelling, way to address this concern is to conduct an experiment where every person who is reached out to tells us how it made them feel. Flip back to the main text to read about that experiment next. Dungan, Munguia Gomez, & Epley (2022). Too reluctant to reach out.
13. Indeed, when we asked people to vividly imagine either expressing support to someone or receiving support from someone, 76 percent of expressers reported that their first thoughts would be about their competence (such as how capable they would be of fixing the recipient's issue or how exactly they'd support the person), whereas 75 percent of support recipients said their first thoughts would be about the expressers' warmth (how genuine and sincere they were and how caring and concerned they were). Dungan, Munguia Gomez, & Epley (2022). Too reluctant to reach out.

14. Dunn, Aknin, & Norton (2014). Prosocial spending and happiness.
15. Regan, A., Radošić, N., & Lyubomirsky, S. (2022). Experimental effects of social behavior on wellbeing. *Trends in Cognitive Sciences, 26*(11), 987–98.
16. The kindness experiments described in the rest of this section are all reported in Kumar, A., & Epley, N. (2022). A little good goes an unexpectedly long way: Underestimating the positive impact of kindness on recipients. *Journal of Experimental Psychology: General, 152*(1), 236–52.
17. This phrase is attributed to William Hewlett in Collins, J., & Lazier, B. (2020). *BE 2.0 (beyond entrepreneurship 2.0): Turning your business into an enduring great company.* New York: Portfolio/Penguin.

9. Choosing Honesty

1. Ben Franklin was surely not the first person to have thought of this maxim about honesty or even to have written it down, but he's the one commonly credited with spreading the advice multiple times in his yearly publication, *Poor Richard's Almanack,* written under the pseudonym Poor Richard from 1732 until 1758. In a rather interesting stroke of irony, the phrase "honesty is the best policy" never actually appears in any of the almanacs. It did, however, appear in some form in at least three of Franklin's writings, so I will continue the tradition of crediting him with the phrase.
2. Indeed, Susan Fiske, a psychology professor at Princeton University and the world's expert on the "Big Two" dimensions of warmth and competence in social evaluation, describes warmth as measuring trustworthiness and friendliness. "Warmth [traits]," she writes, "include warm, trustworthy, friendly, honest, likable, and sincere (in order of priority)." Fiske, S. T. (2018, p. 68). Stereotype content: Warmth and competence endure. *Current Directions in Psychological Science, 27*(2), 67–73.
3. Slepian, M. L., Chun, J. S., & Mason, M. F. (2017). The experience of secrecy. *Journal of Personality and Social Psychology, 113,* 1–33.
4. Slepian, M. L., & Jacoby-Senghor, D. (2021). Identity threats in everyday life: Distinguishing belonging from inclusion. *Social Psychological and Personality Science, 12,* 392–406.
5. Levine, E. E., & Lupoli, M. (2022). Prosocial lies: Causes and consequences. *Current Opinion in Psychology, 43,* 335–40; Jampol, L., & Zayas, V. (2021). Gendered white lies: Women are given inflated performance feedback compared with men. *Personality and Social Psychology Bulletin, 47,* 57–69.
6. Talwar, V., & Crossman, A. (2011). From little white lies to filthy liars: The evolution of honesty and deception in young children. *Advances in Child Development and Behavior, 40,* 139–79.
7. Slepian, M. (2023, Feb. 16). Secrets hurt their holders. Available online at www.Aeon.co.
8. Slepian, M. (2022). *The secret life of secrets: How our inner worlds shape well-being.* New York: Crown.
9. Slepian, Chun, & Mason (2017). The experience of secrecy.
10. In fact, when Michael Slepian and Edythe Moulton-Tetlock asked people about the secrets they had shared (compared with secrets held back), they found that sharing increased their well-being because it connected them more positively with the person they confided in. Sharing the secret led people to feel as if they had bet-

ter social support, and also led them to think about the secret less after sharing it with another person, thereby reducing its burden and increasing their well-being. Slepian, M., & Moulton-Tetlock, E. (2019). Confiding secrets and well-being. *Social Psychological and Personality Science, 10*(4), 472–74.

11. Kardas, M., Kumar, A., & Epley, N. (2024). Let it go: How exaggerating the reputational costs of revealing negative information encourages secrecy in relationships. *Journal of Personality and Social Psychology, 126*(6), 1052–83.
12. Hrala, J. (2017, Dec. 25). This Princeton professor's CV of failures is something we should all learn from. *Science Alert.*
13. Guardian Staff (2016, April 29). CV of failures: Princeton professor publishes résumé of his career lows. *Guardian.*
14. Haushofer published his CV of Failures on his website (johanneshaushofer.com) on April 23, 2016.
15. In one experiment, for instance, my colleagues and I introduced one person to another through either a short or a long text that we created based on how the person being introduced answered a short survey. In this introduction, we revealed one bit of unflattering information. This information mattered much less when it was embedded within a long introduction than when it was in a short introduction, with a more favorable impression coming in the longer introduction that included more positive details about the person. That seems obvious. It wasn't, however, obvious to the people being introduced, who expected that they would be evaluated somewhat negatively regardless of whether it was included in a long or a short introduction.

    This phenomenon is referred to as focalism: the tendency for our attention to focus too narrowly on one piece of information while neglecting the broader context in which it sits. If, for instance, you're thinking about how you'll feel the day after an election when your favored candidate wins or loses, then you're likely to overestimate how much impact the election outcome will have on your emotions the following day if you forget that you'll also be at work doing dozens of other things that will also affect (and thereby mitigate) the impact of the election on your mood. If all you're paying attention to is the negative information you're revealing when you open up and share what you've been concealing, then it can be hard to recognize that this probably isn't the *only* thing about you that someone else is paying attention to. Savitsky, K., Epley, N., & Gilovich, T. (2001). Do others judge us as harshly as we think? Overestimating the impact of our failures, shortcomings, and mishaps. *Journal of Personality and Social Psychology, 81,* 44–56; Wilson et al. (2000). Focalism.
16. This phenomenon is referred to as empathy neglect: failing to consider the extent to which another person might empathize or understand our circumstances, thereby leading them to judge us less negatively when we make a mistake or suffer some mishap than we would anticipate. In one experiment that I think illustrates empathy neglect well, we asked students at Cornell University to solve a series of ten challenging word puzzles in front of one of their peers. Each puzzle included three words, and they were asked to think of the fourth word that these three had in common. One item, for instance, was "jump, kill, bliss." Another was "chamber, staff, box." Can't think of the fourth word that these three had in common? Don't worry, you're not alone. Even these Ivy League students could only answer two or three out of the ten we gave them correctly.

The puzzles are hard. But here's the trick: They only seem hard when you're in the same position as the person trying to solve them, and don't know the answer beforehand. If you were shown the answer to these questions immediately—unlike those who were trying to solve them—then you wouldn't struggle for a moment and the answer would seem easier to you. So if you knew that "joy" was the fourth word that "jump, kill, and bliss" had in common, and that "music" was the fourth word for "chamber, staff, and box," then someone who couldn't solve the item might not seem as bright to you because the answer seems easier.

Indeed, when we asked audience members to judge how intellectually capable the person struggling to solve the puzzles was, those who didn't know the answers and hence could empathize with the solver rated them as more intellectually capable than audience members who got the answers right along with the questions. However, when asked to predict how they would be judged by the audience members, the people struggling to answer the questions expected to be judged similarly harshly, regardless of whether the audience member could empathize with them or not. This meant that those who were struggling in front of someone who could empathize with them were also the most overly pessimistic about how they would be seen in the eyes of another person. Epley, N., Savitsky, K., & Gilovich, T. (2002). Empathy neglect: Reconciling the spotlight effect and the correspondence bias. *Journal of Personality and Social Psychology, 83*, 300–312.

17. For example, in one experiment, we asked people to imagine that they had been stealing their roommate's food from the cupboard and were about to reveal this secret to their roommate. We then asked them to choose three thoughts (out of a list of ten) that they believed would come to mind for someone who heard them reveal a secret they had been concealing. Of the ten possible thoughts, five were negative, such as that they're selfish or that they're hiding other secrets as well. The other five thoughts were positive, such as that they'd be more trustworthy in the future or that they're an honest person.

    Most of those who imagined revealing their secret (77 percent) chose negative thoughts. In contrast, most of those in a separate group, whom we asked to imagine being on the receiving end of the secret (64 percent), chose positive thoughts. Imagining that a roommate had taken their food but then fessed up to it led people to focus on their hypothetical roommate's honesty, rather than on their selfishness, as those imagining fessing up to stealing food feared. As we've seen in many cases throughout this book, those reaching out to connect positively with another person (this time through honesty) simply had a less positive perspective on their own behavior than the people they were reaching out to.

    In other conditions in this same experiment, we learned that asking people to consider only the positive thoughts also made them think they would be evaluated more favorably for revealing their secret (and more in line with the recipients' reported evaluations). In contrast, shifting people's expectations in a negative direction by asking them to consider only the negative thoughts had no influence on how they expected to be evaluated compared with the control condition that considered all ten thoughts (five positive and five negative). This is presumably because negative thoughts are already what we expect will naturally come to mind when we reveal something negative about ourselves. Kardas, Kumar, & Epley (2024). Let it go.

18. Leunissen, J. M., De Cremer, D., van Dijke, M., & Reinders Folmer, C. P. (2014). Forecasting errors in the averseness of apologizing. *Social Justice Research, 27*(3), 322–39.
19. Kachalia, A., Kaufman, S. R., Boothman, R., Anderson, S., Welch, K., Saint, S., & Rogers, M. A. (2010). Liability claims and costs before and after implementation of a medical error disclosure program. *Annals of Internal Medicine, 153,* 213–21.
20. Chen, P. W. (2010, Aug. 19). When doctors admit their mistakes. *New York Times.*
21. Ho, B., & Liu, E. (2011). Does sorry work? The impact of apology laws on medical malpractice. *Journal of Risk and Uncertainty, 43,* 141–67.
22. Roberts, A. R., Levine, E. E., & Sezer, O. (2021). Hiding success. *Journal of Personality and Social Psychology, 120*(5), 1261–86.
23. Sezer, O., Gino, F., & Norton, M. I. (2018). Humblebragging: A distinct—and ineffective—self-presentation strategy. *Journal of Personality and Social Psychology, 114*(1), 52–74.
24. Rogers, T., Zeckhauser, R., Gino, F., Norton, M. I., & Schweitzer, M. E. (2017). Artful paltering: The risks and rewards of using truthful statements to mislead others. *Journal of Personality and Social Psychology, 112*(3), 456–73.
25. In one experiment that makes this point clearly, people were asked to imagine that they were applying for a job and were given a questionnaire beforehand asking if they had ever used illegal drugs. They were asked to imagine that they had, in fact, used illegal drugs and were asked to indicate whether they would choose to reveal that fact on a survey or conceal it by checking the option "choose not to answer." Overwhelmingly, people preferred to conceal this fact, with 70.5 percent indicating that they would select "choose not to answer" rather than indicating "yes," they had used drugs before. However, those who imagined learning that someone either had revealed prior drug use or had chosen to conceal it actually preferred the revealer to the active concealer.

    In another experiment, those who read two dating profiles preferred the person who revealed having a list of five pretty significant personality flaws over someone who admitted to having three of the same personality flaws but then chose not to answer the remaining two questions. The person who actively concealed negative information was judged to be worse than the person who chose to reveal the worst possible character deficiencies. So focused on the negative content we might be revealing, we might miss that concealing reveals dishonesty that might look even worse. John, L. K., Barasz, K., & Norton, M. I. (2016). Hiding personal information reveals the worst. *Proceedings of the National Academy of Sciences, 113*(4), 954–59.
26. Levine & Lupoli (2022). Prosocial lies.
27. Pilot study presented in Abi-Esber, N., Abel, J. E., Schroeder, J., & Gino, F. (2022). "Just letting you know . . .": Underestimating others' desire for constructive feedback. *Journal of Personality and Social Psychology, 123,* 1362–85.
28. Abi-Esber et al. (2022). "Just letting you know . . ."
29. Abi-Esber et al. (2022). "Just letting you know . . ."
30. Other examples haven't been hard for researchers to find. Honestly saying no to a request that you'd rather not agree to tends to be received more favorably than expected. Having an honest conversation with your romantic partner about something they could improve goes better than romantic partners predict beforehand. And patients tend to prefer just getting the cold hard facts over paternalistic lies

that doctors can be tempted to tell to spare a patient's feelings. In all these cases, those being honest assume it will cause more harm to the person receiving it, on average, than it actually does. Saying no is surprisingly well received: Givi, J., & Kirk, C. P. (2024). Saying no: The negative ramifications from invitation declines are less severe than we think. *Journal of Personality and Social Psychology, 126*(6), 1103–15. Having an honest conversation: Levine, E. E., & Cohen, T. R. (2018). You can handle the truth: Mispredicting the consequences of honest communication. *Journal of Experimental Psychology: General, 147*(9), 1400–429. Doctors delivering the cold hard truth: Lupoli, M. J., Levine, E. E., & Greenberg, A. E. (2018). Paternalistic lies. *Organizational Behavior and Human Decision Processes, 146,* 31–50.

31. Diermeier, D. (2011). *Reputation rules: Strategies for building your company's most valuable asset.* New York: McGraw-Hill.
32. Levine & Cohen (2018). You can handle the truth.
33. This experiment from Levine and Cohen asked different people to report their expectations or their experiences, but another experiment they conducted asked the same people to report both their expectations and their experiences in these conditions and yielded the same general pattern of results.
34. In the book *Giving Hope,* the clinical psychologists Elena Lister and Michael Schwartzman describe how parents' fears that their children can't handle the truth about some of the most painful experiences in human life can lead them to struggle with being honest with their kids. And yet they describe time and time again how surprisingly well children can actually process the truth when it is genuinely shared and discussed with them in times of grief. Keeping the truth from our children due to misplaced fears about how well they will respond to it diminishes trust and creates unnecessary distance between parents and their children, just as it does between adults. The authors suggest that it's hard to share the truth but its positive consequences aren't that complicated: "Children can sense when something sad is happening with the adults in their lives and will worry less if you tell them what it is." Lister, E., & Schwartzman, M. (2022). *Giving hope: Conversations with children about illness, death, and loss.* New York: Avery.

10. Being Wisely Social

1. Schopenhauer, A. (1851/1964, p. 226). *The pessimist's handbook* (T. B. Saunders, Trans.). Lincoln: University of Nebraska Press.
2. Hofmann estimates the figure to be about 13 percent, based at least partly on a study of eight thousand Americans from thirty-four states that found 13.3 percent of respondents fitting the diagnostic criteria for social anxiety disorder. This rate makes SAD the third most commonly diagnosed mental disorder in the United States, with only depression and problems stemming from alcohol abuse being more common. Hofmann, S. (2023, p. 42). *CBT for social anxiety: Simple skills for overcoming fear and enjoying people.* Oakland: New Harbinger Publications.
3. Hofmann (2023, p. 114). *CBT for social anxiety.*
4. Hofmann, personal communication, Jan. 9, 2025.
5. Hofmann (2023, p. 90). *CBT for social anxiety.*
6. Polimeni, E., Hirschi, Q., & Epley, N. (2025). Unpublished data, University of Chicago.

7. This mantra comes from Richard Thaler and Cass Sunstein's book, *Nudge.* Thaler, R., & Sunstein, C. (2008). *Nudge: Improving decisions about health, wealth, and happiness.* New Haven, Conn.: Yale University Press.
8. Researchers consistently confirm what I think almost everyone who spends any time in the presence of cell phones knows well: Cell phones distract attention and disrupt social interaction.

   With unlimited access to information and entertainment in a device that's never awkward to connect with and is often clamoring for your attention with texts from friends or notifications from social media, it's hard to look away. When you're not looking away from your phone, it's hard to interact well with those around you.

   In one experiment at a café, friends and family members who were eating together reported enjoying their meals more when researchers asked them to drop their cell phones into a box compared with when they left their phones out on the table. In another, people working together in an experiment felt less connected when one of them (actually an actor in the experiment) occasionally pulled out their cell phone and used it compared with when the cell phone never made an appearance. If you've ever been "phubbed" before—ignored by someone paying attention to their phone instead—then this effect will readily resonate with you.

   Sometimes the costs of having our attention drawn to phones and away from people can even be surprising to researchers. In one experiment, researchers assembled small groups of undergraduates in a waiting room and gave them twenty minutes to themselves. Before entering the room, one group was asked to leave all of their belongings—including their cell phones—outside the room while the other group was told that they could keep their phone with them (along with their wallet and keys in order to disguise the true purpose of the experiment). The researchers thought that the group who had their cell phones would have a more positive experience in the early minutes because they'd quickly turn to their phones for entertainment while those without their phones would have to stumble through the early awkward and unpleasant moments of figuring out what to do with these strangers. They thought that the social costs of phones would only become apparent at the end of the twenty-minute session, after those without their phones had time to connect with each other a bit in conversation.

   This is not what they found. Instead, when asked to look back at the end of the twenty-minute period, those who had their phones reported each five-minute increment of time to be somewhat less enjoyable than those without their phones. When the undergraduates were asked to look back on the entire twenty-minute period, the researchers found that "phones had a negative impact on nearly every other outcome we measured," leaving those who had their phones thinking that the time was less meaningful and productive and feeling less connected to others in the group. Cell phones are remarkable tools for many different things, but making it easy for you to connect in person to people around you is not one of them. Barrick, E. M., Barasch, A., & Tamir, D. I. (2022). The unexpected social consequences of diverting attention to our phones. *Journal of Experimental Social Psychology, 101,* 104344; Dwyer, R., Kushlev, K., & Dunn, E. W. (2018). Smartphone use undermines the enjoyment of face-to-face interactions. *Journal of Experimental Social Psychology, 78,* 233–39; Dwyer, R. J., Zhuo, A. X., & Dunn, E. W. (2023).

Why do people turn to smartphones during social interactions? *Journal of Experimental Social Psychology, 109.*

9. As Ed Diener, the psychologist who discovered the importance of frequency rather than intensity, put it, "Feeling pleasant emotion most of the time and infrequently experiencing unpleasant emotions, even if the unpleasant emotions are only mild, is sufficient for high reports of happiness." Diener even went further and discouraged the pursuit of extremely positive experiences, including in relationships. "One lesson from these findings is that if people seek ecstasy much of the time, whether it be in a career or a love relationship, they are likely to be disappointed. Even worse, they may move to the next relationship or job, seeking intense levels of happiness, which in fact are rarely long-lasting and are not necessary for happiness. People need to understand that intense experiences are not the cornerstone of a happy life." Diener, E. (2000, p. 36). Subjective well-being: The science of happiness and a proposal for a national index. *American Psychologist, 55*(1), 34–43.
10. Woolley, K., & Fishbach, A. (2019). Shared plates, shared minds: Consuming from a shared plate promotes cooperation. *Psychological Science, 30,* 541–52; Woolley, K., Fishbach, A., & Wang, R. M. (2020). Food restriction and the experience of social isolation. *Journal of Personality and Social Psychology, 119*(3), 657–71.
11. Townsend, D. J., & Bever, T. G. (2001, p. 2). *Sentence comprehension: The integration of habits and rules.* Cambridge, Mass.: MIT Press.
12. Durant, W. (1962, p. 74). *The story of philosophy: The lives and opinions of the greater philosophers.* New York: Simon & Schuster.
13. Hudson, N. W. (2018, Oct. 29). You can change your personality. TEDx Talks; Hudson, N. W., Fraley, R. C., Chopik, W. J., & Briley, D. A. (2020). Change goals robustly predict trait growth: A mega-analysis of a dozen intensive longitudinal studies examining volitional change. *Social Psychological and Personality Science, 11*(6), 723–32.
14. Hudson, N. W., Briley, D. A., Chopik, W. J., & Derringer, J. (2019). You have to follow through: Attaining behavioral change goals predicts volitional personality change. *Journal of Personality and Social Psychology, 117*(4), 839–57; Sun, J., & Goodwin, G. P. (2020). Do people want to be more moral? *Psychological Science, 31*(3), 243–57.
15. Duhigg, C. (2012). *The power of habit: Why we do what we do in life and business.* New York: Random House.
16. Philpott, M. L. (2022, March 4). Exclusive! Dolly Parton and James Patterson on their "down-to-earth" personalities, mega-successful careers, and writing a novel together. Parade.com.

Index

Page numbers in *italics* refer to figures and tables.
Page numbers followed by *n* indicate end note.

A NOTE ABOUT THE AUTHOR

Nicholas Epley is the John Templeton Keller Distinguished Service Professor of Behavioral Science and Faculty Director of the Roman Family Center for Decision Research at the University of Chicago Booth School of Business. He is the author of *Mindwise: Why We Misunderstand What Others Think, Believe, Feel, and Want.* He lives with his family in Chicago.

A NOTE ON THE TYPE

This book was set in Minion, a typeface produced by the Adobe Corporation specifically for the Macintosh personal computer and released in 1990. Designed by Robert Slimbach, Minion combines the classic characteristics of old-style faces with the full complement of weights required for modern typesetting.

Composed by North Market Street Graphics,
Lancaster, Pennsylvania

Designed by Cassandra J. Pappas